P9-CLP-968

ISLAMIC POLITICS AND THE MODERN WORLD

edited by ANDREW C. KIMMENS

THE REFERENCE SHELF

Volume 62 Number 5

THE H. W. WILSON COMPANY

New York   1991

THE REFERENCE SHELF

The books in this series contain reprints of articles, excerpts from books, and addresses on current issues and social trends in the United States and other countries. There are six separately bound numbers in each volume, all of which are generally published in the same calendar year. One number is a collection of recent speeches; each of the others is devoted to a single subject and gives background information and discussion from various points of view, concluding with a comprehensive bibliography that contains books and pamphlets and abstracts of additional articles on the subject. Books in the series may be purchased individually or on subscription.

Library of Congress Cataloging-in-Publication Data

Main entry under title:

Islamic politics and the modern world / edited by Andred C. Kimmens.
    p. cm. — (The Reference shelf ; v. 62, no. 5)
    Includes bibliographical references.

    ISBN 0-8242-0784-7
    1. Islam and politics.   2. Middle East—Politics and
government—1945- .
    I. Kimmens, Andrew C.   II. Series.
    BP173.7.187   1990
    320.917´67109045—dc20   90-47495
                                                           CIP
                                                           AC

Cover: Shiite Moslem Sheiks lead Hezbollah zealots during a farewell parade through the streets of Beirut, Lebanon. The seventy-five thousand marchers were mourning the death of the Ayatollah Khomeini, founder of Iran's Islamic Republic.
Photo: AP/Wide World Photos

Printed in the United States of America

CONTENTS

PREFACE

Compiled shortly before the Iraqi invasion of Kuwait on August 2, 1990, the selections in this book are intended to shed light on the realities of Islamic politics so often misunderstood by Western observers. The articles—drawn more from books than from current journals—are in the main thoughtful and informed analyses of the subject and its long-term effects, and they may be read to gain a greater appreciation of the force and complexities of Islamic political activism over the past three decades, a better understanding of the grievances and aspirations of political Islam, and a clearer recognition that Islamic political activism is a permanent feature of the world scene.

Before World War II, the Islamic countries of North Africa, the Middle East, and Asia were by and large politically quiescent—and faced by the power of Western imperialism, acquiescent. Political inertia was encouraged by the royal dynasties, then nearly everywhere in control, which vigorously suppressed all forms of activism and discouraged even moderate moves toward political awareness. The various European colonial powers, though less rapacious and cruel than in their dealings with central and southern Africans, had firmly established their power in the Islamic world and were determined to extract the commercial advantages which went along with political hegemony.

The militant Islamic awakening of the 1970s and 1980s not only shook Western complacency to its foundations but also seemed to reaffirm and encourage a deep antagonism in the West. The rise in Iran of a powerful religious-political leader coincided perfectly with (and seemed in such a large part to satisfy) the inchoate urges of militant Muslims throughout the world, but Western explanations of the Ayatollah as a theological throwback or a conservative anomaly were exactly the kind of wishful thinking that had led to political disaster in the past. Yet the real thought and study needed to change Western perceptions are still almost nowhere in evidence. The confusion and misunderstanding apparent throughout the West in response to the Salman Rushdie affair carried the profound lack of sympathy between the West and Islam a new and dangerous step further.

In the main, this book gives an account of the supplanting in the Muslim political world of a leftist, imported nationalism by a conservative, indigenous radicalism firmly underpinned by Islamic precepts. The selection of articles is meant as much as possible to allow those of Muslim background to explain the complexities of Islamic militancy. One restriction apparent in this volume is that the pieces are devoted to Islamic politics only and do not attempt to cover the vast array of economic, religious, and social topics.

The editor wishes to than the authors and publishers who have granted permission to reprint the material in this compilation.

ANDREW C. KIMMINS

September 1990

I. ARAB NATIONALISM:
THE FAILURE OF THE SECULAR IDEAL

EDITOR'S INTRODUCTION

The Arab nationalism which flourished during the 1950s and 1960s in Egypt and elsewhere under the principal leadership of the charismatic Gamal Abdel Nasser was for a time the pride of Islam, the vehicle by which Muslim peoples intended to gain their freedom from Western imperial domination and stand on their own as respected, free citizens of the world. The humiliation of Britain and France, the major Western colonial powers in Muslim eyes, at the time of the Suez debacle in 1956 was the high water-mark of Arab nationalism. Yet by 1970, Nasser, at the end of his absolute sway over the most important Arab power, had become for many of his erstwhile admirers a hollow shell of pretense, almost a figure of evil in his unwillingness to accept the guidance of Islam in running the state. What caused this reversal? Why did the Muslim world so thoroughly abandon nationalism, a liberation movement that had almost universally seemed so promising?

The standard answer, one that still holds, though with many qualifications needed, is that nationalism possessed exclusively Western intellectual antecedents, was incorrigibly secular in its operations, and thus could not but find itself in fundamental conflict with Islamic precepts. Muslim peoples have always sensed that only through Islam would they find their deliverance; the antagonism of the clerics and their followers in the Muslim Brotherhood to Nasser and his successor, Anwar Sadat, was the death knell for leftist nationalism, the sign that the Islamic masses were looking elsewhere for their salvation. The attachment of these masses to their religious leaders was unshakable, one that no national leader has ever been able to overcome.

This section examines the nature of nationalism in the Muslim world and the reasons for its decline as a potent political force. The first article, by a Muslim political scientist, demonstrates the economic importance of oil, in particular for creating and sustaining the setting for the confrontation between Islam and the West. The next article, by an Iranian-born U.S. academic, is an analysis of the relations among state, society, and ideology in various countries with substantial Muslim populations, including several where 'Islamism', as she terms it, is apparently not a strong factor. The third article is a study of the effect on Islamic militancy and the development of a supranational Islamic political identity of the Nasserist movement and the wars with Israel. The final article is a careful analysis by a senior Middle East expert of how nationalism, a "new imported ideology," "had to be wedded to the indigenous . . . political ideology of Islam," and how unsuccessful this marriage really was.

OIL, ARABISM AND ISLAM:
THE PERSIAN GULF IN WORLD POLITICS[1]

In the popular Western perception the strategic importance of the Persian Gulf region has risen manifold during the last decade. Although the Gulf had produced most of the exportable oil for almost three decades before the 1970s, it was in that decade that its importance as the leading surplus producer of the most vital source of energy was adequately recognised. Therefore, it is not sufficient to state, as most analysts have tended to do, that the quantum of oil produced for export by the Gulf countries was almost the sole reason for its strategic importance. While it is true that approximately 60 per cent of the world's oil reserves is located in the Persian Gulf, that in terms of actual production the Gulf countries produce approximately 20 million barrels daily (mbd) (1977 figures) out of the 30 mbd produced by OPEC and approximately 54 mbd produced by the entire world put together, and that Middle East oil (the bulk of it from the Gulf) accounts for 75 per cent of the oil in world trade, these simple statistics do not tell the whole story.

The missing link (or rather, the unstated assumption) that makes the Gulf so important strategically to the Western in-

---

[1]By Mohammed Ayoob, political scientist, from his book *The Middle East in World Politics*, pp. 118–135. Copyright © 1981 Australian Institute of International Affairs. Reprinted with permission.

dustralised countries is their increasing inability to control the price, the output, and the most crucial of all variables in this context, the political (including the foreign policy) orientation of the major oil exporters. It is this critical variable that underwent radical change in the 1970s and particularly in its closing years. For in the earlier decades (with the partial exception of Iraq following its revolution in 1958) all the major Gulf exporters of oil were, in matters of output, pricing and political orientation, under the control and direction either of Western government or of the Western oil monopolites—the Seven Sisters as they are commonly known. It was the gradual erosion of the Western control over the politics and economics of oil (foreshadowed dramatically by Mossadegh's unsuccessful attempt in the early 1950s to demonstrate Iran's independence of oil monopolies and the Western governments supporting them) in the 1970s that brought on "the energy crisis" in psychological terms which in turn transformed Western apprehensions into a self-fulfilling prophecy.

That this variable is so critical is demonstrated above all by the fact that it had been known for decades that the Gulf was the major source of oil (indeed of energy) for the Western world and that the West's dependence upon this source had been increasing in geometric progressions over the years; but no one in the major capitals of the industrialised countries had lost much sleep over this issue. In fact, in 1980 it appears shocking that despite all these factors and the generally escalating demand for oil in the industrialised countries, the major oil companies could in 1959, and again in 1960, decide to cut the price of oil by an average of 18 cents and 9 cents a barrel, respectively, and that also without prior consultation with the governments of the producing countries. In fact, it was this short-sighted decision aimed at providing the West with cheaper oil ("dirt cheap" to be precise) in a temporary period of glut in the oil market, that, in the words of one analyst, "generated a feeling of economic insecurity in oil exporting countries and emphasised the need for a collective defense to arrest the downward drift of prices." It was this sudden and arbitrary decrease in petroleum prices that acted as the catalyst for the establishment of OPEC, which came into being in September 1960.

But even the formation of OPEC did not tilt the balance against Western interests, governmental and commercial; for despite the ostensible cooperation among the oil exporters, there were many factors, including each exporter's desire to corner a larger share of the market, which kept their bargaining power weak. It was not until the Libyan Revolution of 1969 which brought Qaddafi and his colleagues to power, and the subsequent tough stance adopted by the new Libyan government *vis-à-vis* the oil multinationals on the pricing issue, that the tide began to turn. The Gulf producers, taking a leaf out of the Libyan book, were able to persuade the companies in 1971 at Tehran to agree to an increase of 30 cents per barrel on the posted price, escalating to 50 cents by 1975. Although this was a miniscule increase compared to what happened later, it was the first definite sign that the balance of power between OPEC and the oil majors was beginning to tilt in favour of the former. Therefore, it was the Tripoli and Tehran agreements of 1970 and 1971, for Mediterranean and Gulf oil respectively, that represented the major turn about in the politics and economics of oil and not the 1973 price hikes which coincided with the Arab oil embargo in the wake of the October war.

The Shah of Iran was instrumental to a large extent in persuading the oil companies to face changing realities. His own interest in expanding Iran's revenues for the ambitious economic and military plans he had for his country coincided with several other factors which, taken with the changing balance between OPEC and the oil companies, and, therefore, by extension the major oil consumers of the industrialised West, transformed radically the Western perception of the Gulf. From an almost exclusive Western preserve, with docile governments who did the biddings of Exxon and Shell on the one hand and Washington and London on the other, the oil heartland of the world was suddenly transformed into an area of strategic vulnerability (or so it was perceived) with Arab sheikhs in their flowing robes and outlandish headgear dictating oil prices to meek oil company executives who humbly carried out their orders more than faithfully, by not only passing on the price increase to the consumers but by making several extra millions of dollars themselves in the process.

The other factors which dictated this change of perception (and indeed of the corresponding reality in the Persian Gulf itself) included the British decision in 1968 to withdraw from East of Suez (a decision that was implemented in the fall of 1971), the enunciation of the Guam Doctrine by President Nixon as a result of the American experience in Vietnam and its corollaries of the "twin pillars" (Iran and Saudi Arabia) policy for the Gulf which in the process of implementation was transformed into a "local gendarme" (Iran) strategy; but, above all, the culmination of the process of decolonisation with the independence of the Arab countries of the Gulf littoral and the greater autonomy of action demonstrated by those already independent.

Although most of the governments of the Gulf (with the almost single exception of Iraq) continued to be pro-Western in their orientation, the changing ethos of the 1970s forced them to be more responsive to popular opinion both in terms of control of their economic and natural resources, particularly a non-renewable and fast depleting resource like oil, and on questions of regional politics, especially those that touched the very core of the Arab character of most of these countries.

With the general erosion of the legitimacy of the monarchical system, the sheikhs and kings (and indeed the Shahinshah himself) of the Gulf were under tremendous pressure to adopt visibly nationalistic stands, particularly on the issue of oil (on prices and later on output), if their own residual legitimacy was to be preserved and their nationalist credentials were not to become open to increasingly severe challenges. To add to this, the general strategy of building surrogates for British and American power in the Gulf required the infusion of great quantities of arms of increasing sophistication and this, in turn, needed considerable local resources if it was not to become a major financial drain on Western treasuries, above all on the US Treasury. Increasing oil prices, whereby accumulated petrodollars could be recycled into Western economies in payment for military hardware and training missions, was one obvious way of achieving this end. Oil price hikes, therefore, were not such unmitigated disasters for the industrialised West as they were made out to be by the popular media.

However, what the great Western powers had not counted upon was that once their control over the pricing mechanism was demonstrated, the next logical step for the OPEC members was to assert their control over the volume of oil to be produced for export. It was this question of the volume of output rather than that of price which reflected the real divergence of interests in regard to oil between OPEC members (and two-thirds of OPEC production is concentrated in the Gulf) and the industrialised nations of the West.

The Ramadan or October War of 1973 and the consequent Arab oil embargo both highlighted and exacerbated these differences. It demonstrated dramatically that the West had lost control of the oil situation for the first time. The ineffectual and partial embargoes of 1956 and 1967 had demonstrated the economic and political impotence of the Arab oil producers *vis-à-vis* the oil majors (and their home governments) who controlled the oil market totally in terms of pricing, output, exploration, transportation, etc. The 1973 embargo, on the other hand, coming as it did after the Tehran and Tripoli agreements and coinciding with the 1973 oil price rises in a context of oil shortage rather than one of glut, demonstrated the increasing political and economic clout of OPEC and particularly of OAPEC (Organisation of Arab Petroleum Exporting Countries), which had been established in 1968.

The OAPEC embargo was significant not only in the context of the control of output, which was demonstrated by the Arab producers' decision to cut back production incrementally if Israel did not withdraw from the territories it had occupied in 1967, but also in their attempt to control the direction or final destination of the flow of oil. The total embargo placed on oil shipments to the US and the Netherlands demonstrated the Arab world's resolve to use the only effective weapon at its command to redress its grievances *vis-à-vis* Israel and its Western supporters, above all the United States.

This use of the "oil weapon," as it came to be called, added a new dimension to the politics of the Middle East, including that of the Persian Gulf. For although the Arab countries had tried to use oil for political ends during the Anglo-French-Israeli invasion of Egypt in 1956 and the Six Day War of June 1967, it was not until 1973 that the effectiveness of this instrument was clearly demonstrated. This was particularly true as far as the impact on the US was concerned. For even in 1967 the US imported

very little Arab oil and the shut-in capacity of United States oil fields was considerable. By 1973, however, the situation had changed dramatically: the United States was using, either at home or in supplying military forces abroad, some 2.5 million barrels of Arab oil per day, and American production had gone up to 100 per cent of capacity in order to supply American demand. (R. Ramazani, *Persian Gulf and the Strait of Hormerz*, p. 58)

What gave an added edge to the 1973 embargo as well as the decision to reduce oil output was the fact that it was Saudi Arabia, one of the "twin pillars" of US regional strategy in the Gulf, which was one of the leading proponents of this policy. Although Kissinger, during his shuttle diplomacy, tried his best to dissociate the issue of oil supplies from the Arab-Israeli (and particularly the Palestinian) issue, it should be noted that this very shuttle was prompted above all by the Saudi decision to use oil as a political weapon. Moreover, although Kissinger claimed that he was successful in separating the two issues, the communique announcing the decision of the Arab producers in March 1974 to life the embargo clearly implied the linkage between the two issues. Moreover, in December 1976, Saudi Arabia, going a step further, explicitly linked the issue of oil prices with that of the Arab-Israeli conflict in general and the Palestinian issue in particular. While announcing the Saudi decision to hold down OPEC price increases to only 5 per cent as compared to the 15 per cent advocated by other OPEC members, the Saudi Arabian Petroleum Minister, Sheikh Yamani, put the West, and particularly the US, on notice that his country expected a *quid pro quo* from the Western powers in terms of "responsive" measures on both the Arab-Israeli conflict and the North-South dialogue.

On the American side also this linkage was widely accepted. This acceptance was represented by the various statements by the US President, the Secretary of State and the Secretary of Defense threatening reprisals against Gulf oil producers if they threatened to cut off oil supplies to the West following the outbreak of another round of Arab-Israeli hostilities. Any number of articles in popular and learned journals (with Robert Tucker in *Commentary* leading the pack) implicitly or explicitly accepted this linkage. Several studies, including those by the Congressional Research Service, were undertaken and some published, regarding various scenarios and outcomes of attempted takeovers of Gulf—and particularly Saudi—oil fields in case an embargo was repeated.

All this merely goes to prove that the West woke up to the strategic importance of the Gulf only when its control over Gulf resources and Gulf governments began to slip and local forces and governments began to demonstrate their political and economic autonomy from the traditionally dominant powers.

Another reason which led to the recognition of the Gulf's strategic importance, and which has been implied in the discussion so far, was related to the fact that the increasing political and economic clout of the Arab oil producers and their actions during times of crisis in the Middle East also demonstrated that the Gulf could not be artificially divorced from its parent Middle Eastern region, and particularly from the Arab heartland of the Middle East. If anything, during the 1970s this linkage grew stronger, especially in the conservative monarchies of Saudi Arabia, Kuwait and the UAE as well as in Qatar and Bahrain. Iraq, the odd man out in the Gulf since 1958, had been following a radical anti-Western course through most of the 1960s and had always considered itself a confrontation state *vis-à-vis* Israel. But it was the hardening of the Saudi, and to a lesser extent the Kuwait and UAE, stance on the Arab-Israeli dispute, and particularly on the question of Palestine, that apparently caught Western policy-makers unawares. But, as has been argued earlier, given the changing ethos of the 1970s in the Arab world (including the Gulf), even the most unrepresentative of the Arab rulers had to be responsive in some degree at least to popular demands/desires if they were not to lose legitimacy totally. And, if there is one issue on which popular Arab sentiment is united it is on the issue of Palestine, especially on the question of the removal of Israeli occupation forces from the West Bank and Gaza (of course, in addition to the whole of Sinai and the Golan Heights).

Moreover, despite the existence of several sovereign Arab states and the continuous squabbling among them, there is a certain basic affinity among the Arab peoples which makes it very hard for their rulers to stray too far from the Arab consensus, particularly on Palestine. As a leading Arab political scientist has pointed out,

The Arab States' system is first and foremost a "Pan" system. It postulates the existence of a single Arab Nation behind the facade of a multiplicity of sovereign states. . . . The oneness of the Arab Nation had corollaries in the concepts of the dignity of the Nation, and the oneness and therefore the inviolability of its territory. . . . These concepts together constitute the central value system of the Arab states' system. To be sure they are not uniformly manifested in the five great regions that make up the Arab world—the Fertile Crescent, the Gulf, the Peninsula, the Nile Valley and the Maghreb—nor in the countries of each region. But for historical, religious and cultural reasons they find powerful resonance among the vast majority of Arabs at every level of society throughout these regions. . . . The Palestine problem encapsulates the concepts of pan-Arabism. It is not difficult to see why. By definition the Palestinian people are an integral part of the Arab Nation. Therefore, by definition the injustice suffered by the Palestinian people was suffered by the Nation. Again, the loss of Palestine is the de-Arabisation of Arab territory. It is thus a violation of the principles of the unity and integrity of Arab soil, an affront to the dignity of the Nation.

The evolution of a distinct Palestinian nationalism striving for the establishment of its own state on a part of historical Palestine is perceived as complementary to and not in contradiction with the concept of the larger Arab nation or of Pan-Arabism. The former stands in the same relation to the latter as did Egyptian or Syrian nationalism of the early decades of the twentieth century or Algerian nationalism of the 1950s and 1960s in relation to the Pan-Arab ideal. One does not negate, in fact it strengthens, the other.

In addition to this general Arab commitment, particularly at the popular level, to the Palestinian cause, the presence of substantial numbers of Palestinians in oil-rich Gulf states gives the Palestinian nationalists, and particularly the PLO, considerable leverage with the already nervous rulers of these monarchies and sheikhdoms. According to one estimate made by an informed observer, the Palestinians

number 240,000 to 260,000 or 20 per cent of the total population in Kuwait; about 45,000 or 22 per cent in Qatar, more than the native-born Qataris; and 40,000 or perhaps 30 per cent in the United Arab Emirates, where expaztriate workers of all nationalities outnumber the native workers by 18 to one. . . . In Saudi Arabia, Palestinians and Jordanians together total around 110,000. . . . There are perhaps a total of 480,000 Palestinians in the entire Arabian Peninsula.

What is even more important is the fact that the Palestinian presence in the Peninsula is felt

in qualitative, rather than quantitative terms: the Palestinians of Arabia are *not* helpless, jobless refugees, like so many of their brothers and cousins in the camps of Jordan, Syria and Lebanon. Many hold important posts in the civil service, even as advisers to Gulf rulers (especially in Qatar and the U.A.E.), and more work in the oil, banking and contracting sectors. Some have acquired local citizenship. There are also Palestinians serving in the regular armed forces of some of the Gulf and Arabian Peninsula states. Palestinians who are naturalised Kuwaiti citizens are numerous in the Kuwait officer corps in nian despite the strong personal stakes many have built in the local economies, are strongly nationalistic and closely attached to the idea of a Palestinian homeland.

If you put together all these factors, namely the numerically substantial and qualitatively crucial Palestinian presence in the Arab countries of the Gulf, the problem of legitimacy already facing the Gulf monarchies, and the support for the Palestinian cause among the indigenous Arab population of the Gulf, it becomes very clear that even of the Gulf and Arabian Peninsula states. Palestinians who are swim against the Arab mainstream of popular opinion on this issue of a Palestinian homeland and the withdrawal of Israel from the West Bank, including East Jerusalem, and the Gaza Strip.

Even, or more correctly, above all, the House of Saud cannot be immune to these political currents in and around the Kingdom. More particularly, because of its huge oil wealth, its traditional pro-American policy, its role as the largest Arab supplier of oil to the US, its huge purchases of arms from the US and the consequent inflow of US military and civilian personnel into the country, its guardianship of the holy places of Islam (and the legitimising role for Saudi rule that fundamentalist Islam has played since the inception of the state), the Saudi Kingdom is now under tremendous pressure to prove its Arab credentials. It can maintain its generally pro-Western and conservative stance and yet demonstrate its commitment to the Arab cause only by adopting a firm position on the issue of Israeli withdrawal and the establishment of a Palestinian state. If the current rulers of Saudi Arabia fail to reconcile their twin strategies (pro-Western and pro-Arab) soon they would be in increasing danger of being supplanted either by the more "radical" members of the House of Saud who would be willing to jettison the current pro-Western stance in order to save and legitimise Saudi rule, or by a new regime altogether, possibly of the Qaddafi variety, which would be in a better position to bring the various strands of Islam, Arabism and radicalism together and weld them into a single whole.

The recent events surrounding the occupation of the Grand Mosque in Mecca have demonstrated to the Saudis as well as others how deceptive had been the apparent atmosphere of political calm in the Kingdom. Despite Saudi attempts to play down the gravity of the incident, it now appears that elements of the National Guard (the Bedouin Army), recruited from tribes traditionally loyal both to Wahabi fundamentalism and to the House of Saud, took a leading part in that gruesome episode. Since Bedouin tribal loyalty (particularly of the tribes of Nejd) and Wahabism form the twin pillars of Saudi rule, the reverberations of the Meccan affair are expected to be felt far and wide within the Arabian Peninsula. As one senior Western diplomat in Riyadh put it, "For the first time since the house of Saud was built, its foundations have been rocked. . . . The Saudis are dead scared."

The threat to the stability of Saudi rule takes on an even more serious character once we stop to look behind the facade of unity which seemed until recently to pervade both the ruling house as well as the country. Although until now the ruling family has hung together particularly in times of crisis, fissures based on maternal family ties, ideological orientations and personalities may in the not too long a term prove an unbearable load for the Saudi system to cope with. There are already indications of "pro-Arab" and "pro-American" factions jockeying for power within the ruling circles of the Kingdom. The "Saudairi Seven," which include Crown Prince Fahd but not King Khalid, are being increasingly put on the defensive both because of their tendency to cling together and their pro-American policy stances. Prince Adbullah, the Commander of the National Guard, although reportedly under a cloud temporarily following the involvement of elements of his force in the Meccan takeover, seems to rely on his pro-Arab and pro-Palestinian credentials in his effort to present an effective challenge to the Saudairi clique. Moreover, the younger princes, the "Young Turks" as Sheikh Yamani called them, are bound to play increasingly important roles in the 1980s. The most prominent among them, Saud al-Faisal, the Foreign Minister, has made his pro-Arab sympathies clear more than once, particularly on the Palestinian issue.

Other fissures within the Saudi system include the social tensions created by the pace of modernisation and the concentration of oil wealth in the top layer of Saudi society, as well as the underlying divisions between the various parts of the country, particularly the urban, commercial centres of the Hejaz—Mecca, Medinah and Jeddah—and the Bedouin-dominated Nejd. The Hejaz, until the First World War, had remained a part of the multinational Ottoman Empire with a complex legal system and a cosmopolitan tradition. Nejd, by and large, had been outside the Ottoman fold and was steeped in Bedouin tradition and Islamic fundamentalism. It was the Saudi victory which brought Nejdi power to the Hejaz. An undercurrent of resentment against Bedouin domination probably still continues to exist in the Hejaz, which, rather than Nejd, is the religious centre of the Islamic world. The Hejaz, before the Saudi conquest, was largely Hanafi and Shafe, whereas Nejd was steeped in the fundamentalist Hanbali tradition of Abdul Wahab. To add to this, the existence of a 100,000-strong Shia minority in the oil-rich eastern province of

Al-Hasa which has become increasingly restive in the last few years (and particularly since the Iranian Revolution) is another factor which militates against Saudi stability. In fact, there have been reports of an attempted Shia uprising in the eastern province around the time of the occupation of the Grand Mosque in Mecca.

It is, therefore, quite understandable that in the midst of all these actual or potential problems, no government in Riyadh can afford to alienate Arab sentiment on Palestine by endorsing the Camp David agreement and the subsequent Egyptian-Israeli treaty or by giving unconditional approval to the general trend of US policy in the Middle East.

As has been argued earlier, while Kissinger, as a result of his shuttle diplomacy, had been successful in getting the OAPEC countries to lift their oil embargo, this did not mean that OAPEC, and Saudi Arabia in particular, had accepted the delinking of the two issues of oil and the Arab-Israeli conflict. It is no wonder, therefore, that a Saudi ruling elite, increasingly nervous and under mounting pressure both at home and in the region to prove its Arab credentials, has once again stepped up its campaign explicitly to link the two issues and to prod the US towards some genuine action on the issue of Palestinian self-determination. This Saudi stand (which is also supported by the other Arab states of the Gulf) has been thrown into sharper relief following the Soviet intervention in Afghanistan and US attempts, in the shape of the "Carter Doctrine," to respond to Soviet moves in the region. Saudi Arabia, while basically in sympathy with the US on this issue and distrustful of Moscow, has made it clear that, while it is willing to go along with the US in helping Pakistan financially to meet the presumed Soviet threat, it feels there are obvious limits to such co-operation. As the Saudi Foreign Minister put it, "There is no limit to compromise and pragmatism. But once it reaches the stage of avoiding such issues as self-determination for the Palestinians, it is no longer compromise and pragmatism: it is injustice." The Kuwaiti Minister of Cabinet Affairs echoed Prince Saud's views: "The crisis of Afghanistan should not divert our attention from the real problem. Jerusalem is more sacred to us than Kabul."

In a similar vein Saudi officials have throughout 1979 off and on floated ideas about a cut back in their oil production from their current level of 9.5 mbd to 8.5 mbd in the absence of a solution of the Palestine problem. Riyadh had decided to increase its output in July 1979 on a temporary basis to make up for the West's loss of oil following the Iranian Revolution. In fact, the move was at least partly in response to requests from President Carter himself. Saudi decision-makers, under pressure from pro-Arab elements and from nationalist technocrats who see no reason for the depletion of the country's non-renewable resource in the absence of adequate American *quid pro quo*, have found it increasingly difficult to justify the present level of production. In a briefing in the Saudi capital in February 1980, a senior Saudi official, "a policy-maker in the government who asked to remain anonymous," once again reiterated the Saudi decision to cut back production to 8.5 mbd sometime during the course of 1980. He "portrayed the decision on curtailing oil production as part of a carefully balanced course that Saudi Arabia is trying to steer between its ties with the West and its obligations as a major power in the Arab, Islamic and Third Worlds." It is interesting to note that his briefing was given soon after Brzezinski's visit to the Kingdom and just days before the scheduled arrival in Riyadh of the US Secretary of Energy, Charles Duncan, Jr. The senior Saudi official went on to say that "one of the major concerns of the Kingdom is the slow pace of progress in the autonomy talks on the fate of the Palestinians and the failure of these talks to offer the Palestinian Arabs an acceptable option within a Middle East peace agreement." Another Saudi official (also unnamed) commented that the issue was "opening the way for more Soviet interference and meddling in this region."

From the foregoing analysis it becomes clear that the importance of the Palestine issue in shaping the policies of the Arab countries of the Gulf, and particularly of Saudi Arabia, is likely to increase (and possibly quite dramatically) in the near future. This would have considerable repercussions on the output, pricing as well as the flow of oil to the West in general, and the US in particular. Oil and Palestine are more intricately enmeshed in the politics of the Arab littoral of the Gulf today than they were ever before and the regional politics of the 1980s and their global ramifications would to a large extent be directed by what happens on the Palestinian front.

The third major factor which is likely to dominate the politics of the Persian Gulf in the 1980s is a politically resurgent Islam. Although Ayatollah Khomeini's Iran forms the major symbol of this resurgence, the Arab side of the Gulf has not remained unaffected by the new vitality shown by Islam when used as a revolutionary ideology in the political arena.

While experts on Iranian polity and economy have told us, and correctly so, that the revolution in Iran was the result of many political and economic factors ranging from the oppression of the Shah's regime to the critical downturn in the Iranian economy in the last couple of years of his rule, the most important lesson of the Iranian experience for the Third World, for its Muslim component, and especially for Iran's neighbours, lies in the fact that it demonstrated that a revolution—in both its internal and external dimensions, namely, the restructuring of the domestic order and rejection of foreign domination—could take place in "native" terms and without the help of external agents of influence and legitimacy. This has had far reaching effects on the ethos of the region, not only in the Gulf but in the Middle East as a whole. It has not only increased the sense of insecurity of other monarchical regimes in the area, it has also made traditional Islamic regimes, like the one in Saudi Arabia, sharply aware of the fact that Islam as a political force can be a doubled-edged weapon. While in the case of Saudi Arabia it has so far provided an important basis for the legitimacy of Saudi rule, the concept of Islamic polity if operationalised in the revolutionary tradition of political Islam can perform an extremely destabilising role as far as the traditional rulers of the Arabian side of the Gulf are concerned. For, as Bernard Lewis has pointed out, while "the Western doctrine of the right to resist bad government is alien to Islamic thought . . . there is an Islamic doctrine of the duty to resist impious government, which in early times was of crucial historical significance.

While obviously the political and religious development of Shia Iran through the centuries has been somewhat different from its predominantly Sunni neighbours, and Saudi Arabia is certainly not Iran, the concept of "impious government" can in the late twentieth century be translated by Muslim (Islamic or secular) revolutionaries to encompass not merely the concept of "bad government" defined in its traditional sense, but also an unjust and inequitable economic and political order. The Quran and Marx can, on occasion, be made to appear as two sides of the same coin (as the Islamic-Marxists of Iran, the *Mujahedin-e-Khala*, have successfully demonstrated).

Moreover, although the role of the Shia *ulama* in Iran as the "potential opposition," to use Nikki Keddies's term, to the monarchy has been unique in the Muslim world, the traditional Sunni doctrine of support by the *ulama* for the *Hakim-i-Waqt* (the ruler of the time) is no longer free from challenge. While *Al-Azhar* and the *ulama* of Saudi Arabia are the prime examples of this Sunni tradition in their unswerving support for the rulers in Cairo and Riyadh, Qaddafi's revolution in Libya and the Muslim Brotherhood's (and similar other parties') opposition to various governments of different hues in the Muslim world has made it clear that Islamic ideology (or ideologies) can be used for anti-*status quo* ends in the Sunni as well as the Shia countries.

As far as the larger international system is concerned, the Iranian experience of 1978-9 demonstrated the major role performed by Islam in providing the theoretical basis for the rejection of foreign domination and influence. The experience of foreign domination—direct or indirect, economic, political or military—is one that Iran has shared, and continues to share, with most countries in the Third World. However, particularly in the context of the projected Iranian role as the local gendarme for the US in the Gulf in conformity with the Guam Doctrine, and the fact that both economically and strategically Iran was securely plugged into the economy and strategy of the US and its allies, the Iranian rejection in its Islamic garb of foreign domination assumes great importance. At the same time, the character of the Iranian Revolution and the composition of its leadership can give little cause for celebration in Moscow. In fact, the revival of the revolutionary tradition in political Islam just across the Soviet frontier would, if anything, be cause for dismay in the Kremlin. Given the concentration of Muslim (and, in places like Soviet Azerbaijan, Shia) populations in close proximity to Iran, Soviet misgivings could be well placed. For once, Moscow must have realised that ideas and ideologies can cross political boundaries in both directions and that a politically revived Islam can become a focus for allegiance on the part of disgruntled elements in the Muslim Republics of the USSR.

If you add to this the fact that vast territories of Soviet Central Asia, acquired by Tsarist Russia only 100 or 150 years ago, had for centuries formed in one way or another part of Persian or other Muslim polities and that names like Samarkand and Bokhara evoke for many Muslims even today the not so remote glorious past of Islam, it is bound to add to Soviet worries, if not apprehensions. The radicalisation of Iranian politics in Islamic terms does not seem likely to redound to Moscow's benefit (as was commonly assumed in the West during the crucial phase of the anti-Shah struggle). In fact, it may reopen questions—territorial, ethnic and ideological—that Moscow had assumed were closed a century ago.

The change of regime in Iran has, of course, had a more immediate impact on the issues of oil and Palestine—both of which have formed the major themes in the earlier portion of this paper. The highly nationalistic and anti-American new rulers of Iran have found no particular reason to maintain the high level of oil production that had prevailed under the Shah. Moreover, because of technological and political problems (due to the fact that Iran's major oil fields are located in Khuzistan, which has a substantial Arab population) even the modest output target of around 3 mbd has not been always maintained. The effect of this reduction in oil production has been reflected in oil prices also. It has strengthened the hands of those countries within OPEC, like Libya, Iraq and Algeria, that had been advocating still higher prices. Correspondingly, it has weakened the position of Saudi Arabia and its camp followers in OPEC, particularly the UAE, who had argued for less steep increases in price. Although the differences within OPEC over pricing have not been completely resolved, the Saudis have, for all practical purposes, at least for the time being, considerably muted their opposition to oil price rises. This has suited Riyadh's own ends also, because it helped to demonstrate not only its nationalist credentials at home, but also its displeasure over the American failure to convert the autonomy talks on Palestine into a more meaningful exercise.

The Iranian Revolution has also directly affected the balance of regional forces as far as the Palestine problem is concerned. Iran under the Shah had remained aloof from the Arab countries' stance on the Arab-Israeli issue. In fact, Tehran had supplied Israel with the bulk of its oil requirements. The revolution has changed all that. Iran is now firmly committed to the Palestinian cause and the erstwhile Israeli Embassy in Tehran has been handed over to the PLO for its use. Yasser Arafat was the first notable political figure to visit Tehran after the revolution and he was accorded treatment befitting a head of state or government. All oil supplies to Israel were cut off in late 1978 and one of the popular slogans during the closing stages of the Iranian Revolution was: "Today Tehran, tomorrow Jerusalem."

This change in the regional balance on the issue of Palestine could be crucial both to the regional actors and to the great powers. Although the official US stance on Palestinian statehood is still dictated to a large extent by Israeli policy (and the corresponding pressure brought on the US Congress and the White House by the Jewish lobby in America), there are indications that in the light of the Iranian reversal and the increasing political salience of Islam and Arabism and, above all, the cumulative impact of all this on the issue of oil supplies, the importance of the Palestinian factor in the context of Gulf and Middle East stability is better recognized in the US today than it was ever before. Among those eminent Americans who are able and willing to appreciate this linkage is former US Under-Secretary of State George Ball. In a recent article in the *Washington Post*, Ball put the issue in his characteristically blunt fashion:

So far we have persistently approached the Middle East problem from the wrong side, spending enormous political capital to settle the Israeli-Egyptian quarrel, which has little to do with oil, while in the process inflaming the Israeli-Palestinian dispute, which critically affects U.S. relations with oil-producing countries. But we cannot realistically expect those Arab nations to risk close identification with us by giving the United States bases on their soil or cooperating in military planning while we continue to subsidise Israeli colonialism on the West Bank and the Gaza Strip and condone by inaction the Begin government's cynical effort to absorb those areas. Let there be no mistake about it: so long as the United States delays a frontal attack on the Palestinian issue, it is alienating the whole Moslem world, as shattered U.S. Embassies have demonstrated.

The fall-out effects of the developments in Iran have, therefore, only strengthened the trends both on the question of oil and of Palestine that we had discerned in relation to the Arab littoral of the Gulf.

Recent Soviet moves in the region, particularly the massive intervention in Afghanistan, have made it all the more imperative that the Western powers, and particularly the US, should respond to the evolving situation in the Gulf in a carefully calculated manner after fully taking into consideration the changing realities of the regional scene. This would involve first of all a genuine effort to understand the actual political dynamics of the Gulf (and its parent region, the Middle East). Unless and until the US is able to understand those dynamics—weighted in favour of social and political change, however unpalatable many of these changes might temporarily appear from a Western perspective, and inextricably interwoven with the Palestinian quest for justice and self-determination—it will continue to face reverses in that strategic region. For it is not the Soviet Union, despite its presence in Afghanistan (which might actually be a blessing in disguise for the West), from where the major threats to Western economic and strategic interests in the region are likely to emanate; it is from dissatisfied local forces, temporarily thwarted in their efforts to achieve political justice and social change, that these major threats are likely to arise. In fact, the Soviet Union—despite, or rather because of, the fact that it might become a net importer of oil before the decade is over—would be as interested in maintaining the free flow of Gulf oil as the Western powers would be. However, the same cannot be said of local forces, Arab and/or Islamic, who would have few, if any, qualms about turning off the oil tap (or at least reducing its flow drastically) if those who benefit most from the Gulf oil do not show adequate responsiveness towards their political and economic demands. Scenario-building about the US takeover of Gulf oil fields in case of another oil embargo or drastic reduction in oil supplies, while it may serve as a psychological palliative for some people in Washington, does not serve long-term (for even short-term) Western interests; for as various studies have demonstrated, these attempts would be far from cost-effective in terms both of military costs and the economic and political fall-out effects of such adventures. In fact, they may achieve exactly the opposite results.

Oil, Arabism and Islam have come together to form a unique nexus in the Gulf. It would, therefore, be extremely shortsighted for the leading consumers of Gulf oil and the great powers of the West with major strategic and economic interests in the region to be oblivious to the central concerns of the decision-makers (and by extension the people whom they represent and/or govern) in that strategic region. For if these grievances are not redressed, they might lead to an explosion of catastrophic proportions in the Gulf and in the larger Middle East region as a whole which would have grave repercussions on the international political and economic structures as they are constituted today.

IDEOLOGY, SOCIETY AND THE STATE
IN POST-COLONIAL MUSLIM SOCIETIES[2]

This essay will deal analytically with the relations between state, society and ideology in certain post-colonial muslim societies. The emphasis will be comparative, with the aim of using comparison to shed light on each society and on the differences and similarities among them. For the purposes of this discussion "post-colonial" is taken to begin with the Ataturk and Reza Shah regimes in Turkey and Iran, when important political and economic breaks were made with Western power, and to begin with the achievement of independence from colonialism in the other countries discussed. Hence there is a gap of twenty-five years or more between the two categories.

Islam and Secularism: The First Phase

As others have noted, without sufficient effect, "Islam" is not a concept that should be reified, but like other religions, it has varied with time, place, social class, ethnicity, gender, and other variables. The varieties of Islamic trends before colonial conquest or influence differed from what developed after, and both differed from what developed after independence. Pre-colonial Islamic trends, at least outside Saudi Arabia, differed greatly from what is preached by Islamist movements today. As a gross generalisation, pre-colonial Islam stressed law and practices led by an ulama who were normally in general alliance with their governments to maintain the status quo. Contrary to some writers, there was major differentiation between the sphere of the ulama and that of rulers. Most of the time, Islam tended to be conservative rather than militant or exclusivist. With Western influence or conquest in the late nineteenth and early twentieth centuries there grew up schools of Islamic reformism, associated chiefly with the Young Ottomans, Jamal ad-Din' al-Afghani', Muhammad Abduh, Rashid Rida and the Salafiya movement, and Syed

[2]By Nikki R. Keddie, professor at the University of California at Los Angeles, from Fred Halliday and Hamza Alavi, eds., *State and Ideology in the Middle East and Pakistan* pp. 9–30. Coypright © 1988 Nikki Keddie. Reprinted by permission.

Ahmad Khan. These trends tried to make Islam compatible with many Western scientific, economic, and political concepts in order to strengthen Islamic countries against the West, and adapt Islam to the needs of modern bourgeois society. In addition, there were other modernist movements that stressed national rather than Islamic identity—radical Iranian nationalism stressed by the freethinking nineteenth-century Mirza Aqa Khan Kermani and the twentieth-century Ahmad Kasravi; pan-Turanianism in pre-Ataturk Turkey, and Arab nationalism, which had a special appeal for Christians and other minorities. The nationalist movements were more secular than Islamic ones, although Arab nationalists usually paid obeisance to Muhammad and Islam, partly as Arab phenomena.

If one looks at popular movements in the period before the end of colonial rule, as defined above, it seems clear that for the bazaar class or petty bourgeoisie, and for the masses of the population, Islam, without a particularly reformist content, remained a focus of identity and aspirations. The Iranian revolution of 1905–11 was fought by its popular leaders in the name of Islam and got much of its power from support by some of the ulama. On his way to power in 1921–5 Reza Khan was careful to court ulama support. Similarly Ataturk fought his popular war of liberation in the name of Islam, which is frequently invoked in his early speeches. In Egypt the popular nationalist Mustafa Kamil successfully invoked traditional Islamic practices, including veiling and seclusion, in his attacks on the British, while modernist opponents appealed to a more restricted bourgeois group.

One may roughly say that in both the colonial and post-colonial periods Islam of a fairly traditional kind continued to appeal to the masses, to those of the bourgeoisie who were tied to the traditional economy, and to the ulama, while modernism, nationalism, and secularism had their greatest appeal among classes tied to the West, the new army and bureaucracy. In both cases ideas suited interest.

The post-colonial states, whose leaders wished to centralise power and to build a stronger economy, were logically moved to weaken the classes most indentified with Islam, especially the ulama, and to establish what is often called secularism, although state control over religion would be a more accurate designation. This was not exclusively a post-colonial trend: already in the nineteenth century those states most influenced by the West, notably the Ottoman centre, Tunisia, and Egypt, had taken steps to weaken the power of the ulama. With Ataturk and Reza Shah, however, the steps were much more dramatic. Ataturk abolished the caliphate, outlawed the use of the Arabic alphabet, ended the religious school system, gave women equal legal rights, encouraged unveiling, and so forth. These steps were emulated by Reza Shah somewhat less radically, though it was he and not Ataturk who actually outlawed veiling, in 1936.

Both rulers encouraged an ethnic nationalism which had its roots in the past but now took new forms and strength. While Iranian nationalism had started as a radical idea, praising the pre-Islamic religious socialist Mazdak, Reza Shah and his son favoured a monarchist version, stressing great pre-Islamic kings–Cyrus, Darius, and the Sasanians. Existing anti-Arab feeling was encouraged so that most educated Iranians came to feel that the inferior Arabs had caused Iran's backwardness by imposing their religion and ways. The break between the bourgeois-nationalist culture of the elite and the Islamic culture of the masses and bazaar classes increased with time. Radical nationalism *a 'la* Kasravi remained a trend among the educated classes.

Ataturk and his followers encouraged an ethnic nationalism which lost nothing in force from the fact that it was based on shaky intellectual foundations. Ataturk's Turks in Turkey had to adjust to the loss of empire and to the idea, new to most of them, that "Turks" were not just unlettered countryfolk, but a nationality with a proud history. Not having pre-Islamic glories of an Iranian kind, Ataturk and his followers substituted pure inventions—such as the idea that the Anatolian Hittites were Turks, and that Turkish was the root of all human languages. The "artificiality" of these ideas did not bring discontent or instability. Turkey, in fact, has had several advantages in maintaining itself in the modern world. Among these are its long history of Western contact and internal reform; the unique role of Ataturk as *gazi* (significantly, an Islamic term)—the hero who beat the foreigner-infidel in the post–First World War fighting; and the relative homogeneity of modern Turkey and its overwhelming Turkish-speaking Muslim identity. For all the recent rise of Islamic counter-movements, Turkey remains the most secular of Muslim states, and none of its secular law codes has yet been repealed.

None the less, the masses, especially in rural areas and among recent urban migrants, continue to identify strongly with Islam, regarding the Muslim marriage rather than the civil one as important, for example. While opposition has arisen from both the Marxist left and from Islamic movements, the latter appear to have a wider appeal, and Islamic politics have had a growing influence, both in the opposition and in the government.

The state-backed ideologies of Ataturk and Reza Shah, including strong national identification, indentification with the leader, a downplaying of traditional Islam and its leaders, new freedoms for women, and stress on self-strengthening, were highly appropriate to their building of a modern, centralised national state, complete with new armies, bureaucracies, school systems, and so forth. They were also appropriate to the state or state-backed capitalism which encouraged the growth of factory industry and the end of capitulations (tariff privileges and extra-territoriality for Western countries). The partial liberation of women allowed them to enter parts of the modern labour market as teachers, nurses, secretaries and in certain other positions. Although Reza Shah was more authoritarian and less lettered than Ataturk, and hence less popular with intellectuals, he had much more intellectual and professional support than later Iranian writers usually claim. While his Iranian nationalist ideology was more "natural" than Ataturk's Turkish one, being based on several prior Iranian dynasties, it was ultimately less successful among the people as a whole than Ataturk's "artificial" ideology, mainly because Reza Shah lacked Ataturk's past as a national hero. The Iranian ulama also retained under Reza Shah powers that the Turkish ulama lost under Ataturk or even before—the economic power given by their direct collection of *zadat* and *khums* taxes (a Shi'a feature), more control over *vaqf* property and income, and more retention of Islamic schools and religious powers. Hence, the Iranian ulama, long more powerful than the ulama elsewhere in the Middle East, remained in a position to stage a comeback after Reza Shah was forced by Britain and Russia to abdicate in 1941.

The official ideologies of Reza Shah and Ataturk contained features already found in the Muslim modernists (rationalised and partly secularised Islam) and in early nationalists (stress on the national pas t and the superiority of one's own nation), but like other state or governmental ideologies they did not simply adopt intellectual systems from pre-existing intellectuals. Rather, those features of earlier systems of thought that were appropriate to the goals of the state were chosen, whether consciously or unconsciously. Both Islamic modernism and nationalism in fact borrowed heavily from Western liberal and nationalist thought systems. Modernism found new values in the Islamic past, just as less liberal Muslims are doing today. In the case of nationalism, such values were found in the national past, and it was natural not to acknowledge a debt to the West, as each nation tried to convince itself of its own superiority.

What Defines Ideology

An important, and insufficiently studied, aspect of ideology is the question "Who is the Enemy?" against whom a given ideology is chiefly directed. In a classic study of medieval Islamic ideologies, Claude Cahen has noted that the same intellectual movement may have had opposite social meanings according to who was the powerful enemy the movement opposed—and opposite-seeming ideological trends may similarly have allied social roles in relation to rulers with objectively similar roles but different ideologies. In the post-war Muslim world the strength among intellectuals of Islamist ideologies is often in inverse proportion to its strength in ruling groups opposed by most intellectuals. Notably in Pakistan today, even though Islamic terminology is *de rigueur*, there are very few intellectuals with a really Islamist outlook, and this is largely because of the unpopularity of a government that calls itself Islamic. On the other hand, in Egypt, Tunisia, and pre-revolutionary Iran Islamism is or was on the upswing, largely because the government opposed by intellectuals and others was or is largely secular, and also seen as subservient to the secular West.

The papers in this book mostly stress another important aspect of ideology, its class basis, which is crucial, but which does not in itself allow us to predict or understand what ideology will be followed by a given class at a given time and place. The petty-bourgeoisie, for example, is notorious for switching ideologies, yet these switches are not random, but reflect given time situations. The petty bourgeoisie as well as what Alavi calls the "salariat" and also the big bourgeoisie tended to rally round nationalist, secularising, national unity ideologies when these were seen as the most effective way to overcome weak monarchies dependent on the West and backed by old land-owning and clerical classes, and to set up strong nation-states. This was the case in Pahlavi Iran, Ataturk's Turkey, and Nasser's Egypt. All three brought in significant reforms from the top, promoted private and/or state capitalism, and brought landlords and religious institutions under state control. As noted above, it is state control of religion rather than separation of church and state that constitutes what is often misleadingly called the "secularism" of these regimes. Although Nasser's rule is with reason considered more radical and socialist than were Ataturk and the Pahlavis, the difference is smaller than rhetoric would suggest. The land reforms of the late Shah were as extensive as Nasser's, while Nasser's nationalisations did not result in permanent dispossession of the local bourgeoisie. What ties the Ataturk, Pahlavi, and Nasserist ideologies and movements together is their stress on national unity, on reform, on centralised bureaucratic controls, and on opposition to a prior weak monarchy that was complaisant to foreigners. The importance of overcoming weakness and foreign control while playing down internal class differences that might lead to internal strife brought forth totalistic and radical-sounding ideologies. The Islam faced by the three regimes, at least at the beginning of their rule and even later, found its representatives in an ulama who had ties to traditional ways and to traditional landlords (ulama were often large landlords themselves, or guardians of large landed *waqf* properties). A regime that wanted, as all three did, to expand secular education and a modern unified judicial system, and to introduce other modern institutions, would naturally want to control the ulama as much as possible. Nasser's ideology differs from the secular nationalism of Ataturk and the Pahlavis in stressing Arab unity, and even larger Islamic and African spheres, but as time went on Nasser had to fall back increasingly on Egyptian national conditions and interests.

The rise of Islamist movements in the Middle East, beginning especially in the 1960s and growing in the 1970s and 1980s, is not at all a traditional phenomenon or a return to the medieval, as some think, but is largely a reaction of dissatisfied groups and classes to the areas of failure of secular nationalism. As secular nationalism may be seen as a response to weak foreign-backed old regimes on the part especially of several educated classes, so Islamism is largely a reaction to successor nationalist regimes, like the three mentioned above. As Alavi's paper suggests, this is true even in Pakistan, whose founders were secularists, as was Zulfiqar Ali Bhutto, against whose secularising populist regime an Islamist movement broke out. In the case of Pakistan Islam has a special role as the *raison d'être* of the state and the only apparent glue holding together ethnic groups, but the country is, none the less, less unique than it may seem.

Reasons for the Variable Strength of Islamism

The term "Islamism", which apparently originated in both Arabic and French in North Africa, and has begun to be used in English, is used in place of the inaccurate and resented "fundamentalism" and the overly vague "Islamic Revival" and the like. Although some dislike "Islamism," it has the great practical value of being the term most acceptable to Muslims. "Islamism" refers to twentieth-century movements for political Islam, usually aiming overtly or covertly at an Islamic state that would enforce at least some Islamic laws and customs, including those related to dress, sex segregation, and some economic measures and Qur' anic punishments. Outsiders and even insiders often have the impression of a trend sweeping the entire Muslim world, but my own extensive travels from Indonesia to Senegal in the summer of 1983 through late 1986 (three long summers plus all of 1985) do not support the view of Islamism as a major force everywhere. I here recount some of my experiences, impressions, and readings, all of which suggest that Islamism tends to be strong in certain specific circumstances, and weak in others.

To begin with, Islamism is not strong in states which are *really* largely traditional and have not experienced a major Western cultural impact, though such states are increasingly rare as Westernisation impinges almost everywhere. The people in such states may still follow a number of Islamic laws, but militant mass movements calling for an Islamic state and the end of Western influence are relatively small. The prime example of such a state in my travels was the Yemen Arab Republic (North Yemen), as of 1983, though Islamism has developed considerably since then. In North Yemen republicans overthrew a traditionalist Imam (leader of the Zaida Fiver Shi'a line) in 1962, and still had to fight for several years with Nasser's help against the Saudi-backed monarchists. The Imam of Yemen had tried to keep out Western influences, and though he was not wholly successful, he was largely so. Yemeni emigration to Saudi Arabia, the US, and elsewhere has brought in large remittances, so that Japanese cars, trucks, VCRs, video cameras, and so forth, are plentiful, but major elements of law and custom remain traditional and are considered Islamic. Law is a codified sharia; most women veil; and many are secluded in the home. Even within "tradition" there are changes, as unveiled village women have been made to veil by their religious leaders once modern roads brought in strangers, and many urban women sport the top-to-toe black skirt, cape and face veil that used to be reserved by the Imam's family. Its rapid spread after the Imam's overthrow led it to be called "the banner of the revolution." The spread of such veiling differs from Islamism's conscious "return to Islam." The most "modern" female costume, worn by students and some professional women, is called the *balto* (a word of Franco-Russo-Egyptian derivation). This is a long, unbelted raincoat worn over blue jeans, topped by a headscarf. When I was in Yemen, students were turning to this "modern" dress, not to the veil. Yemen (as of 1983) had neither the large, alienated, educated class, nor the extensive break with traditional culture that would encourage a major Islamist movement, although elements of socio-economic change and the forced return of emigrant workers as a result of declines in oil production and world-wide recession may be bringing in a significant alienated class. It is not certain that under Yemeni conditions such a class would turn to Islamism, but could. Eye-witness reports in 1986 say that the Muslim Brethren have grown, encouraged by Egyptian teachers and intellectuals.

The profile of countries with strong Islamist movements nearly always includes the following. The country should have had one or more nationalist governments which tried to unify the country by relying more on national than Islamic ideology. It should have experienced rapid economic development and dislocations, which have brought rapid urbanisation and visibly diffential treatment for the urban poor and the urban rich. Although not all such countries have oil income, virtually all have profited from oil economies at least at second hand, and oil income has hastened the urbanisation and income gaps, corruption, and visible wealth for the few that have made many responsive to the Islamists' call for unity, simplicity, and honesty. In addition, countries ripe for Islamism have experienced a longer and more radical break with an Islamically-orientated past government and society than is true of a country like Yemen. Most have experienced a heavy Western impact and control and Western and secularly orientated governments.

The above characteristics are derived from reading and observation, though naturally to generalise meaningfully one must be able to see which of the multiplicity of trends within each country would be likely to encourage Islamism. Since the generalisations were derived from experience, however, it is not surprising that they fit experience. Iran, for example, is a prime case of a country where the rulers tried to suppress Islamic and customary ways and laws, where a huge oil income allowed rapid economic change and over-rapid urbanisation, and where Western influence was acutely felt. Also, on the ideological level, Islamism was encouraged by the late Shah and his father actively suppressed Islamic ways and were thoroughly identified with Western, non-Islamic powers. Egypt is another country ripe for Islamist trends and movements, which have been growing. Although not an oil economy, Egypt in recent decades has been almost a "*rentier* state," living not on the production and export of goods, but on the export of workers and professionals, primarily to oil countries, and on foreign aid. Sadat was seen by many Egyptians in much the same way as the late Shah was by many Iranians—as an American-supported collaborator with Israel whose economic policies benefited old and new elites while bypassing the needy. Mubarak has tried to steer a more Arab-orientated course, but it is unclear if this will help him solve Egypt's overwhelming economic problems, especially in a period of worldwide oil slump and economic difficulties.

The influence of moderate or radical Islamism in Egyptian cities is striking to a visitor who had not been there between 1964 and 1985. While in 1964 very few women showed concern for Islamic dress, now most do, although covering-up takes numerous forms. It ranges from the top-to-toe gloved outfits of Islamist students, to the modified look of calf-length skirts and long-sleeved, high-necked blouses, with scarves worn tied behind the hair which is the minimum costume. Even foreign residents often adopt the latter dress as it generally keeps one from being hassled or annoyed. Many women in Egypt and elsewhere defend Islamic dress by saying that it keeps male co-workers from seeing and perceiving them as sex-objects, which may be true, but I have yet to hear any of them say that young men should be socialised not to harass girls and women, even if they are not in "Islamic dress."

More dramatic has been the continuation of extremist Muslim movements, some of which are discussed in Gilles Kepel's recent book. And even more threatening to some has been what many call "the unholy alliance" between recently permitted opposition groups and parties—specifically the hitherto secular Wafd Party and the Muslim Brethren, today the least militant of Egypt's Islamist groups. A prominent scholar and member of Egypt's Human Rights organisation assured me that the Muslim Brethren, having seen how Human Rights groups defended them when they were persecuted, are now convinced believers in human rights, free speech, and the like. One may be permitted some scepticism, as human rights are generally popular with persons who follow totalistic ideologies when they are out of power, but are almost never supported by them when in power.

Tunisia is a country with some features favouring Islamism, especially the rule since 1956 of President Bourguiba and his followers, who have enforced a secular, nationalist, and pro-Western orientation. Some of the burden of flight from the country-side has been absorbed by emigration, usually conditional on work, to places like Libya and France. With those countries now making Tunisians leave, Tunisia faces new economic difficulties. A series of riots and risings in recent years, aimed against a rise in bread prices or having more political goals, suggests that ferment may be as great in Tunisia as in Egypt. In this situation there have been various moves back from secularism somewhat reminiscent of the last years before Iran's Islamic Revolution. Like Egypt and pre-revolutionary Iran, Tunisia has several Islamically-orientated groups. The mildest is a small group of intellectuals, known as progressive Islamists, who put out a journal called 15/21 (fifteenth Muslim, twenty-first Christian century), oppose militant political activity, and favour an Islamic dialogue with Western and Christian thinkers. The most militant group is part of an international clandestine organisation, the Islamic Liberation Party, and its members have been arrested and blamed for assassinations of prominent figures. In between, and the most important, is the Islamic Tendency Movement, MTI, led by men with some Islamic training who have also had a Western-style education. Recently the MTI has stressed its moderate and democratic side in the hope, abortive thus far, of gaining a permit to publish legally and to be a political party. MTI leaders were arrested and jailed for a time, but then freed. Their published programme contains nothing illegal, and, as in Egypt, there are some secular Tunisian oppositionists who take the programme at face value and wish to work with the MTI. However, the vagueness of their leader's discourse when he describes the second, Islamic, phase that follows the democratic phase; the militance of the student followers of MTI who won control of the University of Tunis student union; and a secret document that has been published outlining their clandestine goals and tactics, indicate that democracy is just a way-station for the MTI.

MTI leaders are clever in questioning government policies without putting forth Islamic alternatives that might be controversial. They call for a referendum to review Tunisia's reformist Personal Status Code , but do not say what they want in its place. Thus a male MTI leader could tell me that women have more rights than men under the code, while a young woman lawyer in the MTI said review was needed because the code is patriarchal and favours men!

As in many countries, Islamism of the MTI variety has an appeal for many young women. Meeting together they get mutual support and also learn how to argue articulately. They, like Islamist women elsewhere, wear a recognisable "uniform." In Tunisia they wear long dresses in plain colours, usually belted, and a large scarf, tied in front. They consider that this uniform shows that they are Islamic activists and also not open to sexual advances. Some girls actually gain freedom by becoming Islamists: they were formerly never allowed to go out alone, but now can go to mosques or meetings. Also, they can reject marriage partners chosen by their parents on the grounds that they are not sufficiently Islamic. These advantages also apply to many Islamist women outside Tunisia. It seems that Islamism can present a cultural alternative that many men and women do not find in school or in the official discourse, both of which are highly Western and secular. In this way Tunisia somewhat resembles pre-revolutionary Iran. Secular or feminist-orientated Tunisians have a discourse hardly distinguishable from Westerners, and know much more about Foucault or de Beauvoir than they do about Islamic thought, which in general is barely taught in the schools. This creates a gap between the Frenchified group with good secondary or higher education and the masses; in one way the gap is even greater in Tunisia than in Iran, as the educated group may speak French by perference, and often cannot deliver a talk in Arabic, while the masses generally know only Tunisian Arabic.

In both Tunisia and Egypt, it is important to remember that the Islamists are not the only opponents of the regime, and various secular groups and parties exist at different points of the left-right scale. Nevertheless, the Islamists can have a great appeal in an age of cultural and economic crisis, and so they should be taken seriously.

In my travels I spent brief periods in two countries where Islamism has a special point of appeal greater than in Tunisia and Egypt—namely, Nigeria (northern), and Malaysia. Both countries fit the "Islamist" profile of oil-producing countries that have undergone rapid economic and social change and migration to cities, and both have also experienced nationalist governments. It appears to me that the main reason why Islamism is important in these countries is that in both Muslims make up a plurality (or a small majority in Nigeria) who have not been able thus far to impose their will as much as they wish on the large minority populations. In both countries the Muslim plurality is also relatively economically backward, and would like more economic favours to enable them to get ahead of the other communities. In Malaysia the two principal non-Muslim communities are the larger Chinese one and the smaller Indian one, and it has been noted that a Muslim immigrant from Indonesia will immediately be regarded as a native, while a fifth-generation Chinese will not. Although Malaysia's current government has favoured the mainly Muslim Malay community by a variety of economic concessions, this has not satisfied all of them. Early on the Muslims adopted a formula that would give them a fictitious majority; if they had called themselves Muslims, or even Malay-speakers, it would have been clear that they were not in a majority, so the term "Bumiputra" ("sons of the soil") was adopted, which lumped together with its Malay-Muslim majority "natives" of island Malaysia who were neither Muslim nor Malay. The leading Islamist party, PAS, wishes to enforce the sharia in all Malaysia, which could hardly be more felicitous than it was in Sudan. When I was Malaysia in 1984 PAS had referred to the ruling Muslims as unbelievers, and there was talk of a debate between PAS and the ruling party, though each side demanded different terms for a debate. There were also PAS-supported risings in "backward" areas. The government was pleased to have brought some Islamic leaders into its fold, especially—as a minister—the leader of the Muslim Youth Movement, Anwar Ibrahim. This made it hard for PAS to monopolise Islamist sentiment. Government moves to incorporate Islamist leaders, and policies like Islamic banking and home loans, helped reduce PAS's appeal.

Women in Islamist dress were numerous in Malaysia in 1984, but the dress was a world away from that found in Iran. It was a form-fitting sarong and long-sleeved top, both generally in bright colors, and a kind of light cowl headdress, often fastened by jewellery. My Iranian ayatollah informants who noted that the whole point of Islamic dress was for women not to be noticed would not have been pleased, and one Malay specialist called it the dress of "sexy nuns." When I spoke to a women's group at one university I found a clear generation gap; scarcely any of the teachers or other middle-aged women wore Islamist dress, while all students did. The older women said that students were coerced by peer pressure into dressing and behaving in an Islamist way.

Malaysia has features that have reduced the appeal of oppositional Islamism, as demonstrated by the defeat of PAS in the 1986 elections. Besides the incorporation into the government of Islamist leaders and policies (which may, however, have increased the Chinese opposition vote), the government is almost unique in allowing Islamists to have a legal party and contest elections. This made PAS pronouncements *appear* strong, but also allowed the government to gauge the opposition and counter its appeal. Malaysia is significant in showing the oppositional Islamists can be reduced. It is possible that legalising Islamist parties in some other countries might decrease, not increase, their appeal, although only if accompanied by policies to meet mass grievances.

The main comparative point is that Malaysia, like Nigeria, not only meets the general criteria of a country favouring Islamism, but has the added feature that the Islamist path is seen by many Muslims as a way to overcome their backwardness *vis-a-vis* other communities, and to forge ahead economically and politically. As elsewhere, questions about the rights and status of minorities are generally met with vague remarks about Islamic tolerance and the flourishing of minorities under Islamic rule.

Nigeria, like Malaysia, has had Muslim rulers for decades, but as in Malaysia, this is insufficient to satisfy Islamists. Nigeria with its population of about 95 million, about half Muslim, is by far the most populous state in Africa, with by far the most Muslims. Discussion of Nigerian Islamism is difficult, as there is not a single Islamist group, and Westerners often mix up a radical heretical group that was involved in urban risings in the early 1980s; radical Islamist and Khomeinist mainly student groups; and the old Muslim elite, including lawyers and judges, who have been calling for a return to sharia law. To an extent the last two are related, but the last one is in some measure more conservative and traditionalist than Islamist. Under the British protectorate, the sharia did have a larger role in Northern Nigeria, and so those who call for the application of the sharia are not far-out utopians necessarily—they may actually be calling for a return to a system under which they flourished more than they do now. What is newly powerful in the Islamist *Yan Izala* group is its "Wahabi" attacks on the Sufi orders. Also new is the movement to extend the sharia to the South, which is strongly resisted by southern non-Muslims.

Student radical Islam is another matter, and as in many countries Nigerian Islamists are strongest at the universities. Although Khomeini's Iran is the only popular model for many Islamists everywhere, the two places I travelled where Khomeini seemed most popular (not counting the Shi'a of Pakistan who have a sectarian identification with him but are not planning a Khomeinist revolt) were Northern Nigeria and Malaysia. One might guess that Khomeini's popularity increases with the square of the distance from Iran, but this, though it has some merit as an idea, would not account for his apparently lesser popularity in the more distant Senegal and Indonesia. Rather, I would guess that the same factor of economically and educationally backward communities that want to impose an Islamic state so as to put dominant economic and political power in Muslim hands operates in both. Among Nigerian radicals only Khomeini, I was told more than once, is considered a truly Islamic ruler, largely because of his radical Islamic rhetoric and programme and his revolutionary path to power. Islamist students were very angry at a talk I gave at a northern university in which I tried to show that Khomeini's Islamic revolution was not replicable elsewhere, as it was heavily based on the power and independence of Iran's Shi'i ulama, even though other Islamic revolutionary paths might be possible. Not only was I openly accused of being a CIA agent sent in to talk them out of revolution, but I was told that since they had not heard of Shi'ism until a few years ago, it must be an American invention to split the Muslims. (Such a reaction is not exclusive to Nigerian students—some of my Tunisian students in Paris in 1977 were suspicious of my mention of Arab Shi'a.)

In Northern Nigeria I had the privilege of being an observer at a three-day conference of Muslim women. This was one of many experiences that indicated that self-consciously Muslim women's groups and the behaviour they advocate are far from being the wholly negative phenomenon that Westerners often think. For in this gathering educated women Muslim leaders insisted that the large audience, mostly of college students, should insist on such rights as the right to be educated, the right to work and to carry out respectable activities outside the home. In an area where many women are secluded in the home and rarely can go out, this insistence was clearly one that would better the position of women. So too were rights in the family, where a pro-woman view of Islamic injunctions was presented. On the other hand, the leaders stressed that Muslim women should not join inter-faith organisations or follow their programme.

If Islamism is strong in Nigeria and Malaysia, it should be realised that anti-Islamism is also very strong. The secular Muslims of these countries appreciate what tensions would be brought in along with Islamic laws and practices, especially if they were imposed on non-Muslims. So many Muslims and all non-Muslims oppose the Islamist programme, but economic and other difficulties may none the less increase Islamist strength. In Nigeria there have been controversial government moves early in 1986 to join an international Islamic organization, which may have been aimed partly at appeasing Islamists, but alarmed secularists and non-Muslims.

Last, I shall deal with countries where Islamism is apparently not strong, even though, unlike North Yemen, they have moved far from traditional ways. One of these is Senegal, where the weakness of Islamism may be tied to the peculiar interaction of Islam and politics. Instead of having a single class of ulama, as in most Muslim countries, Senegal is still dominated by Islamic orders, especially the large and nearly equally strong Tijaniya and Muridiya (a local twentieth-century order). These orders offer support to politicians in return for patronage and favours, and they are rivals to one another. One might almost say that for many loyalty to Islam in the abstract is replaced by loyalty to an order, and that each order vies for influence. In this situation one has vertical, not horizontal, religious groups and identification, and it would be hard for an all-Islamic movement to get far. The Catholic ex-president, Leopold Senghor, was sometimes ridiculed by Westerners for giving so much attention and patronage to Islamic orders, but in so doing he helped to perpetuate divisions among Muslims and to forestall Islamic unity against Christians and animists; his Muslim successor does the same. Among the highly educated there are movements for greater Islamic orthodoxy and all-Islamic identity, but as yet no major radical Islamist movements. In addition, Senegal has seen less rapid socio-economic change than Islamist-profile countries. A small Islamist current has, however, developed in recent years.

Another non-Islamist area visited was West Sumatra, in Indonesia. Although there have been Islamist trends in Indonesia, I found almost none in West Sumatra, except one from a student of the Technical University of Bandung, Java, which is the centre of student Islamism. (In all countries that I know of, scientific and technical students are the most Islamist—this was dramatically true in Iran and also in Tunisia.) To look only at West Sumatra, an area I know: here is an area which does not have the profile of an Islamist region; it has had very little industry, its cities are not overcrowded with migrants, and living standards are relatively egalitarian (this may be true of Indonesia in general). Most women wear either Western or Indonesian dress and do not cover their hair. In addition, West Sumatra is a matrilineal society, and although its inhabitants are very strict about prayer and the other "5 pillars" of Islam, they would not want to change their matrilineal landholding and inheritance system in order to conform to Islamic law. However, the crucial point is probably the lack of rapid economic change and inequalities.

The figures for Islamist trends versus non-Islamist trends in the countries discussed thus far are four with such trends being important: Egypt, Tunisia, Malaysia, and Nigeria; and three where they are less important or unimportant: Sumatra, Yemen, Senegal. With my last two countries the majority turns in favour of those with weak Islamism, though if one considers Yemen to be borderline as of 1986, it is a draw.

In my brief observation I would say that true Islamism is weak in Syria. The government appears to be generally successful in defending the rights of minorities, which include not only its own Alawi group, but various Christians, Jews, Druze and Shi'a. If it is true, as it appears to be, that many Sunnis identify with the Sunni Muslim Brethren, this does not mean that most of them would like to enforce a Sunni Islamic state. Rather, they would like to see the Sunni majority favoured in politics and economics. In Syria there seems to be considerable appreciation of the problems that may come from stressing sectarian identity, or giving one religious group the chance to enforce religious law. Hence I would doubt that true Islamism is growing in Syria, which also does not seem to have the socio-economic profile of a state that encourages the growth of Islamism. This is said tentatively, as Westerners say that the two questions not to discuss in Syria are religion and politics, and it is difficult to do in a brief visit. Nor must one forget the brutal suppression of a Muslim Brethren–sponsored rising in Hama.

More dramatic is my final instance, the case of Pakistan, which many Westerners, at least until the April 1986 return and huge rallies of Benazir Bhutto, assumed was a supporter of Islamism. Visting Pakistan in the autumn of 1985 and in 1986, I was struck that in conversations with a wide range of intellectuals, including members of Islamic organisations, I found only one man who defended the Zia Government . I met him on my last day in 1985 in Karachi, and that night had dinner with a senior literary figure and his sons and told them about it. They pressed me to say who it was who had defended the government, but I prudently decided not to say; one son burst out laughing and said, "You see what Pakistan is like; she has to protect the identity of someone because he favours our government!"

One may say, with the examples of Zia, Numeiry is Sudan, and probably ultimately Khomeini and his followers, that there is nothing like having a government that calls itself Islamic to discredit Islamism. Zia's government has done this in various ways. For the popular masses he has not brought significant economic or social improvements, and education, health, and social welfare remain at abysmally low levels, despite overall economic growth.

In addition, his policies have offended several key groups, who have generally mounted a more militant and effective opposition than have their counterparts elsewhere in the Islamic world. Pakistan has the most effective and militant women's movement of any Muslim country I know. It originated as a coalition of women's groups, mostly professional, in response to Zia's proposed Islamisation laws that would reduce the status of women. The most important such law fought by the new coalition organisation, the Women's Action Forum, was the law of evidence, which made the testimony of one man equal to that of two women. Women on peaceful marches protesting against this law were beaten and jailed, but that did not stop them. Although the law went through, there seems no doubt that continued protests by women and their male allies slowed down much of the rest of Zia's Islamisation programme. For example, the proposal for separate higher education for women has not got off the ground. The ruling that women television broadcasters must cover their hair brought the resignation of one prominent woman, while the others now wear filmy chiffon scarves over the back of their hair (of Hollywood 1930s glamour style), show the rest of their hair, and wear make-up and jewellery. (Indeed, there are very few women in Islamist dress in Pakistan; those who veil and cover their hair are in a minority and are generally popular class or tribal women in traditional dress.) Women's continued activism was almost certainly largely responsible for making Zia set up an activist "Women's Division" in his government, and also create a Commission on Women, whose 1985 report, under appropriate Qur'anic quotations, was almost entirely egalitarian. It remains unpublished and, like the reports of many US Govenment commissions, unacted upon.

Zia's regime has had what may turn out to be a long-term benefit; as discourse must be Islamic, it has forced many women and other activists to study Islam, and to learn Qur'anic and legal precedents for their programmes. This means that secular or semi-secular oppositionists are not nearly as alienated from the masses and the Islamic petty bourgeoisie as was the case in Iran. It does *not* mean that, like the Iranian Ali Shariati and some contemporary Egyptian intellectuals, Pakistan's intellectuals are compromising on such issues as equal rights for women; rather they are finding Islamic precendents for this. In delivering an endowed lecture at Radcliffe College in 1985, Benazir Bhutto insisted that the Qu'ran was egalitarian for women. This brought negative letters from several Westerners and Muslims, but Benazir was only following the general pattern of Pakistani oppositionists, which is aimed at defending equality and making that defence more acceptable by tying it to Islam. This is the *modus operandi* of the Women's Action Forum, and it seems worse than useless to question its sincerity or its accuracy in depicting what was meant by the Qu'ran in the seventh century.

Another group offended by Zia's Islamisation have been the Shi'a (which in Pakistan and most countries means the larger, Twelver Shi'a—the Isma'ilis are apolitical in accord with the instructions of their imam, the Aga Khan). Every country that has tried Islamisation has found that by enforcing one branch of Islamic Law it offends Muslim minorities—this includes the minority Sunnis in Iran and the minority Shi'a in Saudi Arabia. In Pakistan the Shi'a, like the women's organisations, became more activist as a result of Zia's policies. The first object of Shi'a opposition was Zia's ruling that *zakat* be collected by a 2-1/2 per cent tax on bank accounts. The Shi'a pointed out that their zakat tax did not go to the government, but to religious leaders, *mujtahids*. They had strong enough demonstrations that the govenment was forced to rule that anyone who signed an affidavit that the zakat law was against his or her *fiqh* was exempt from it. The saying in Pakistan was the Zia had done more than anyone to create Shi'a, as a number of Sunnis (in a situation where there are no formalities for conversion to Shi'ism) declared themselves Shi'a to escape the tax. In the autumn of 1985 when I visited Pakistan, Zia was still trying to extend Muslim law (meaning Hanafi Sunni law), and the Shi'a were still objecting that Shi'a law differed on numerous points, and if Sunni law were to be applied to Sunnis, then Shi'a law should be applied to Shi'a. Some of the Shi'a lawyers engaged in finding all the differences between schools that they could were really aiming at killing the whole idea of promoting Islamic law: "Scratch a Shi'a and Find a Secularist" was an apt expression I heard more than once, and one that would apply to most minorities, Muslim and non-Muslim, in the Islamic world.

While middle-class and wealthy Shi'a tended to be secularists, for many this does not preclude admiration for Khomeini as a great anti-imperialist Shi'a. Popular-class Shi'a mostly admired Khomeini, whose name and picture were found in homes in the remotest areas. This should not, I think, be taken as a sign of widespread militant Islamism so much as of admiration of a Shi'i hero who had put Shi'ism on the map and made it more prideful to identify as a Shi'a. There are, however, pro-Khomeini militant Islamists in Pakistan.

The Pakistani Shi'i Westernised middle class had an attitude towards Shi'ism radically different from the Iranian Shi'i Westernised middle class. I asked several educated Pakistani Shi'a what they identified Shi'ism with, both as children and now, and overwhelmingly they spoke of the justice, egalitarianism, and selfsacrifice of Ali and Husain, which they identified with their current democratic (and in one case left socialist) values. When I asked the same question of educated Iranians, they identified Shi'ism with mourning, self-flagellation, fanaticism, and the like. This may be mostly the difference between a minority and a majority community, but is also a general situation that educated Muslim Pakistanis refuse to see Zia's Islam as true Islam, and often study Islam quite deeply to find precedents for a different kind of Islam.

Zia's encouragement of a rigid Sunni Islam has alienated Sunnis and also helped produce Sunni-Shi'a tensions expressed in murderous rioting in the Punjab in Moharram (September) 1986.

Another group in Pakistan who have been militantly active against Zia are lawyers' associations, who in many marches, publications, and demonstrations have taken the place of the banned political parties. Their members have also been beaten and jailed, but they have kept up activity. Much of the press has also been increasingly oppositional as Zia's absolute controls were weakened, and in late 1985 important newspapers like Karachi's *Dawn* and Islamabad's *The Muslim* were largely oppositional, as was the serious popular magazine *The Herald*, whose editors are mostly women. Finally, the political parties continued to exist, and even to be constantly referred to in the press as the "(banned) Pakistan People's Party," and so forth. The latter party, the populist party of Zulfiqar Ali Bhutto, who was overthrown by Zia in 1977 and executed in 1979, remains that most popular party in the heterogeneous opposition coalition called Movement for the Restoration of Democracy. Benazir Bhutto is the PPP's chief leader, and her huge rallies are an indication of her and the Party's support. The popularity of a young, non-Islamist, Western educated woman as the heir apparent of the opposition is one indication of how little popular support Islamism now has.

Although nobody can predict the future, it seems that Islamism at present is not as strong worldwide as is sometimes suggested. It is weak at two ends of the spectrum—places like Senegal, Syria, and Sumatra, which do not fit the Islamist socio-economic and political-cultural profile suggested above, and in countries that do fit the profile, like Egypt and Tunisia, and in a very few countries where a Muslim plurality or slight majority wants to increase its economic and legal power, like Nigeria and Malaysia. Naturally there are specific local situations and traditions that influence and modify the large generalisations made above, but since such general comparisons are rarely made and can be illuminating, it seems worth while to hazard them. Some countries may still have to live through the experience of Islamist government (which has several models—Pakistan is not like Iran) before becoming disillusioned with its excesses, while in others like Sudan and Pakistan, it is or may be on its way out. The frequent Western (or Islamist) picture of a constant growth of Islamism nearly everywhere in recent years is an over-simplification that can be rectified by local and comparative studies of the Islamist phenomenon.

A final point concerns the image of Khomeini and the Iranian Revolution. Although both have dropped in popularity since the early Muslim enthusiasms of 1979, they still represent the *only* Islamic government taken seriously as such abroad, and still evoke various degrees of admiration among educated and urban groups. Their admirers are not Islamists, however, but include many who see Khomeini as the first Muslim revolutionary who has effectively stood up to the West, especially the US, while keeping equally independent of the USSR. This independence plus Khomeini's reputation for simplicity, probity, and egalitarianism, give him an appeal beyond Islamist circles, even among many who dislike some things about the Islamic republic.

THE ARAB-ISRAELI WARS, NASSERISM, AND THE AFFIRMATION OF ISLAMIC IDENTITY[3]

A visitor to the Arab world cannot but note the intensification of Islamic identity that has taken place in the past several

[3]By Yvonne Haddad, political scientist, from John L. Esposito, ed., *Islam and Development*, pp. 107–121. Copyright © 1980 by Syracuse University Press. Reprinted by permission.

years. The Islamic nature of the area is apparent in the flood of conservative religious literature in the bookstores of Egypt, the availability of Muslim Brotherhood publications in Bathist Damascus, the rise in the number of veiled educated "liberated" women, and the general tenor of the society. The militant actions of Jamiyyat al-Takfir wa-al-Hijrah, the attempt to enforce Islamic laws of reform in Egypt and Kuwait, the permission for Maruf al-Dawalibi to visit Syria, the rising academic respectability of writing texts from the Islamic vantage point—these and many other phenomena can be cited as illustrations of the increased measure of Islamic identity.

The writing of texts from a specifically Muslim perspective, of course, is in part due to the competition among faculty at Egyptian universities for the highly remunerative teaching positions at the many new institutions of higher learning in the Arabian peninsula. Also influential are the academic conferences on Islamic subjects sponsored by these Arabian universities and by the Muslim World League. By focusing on Islamic topics, they have directed historical and social science research into specific channels, and have fostered a network of authors and professors committed to the pursuit of such research.

The rise Islamic consciousness is in no small part the result of the Arab-Israeli wars of 1967 and 1973. It is also the result of political and military realities, realignments and perceptions of these confrontations as well as the end of the Nasser regime and its policies. The existence of Israel in the heart of the Arab world has had a dramatic effect on the growth and development of modernity, reform, and Westernization in the area.

Western historians and social scientists will never be able to understand fully the Arab/Islamic interpretation of the current state of affairs in the Arab world as well as the Muslim view of historical process without coming to terms with the meaning of the existence of Israel for Arabs. Although Israel and its supporters may perceive its existence in the heart of the Arab world as a purveyor of modernity and technology for the area, for Arabs both Muslim and non-Muslim it serves as a constant reminder of their impotence and failure. It is crucial to the understanding of the Islamic view of history to see that for Muslims the existence of Israel is a condemnation and a sign that the forces of darkness and immorality, of wickedness and apostasy, have for reasons yet unexplained, taken the ascendancy in the world.

After thirty years of pain and struggle, of sacrifice and suffering, the Arab cannot fathom why Israel continues to prosper and become stronger while his people are weaker and more helpless. Israel is seen as part of the confrontation and effort at domination of the Arab world by the Western colonial powers. Many publications refer to Zionism as a modern version of the Crusades, an insidious conspiracy of the Western Christian world in its continued hatred and enmity toward Islam. Recent publications about the role of the city of Jerusalem and its central place in Muslim piety echo the concerns of medieval writers who saw in the Crusades an infidel incursion against Islam. Jerusalem must be under Muslim domination in order to guarantee the worship of the true God. Both the Christians and the Jews have deviated from the true way; control of this sacred city must therefore be in the hands of Muslims whom God has appointed to be the guardians of His truth.

The religious significance of the Arab-Israeli conflict was enhanced by the loss of the holy city of Jerusalem (al-Quds). This loss was aggravated by Israel's attempts to Judaize the city through the systematic eradication of its Arab influence. This was carried out by the policy of expropriation of Arab land and the demolition of Arab housing, the expulsion of eminent intellectuals and leaders of the Arab community, and the imposition of the Israeli curriculum on Arab schools which distorted the historical claims Arabs have for Palestine. Israeli policies also encouraged Jewish settlement of the area by providing subsidies for settlers as well as the construction of high-rise apartments, "the cement Jungle," around the Arab sector of Jerusalem aimed at truncating it from other Arab communities and rendering it into a ghetto.

The activities and speeches of Rabbi Shlomo Goren of the Israeli armed forces alerted many Muslims to the possibility of the destruction or expropriation of the Muslim holy places. Besides holding services in the Aqsa Mosque, Rabbi Goren affirmed his intent to rebuild Solomon's Temple (on the grounds where the Mosque now stands). These fears were also fanned by the archeological excavations around the mosque which precipitated the weakening of the existent structures and necessitated the installation of supportive beams. The several Zionist conferences calling for the restoration of Jewish places of worship and the highhanded manner in which the Judaizing policy was and continues to be implemented did little to allay the fears in Arab minds that the Israeli government would seek the eradication of Muslim holy places, especially the Aqsa Mosque because of its historical significance. Thus, the burning of the Mosque on August 21, 1969, by an Australian Christian fanatic escalated the fear of what was perceived as part of the Zionist conspiracy.

The religious significance of the Israeli occupation of the Holy Land and the burning of th Aqsa Mosque in 1969 was reflected in a letter written by Nasser to the armed forces in which he said:

I have waited and thought a great deal about the terrible crime inflicted against the holy of holies of our religion, our history and our civilization. At the end, I did not find anything but the new affirmation of the meanings that were evident to all of us from the first day of our terrible experience. There is no alternative, no hope and no way except through Arab force, using all we are able to muster, to allocate and to pressure with, until the true victory of God is achieved.

We have opened every door to peace, but the enemy of God and our enemy closed every door in the way of peace. We left no means untried, but the enemy of God and our enemy obstructed the means, blocked the roads and made evident to the world what was hidden about his nature and intent.

We are before an enemy who was not satisfied by challenging man, but through his arrogance and insanity transgressed by challenging the sacred places that God blessed and willed as houses for Himself.

I want our men, officers and soldiers to understand the feelings of the last two days and be aware of their meaning, to appropriate in their conscience the conscience of their nation and to know in their depths that they shoulder the responsibility not carried by any army since the descent of revelations from heaven as guidance and mercy for the world.

They, in their next battle, are not the soldiers of their nation only, but the army of God, the protectors of His religions, His houses and His Holy Books.

Their next battle is not a battle of liberation only; it has become necessary for it to be one of purification.

Our vision is focused on the Aqsa Mosque in Jerusalem as it suffers from the forces of evil and darkness.

Whatever our feelings at this moment may be, we pray to God as believers, in awe, that He may grant us patience, knowledge, courage and capacity to remove evil and darkness.

Our soldiers shall return to the courtyards of the Aqsa Mosque. Jerusalem will be returned to what it was prior to the age of imperialism which stove to spread its hegemony on it for centuries until it (Imperialism) gave it to those who play with fire.

We shall return to Jerusalem and Jerusalem will be returned to us. We shall fight for that. We shall not lay down our arms until God grants His soldiers the victory and until His right is dominant, His house respected and true peace is restored to the city of peace.

A flood of literature appeared as an essential response affirming the centrality of Jerusalem for Islam. The Fifth Conference of the Academy of Islamic Research of Al-Azhar in 1970 devoted a substantial part of its proceedings to the topic of the Islamic nature of Jerusalem and Palestine. In his opening speech, Muhammad Fahham, Rector of al-Azhar, affirmed that historically, Arabs were the first to inhabit Jerusalem (3000 B.C.). Jewish settlement in the area came later (1200 B.C.). Consequently, if historical precedence is used as an argument for right of possession the Arabs were the original inhabitants.

Moreover, the religious argument that Palestine is the promised land for the Jews is rejected as obsolete since God's promise had been fulfilled in history and the Jews had forfeited their right to the land having broken the covenant and committed evil. Thus, Jerusalem's religious significance for the Muslims is contingent on the Muslim concept of prophecy which sees all prophets as Muslim since they were sent by God to affirm His guidance for humanity which He initiated with Adam and fulfilled in the Quran as revealed to the prophet Muhammad.

Also, of unique importance is the fact that God has blessed Jerusalem with special significance since He has repeatedly chosen it as the place where His revelation was made manifest. In the case of Islam, its centrality is heightened through its being the place from which Muhammad ascended to heaven during the Isra and Miraj.

Crucial to an understanding of the wars with Israel is the perception of victory and defeat within the Quranic context. The Quran is very explicit that victory will be given to those who are with God. Israel's victories then stand as a condemnation of the Muslim *Ummah*. The Arabs apparently have lost because God has forsaken them. This gives rise to a series of related questions: Has God given the victory to Israel because she has been found more zealous in commitment to His purposes? It is possible that Judiasm is the more correct way of life? Has God forsaken the Muslim nation? What are the reasons for the apparent victory; have the Muslims been tested and found wanting? Each war with Israel has elicited different justifications and reasons, depending on the particular perceptions Muslims have had of themselves.

It has been relatively easy to justify the debacle of 1948. The loss of Palestine can be blamed on the colonial powers, especially Britain, that nursed the Jewish immigrants into a sizable commu-

nity in Palestine and provided them with training and armaments, while decimating the Arab resistance and bleeding its
human and material resources during the disturbances of
1936–39. The Jordanian army in the meantime was led by British
officers who deliberately disobeyed the orders of King Abdullah
in favor of England's command to cease fighting once the demar-
cation lines were reached. Jerusalem, which had already surren-
dered to the Transjordan army, was granted as a gift to the
Israelis by Glubb Pasha.

The defeat of the Syrian forces, meanwhile, was clearly due
to their disorganized condition, lack of leadership, and the trea-
sonable behavior of some government officials. During the
French occupation, which had ceased only three years earlier, the
Syrian army was led by Christians, Alawis, and other minorities
due to France's policy of ruling the majority (Sunni Muslims) by
the use of minorities. Upon gaining independence the Syrian government had removed the core of officers, who had been pawns
of the French regime, rendering the army ill equipped with no
trained officers and in no way ready to fight the Israeli forces.
The Egyptian army was in no better condition. Egypt itself was
occupied by British forces, and the King and government were
puppets administering the policies of the resident British High
Commissioner.

Thus, although the 1948 war ended in defeat of the Arab armies by 1949, genuine reasons and excuses were found to cope
with its disastrous impact. Given the condition of the Arab forces,
it has been easy for Arab historians to understand the ease of the
Israeli victory, especially given the duplicity of the colonial powers in providing Israel with arms while denying the Arab troops
any such assistance during the armistice. The defeat was not only
proof of the present military impotence of the Arab nations; it
also provided a dramatic end to the romantic period in which the
West was perceived by many modernizers as primarily representative of a system worthy of emulation in the search for full participation in the modern world.

Events had been leading in that direction for decades. The occupation of the Arab world by Western forces, the failure of Britain to live up to its agreement after the First World War, the
mockery made of parliaments by occupying forces, the travesty
of the human rights of indigenous citizens, and the steady and insistent support of Western nations for the creation of the state of

Israel put an end to the dreams of the romantics. Any student of the careers of literary and reformist figures such as Taha Husayn, Abbas Mahmud al-Aqqad, Sayyid Qutb, and Ahmad Amin can find in their writings the shock of realization that the West they loved and championed had spurned them again as unfit partners. These and other authors turned back to their roots in an attempt to find a more authentic existence and a reliable *raison d'etre*. For each one the creation of the state of Israel was incomprehensible. The West that had promised so much had in the end jilted them, not because they did not measure up to its requirements but for the specific reason that they were Arabs. By treating them as nonpersons the West not only violated Arab faith, but in effect invalidated their very existence.

The revolt of 1952 in Egypt has welcomed by the masses and the army because it eliminated the discredited leadership under King Farouk that was a puppet of the British and had proved impotent in Palestine. Also backing the revolt was the Muslim Brotherhood organization, then in its heyday of power. It rejected the West not because it had failed to live up to its promise as did the romantics; rather it rejected it because of what the West was, alien, and therefore potentially leading Arabs astray from the true path of Islam. The Brotherhood, along with the conservative Muslims, maintained that the Muslims were weak because they had abandoned Islam. The Muslims were in the condition they find themselves in, defeated and backward, because they had ceased to strive for God's purposes and consequently God had abandoned them. For the Arabs to regain their position of leadership, of ascendancy, and of power, they must cease to champion alien ideologies, put away the worship of the gods of materialism and technology, and return to the true faith and a life committed to the way of God in obedience and humility. Only then would God give victory over the enemies of Islam. The Muslim Brotherhood was not opposed to technology. It established factories in different areas of Egypt to provide sources of employment, and was progressive to the point of organizing unions for workers and championing their rights. Its main creed was that to be modern is not to be Western, but to be truly Muslim, recognizing the traditions of Islam and its authority over all aspects of life, seeking answers to today's problems from within the Quranic revelation which is eternally sufficient and valid.

Others reacted to the creation of Israel by calling for a rearmament program that could match Israeli power and be able to replace the foreign rule that was established on Arab land. What was most galling to them was the fact that while most colonies were winning their freedom from colonial rule, the British with the might of the Americans planted an alien people in the heart of the Arab world. The Israelis were seen as tools by which the colonial powers would suppress the hopes and wills of the burgeoning Arab nations.

Rejection of the West, of course, was not the only response to the 1948 war. Some actually called for a renunciation of all Arab culture and the total appropriation of Western technology on the grounds that Israel's victory is the proof that to be modern one has to be Western. In this understanding traditional moral and ethical considerations must be renounced and the "new morality" of might over right adopted. Israel has provided the perfect example of this kind of modern morality in which people count only in so far as they can successfully fight for their rights. The United Nations, on which was pinned all hope for the ushering in of an era of brotherhood, human rights, and equality, turned out to be a tool in the hands of the imperialist Western forces. True justice was ignored in favor of force and the might of arms as thousands of Palestinians were thrown from their homes in order to make room for the European Jews that Europe and the United States did not want.

The second major confrontation between the Arabs and Israel occurred in 1956. It confirmed for the Arabs Israel's role in the area as an agent of imperialism and colonialism. The confrontation came as a result of collusion between the governments of Britain, France, and Israel as a response to Nasser's nationalization of the Suez Canal. Rebuffed by John Foster Dulles because he had purchased arms from Czechoslovakia, Nasser saw no alternative but to seek Russian help in building the Aswan Dam. Once again the Arab world became a victim of the Cold War which was then at its peak.

Although Britain, France, and Israel occupied the Sinai and the Canal areas in a very short time, the outcome of the war was perceived as a victory for Nasser. For centuries the Western powers had pressured the Middle Eastern nations to follow policies that are beneficial to the West. They had removed rulers who refused to do their bidding, formulating legal and economic policies favoring Westerners over the native peoples. They had used their armies and navies to eradicate all resistance. Thus Nasser's ability to stand up to the dictates of the West and insist on making decisions that benefit the interests of the Egyptian people was hailed as a great achievement. Whether he won or not in practical terms was insignificant. The important thing was that he was able to withstand pressure and to tell the aggressors that the Arabs will not be pushed around any longer. Despite the fact that the tripartite aggression resulted in extensive devastation of Egyptian land, and that the army was routed and the economic loss was huge, Nasser came out of the war with the image of a hero who saved the world of Islam from another humiliation. He had led Muslims, therefore, to what was perceived as a moral victory.

Political events following the 1956 war led to the further growth of Nasser's prestige and power and his increasing use of Islam. These included union with Syria and the insistence on a policy of nonalignment between East and West. Nasser was also successful in obtaining Russian aid in building the Aswan Dam and in training and supplying the armed forces. The union with Syria encouraged socialist planning for the United Arab Republic. When Syria broke away, Nasser set in motion socialist reforms that were meant to fashion a new Egypt, a program that was to remove it from its backwardness and bring it into the twentieth century. The landowner class was legislated out of existence through the Land Reform Act that limited the acreage any person could possess. The land was distributed to the farmers and cooperative agricultural societies were initiated.

Western occupation of Egypt provided the opportunity to rid Egypt of its resident entrepreneurs. As agents of Western influence on the economy, they were perceived as a threat to Egyptian interests. Thus Nasser nationalized both Western companies and large indigenous businesses. The effort was concentrated on the development of a new Egypt and its citizens as persons who could proudly raise their heads among other men.

In this brave new world of the revolution that was to lead Egypt to its longed-for goals, there was no room for critics or dissidents. The Muslim Brotherhood was silenced through the execution of a few of its leaders and the imprisonment of a substantial number of its members. Al-Azhar and Islam were reformed by several decrees, leading to virtual nationalization of the religious institution. Thus the religious leaders and most religious literature became an effective agency legitimizing the government and its policies. These reforms were instituted in 1961 under the leadership of Mahmud Shaltut, the new rector of al-Azhar whose reformist ideals coincided with those of the Revolutionary Council. They were expounded in Law 103 that reorganized that venerable institution. A ministry of al-Azhar was begun, making religion one of the areas supervised and maintained by the government. Official academic recognition was extended to graduates of al-Azhar, placing them on a par with graduates of secular institutions of learning. Furthermore, the title Rector was changed to the more religious one of "The Grand Imam and Shaykh al-Azhar." It was also determined that the Vice-Rector and all the college deans were to be appointed by presidential decree.

Through the action of this reform, the Azhar was divided into five institutions. These included:

(1) Al-Azhar Higher Council, which was to function as the general administration of the complex.

(2) The Islamic Research Academy, perceived as the highest body for Islamic research, whose function was "to work to revitalize Islamic culture, purify it from unwelcome foreign accretions and traces of political and sectarian fanaticism, and restore it to its pristine condition."

(3) The Institute of Islamic Missions designed to provide trained religious leaders to help spread Islam abroad.

(4) Al-Azhar University, which was to consist of several colleges concerned with Islamic Studies as well as colleges for Arabic studies, business adminstration, engineering, agriculture, medicine, and industry (Art. 34). The law provided for free education and an equal opportunity to all Muslims.

(5) Al-Azhar Institutes, including the al-Azhar Institute for Women, providing primary and high school education for women in preparation for university training.

Also in 1961 the government nationalized the press and the news media. All writers and authors, even literary artists, as well as any person involved in the dissemination of news, became employees of the government. With this kind of tight control the government was able to censor anything not in line with its own propaganda. In 1962 further consolidation of governmental authority was attempted. A charter entitled *al-Mithaq* was published outlining the guidelines of the revolution and presented to the

National Conference of Popular Forces for deliberation. Whereas the Constitution of 1956 declared Islam as the state religion, the draft of the charter of 1962 advocated religious freedom and gave equal status to all religious faiths:

In their essence all divine messages constituted human revolutions which aimed at the re-instatement of man's dignity and his happiness. It is the prime duty of religious thinkers, then, to preserve for each religion the essence of its divine message. . . . The essence of the religious message does not conflict with the facts of our life; the conflict arises only in certain situations as a result of attempts made by [reactionary elements to explain religion—against its nature and spirit—with a view of impeding progress. These elements fabricate false interpretations of religion in flagrant contradiction with its noble and divine wisdom. All religions contain a message of progress.

Besides elevating other faiths to the status of Islam, the *Mithaq* emphasized national consciousness. The true expression of Arab national consciousness was "unity, liberty, and socialism;" Islam was merely a component of Arab nationalism. It was recognized as an element in the achievements of the revolution in the past ten years, but ranking only fifth in importance. The *Mithaq* also proposed socialism as the direction of the state.

With the al-Azhar reforms of 1961, the government relegated the religious institution to an arm of its own operation. A great number of *ulama* became government functionaries, and a substantial amount of their literary output was a religious justification or apologetic of the regime. An article in *Majallat al-Azhar* explained that "the task of al-Azhar in its new era is to inculcate the new, revolutionary thought and understanding in the people's mind.

Whereas othodox Muslims have always believed that the Islamic state "would protect and propagate Islam, would strive for the realization of Islamic ideas, and would apply Islamic laws," under the Nasser regime its function became one of providing Islamic apologetics and interpretations for the policies of the government in order to propagate socialism and implement its goals.

Nasser's use of Islam to legitimate his Arab nationalist/socialist ideology and to enhance his status as a leader in the Arab world did not go unchallenged. Saudi Arabia was also looked upon by many as a concrete example of God's favor precisely because of its rise in power and prestige. Wealth and progress, as we have seen, are regarded in Islam as signs of God's approval and potency as a gift of His mercy. Thus Saudi success provided an impetus to a re-emerging sense of Islamic identity for all Muslims at the same time as its financial support of other Arab states tempered their socialist zeal. Saudi Arabia did not come into this role suddenly. Faysal's efforts at combating the influence of Nasserism date to the early sixties. The formation of the Muslim World League, Rabitat al-Alam al-Islami, and its efforts at propagating the Islamic way of life through sponsorship conferences and lectures on Islamic subjects were aimed at providing an Islamic alternative to Nasserism.

Nasser's involvement in the war in Yemen set him against Saudi Arabia and its ally, America. His emphasis on "Islamic socialism" enabled Nasser to attack Saudi Arabian Islam as reactionary and stifling. True, Islam was that which would lead to the modern victory of the Arab people and not to retardation and decline, He further criticized King Faysal's calling of an Islamic summit which was co-sponsored by Faysal and the Shah of Iran. Nasser attacked this "Islamic Pact" in a speech on February 22, 1966, and condemned it as an imperialist conspiracy "using religion as a tool with which it can restore its influence." The "Islamic Pact" was portrayed as a move away from Arab unity. "The imperialist reactionary alliance aimed at spreading the idea of Islamic unity to counter Arab unity. It agreed that the Islamic countries of the Baghdad Pact should work for Islamic unity. . . . " Nasser saw this stress on Islamic unity as a threat because it would of necessity include non-Arabs, thus diffusing the efforts that were needed in addressing the immediate problem of the Arab world—Israel.

In the spring of 1965, the Muslim World League held its second conference in Mecca, agreeing to espouse Islam over against nationalistic considerations. This was, of course, contrary to the Egyptian ideology of Arab nationalism. Nasser perceived in the League's goal an imperialist conspiracy to eradicate the gains of the revolution.

Relations between Egypt and Saudi Arabia worsened. While Egypt supported the Yemeni Republicans, Saudi Arabia gave aid to the Royalists. Both nations worked to undermine each other's ideologies. It is as a result of the sharpening of this controversy between the Islamic and the Nationalist ideologies that we find the most intense debate about the present and future of Islam. In the context of this debate, particularly on questions of allegiance and destiny, one finds the focus of the ideological concerns of the seventies. The debate, of course, was in effect the continuation of the 1952 Egyptian revolution, for manning the agencies of the Muslim World League and editing its publications were many of the members of the Egyptian Muslim Brotherhood who had sought asylum in Saudi Arabia when their society was banned.

Egyptian attacks on Saudi efforts continued. Saudis were accused of championing imperialistic causes and of impeding the liberation of the struggling Islamic nations. Besides attacking the reactionary forces (al-rajiyyah), the Egyptian government sought to insure that its employees supported its ideology. Thus it embarked on a thorough program of indoctrination that included the *ulama* to prepare them for their revolutionary role in society.

The fear of subversion or the teaching of unauthorized interpretations of Islam led to the Egyptian government's censorship of the Friday sermon and insistence on focusing on pertinent topics. Among the themes expounded in the literature was the affirmation that the revolution was based on faith, *thawrah muminah*. It did not draw its ideas from posted theories or rational philosophies, but rather was inspired by the *shariah*, "one that is whole, eternal, and valid for every time and place."

The ideology of the revolution was presented as the heart of the Islamic *dawah* (mission). Islam was seen as identical with socialism, and deviation from socialism in Islam as one of the causes of retardation. Other expressions of the intricate relations between socialism and Islam led to interpretations such as that which said Muhammad's message was a socialist response to a capitalist society in Mecca which had a class structure. "Muhammad forbade usury because it is an expression of the capitalist system," thus suggesting that the Quran may be of human rather than divine origin. Even Sufism was seen as socialist in origin by the head of the Sufi orders.

Besides being socialist, Islam was presented as revolutionary. It was seen first and foremost as a revolution against corruption, and the revolution of July 23, 1952, was said to have "materialized the heart and content of Islamic revolutionism in a practical manner. It came into being "for spiritual values and the revivification of the religious heritage of the Arab person." In fact, not only was Islam presented as revolutionary and as a driving force, but Nasser even said that "Islam *is* revolution."

The literature on Islamic socialism is extensive. Various efforts were made to reinterpret the life of the Prophet and his Companions so that one finds titles describing the socialism of the Prophet *(Ishtirakiyyat Muhammad)*, of his wife *(Umm Ishtirakiyyah: Khadijah Bint Khuwaylid)*, of Umar *(Ishtirakiyyat Umar)*, and of Abu Bakr *(Ishitirakiyyat Abu Bakr)*. Typical are works such as that by Ahmad Farraj entitled simply *Islam, the Religion of Socialism*.

Under Nasser Islam continued to provide the aura of divine legitimation and validity for proposed social, political, and economic reforms, Even though the programs failed, Islam survived precisely because of the Nasserite emphasis on the Islamic aspect this brand of socialism which kept radical groups from introducing extreme proposals for change. Through suppression of dissent and a carefully orchestrated propaganda machine (which included the religious leaders and institutions) Nasser maintained a feeling of developing power, or potency, of belonging to the modern world. A sense of pride was growing, an identity as a people who could no longer be described as "the mat over which powerful nations wipe their shoes."

The third Arab-Israeli war in 1967 came at a time of the recapturing of Arab/Muslim pride, of great hope, and of a feeling of maturity. The internal and external causes of the war for both Israel and Egypt are not crucial for an understanding of Arab/ Muslim response. What is important here is that the defeat was total and catastrophic. While the Israelis felt bolstered in confidence and powerful in their strenthened position and holdings, the Arab world, defeated, stood once again naked, vulnerable, the laughing stock of all the world. [Less agonizing than the humiliation of the present defeat was the collapse of faith in the future and despair over any means of survival.

For the conservative Muslims, the war of 1967 proved a vindication of what they had been saying all along. The ways of "Islamic socialism" are not the ways of God. The defeat came as a punishment from God because the Muslims once again had placed their faith in alien systems and devoted their energies to the posited purposes of these systems rather than zealously working for the purposes of God. They had marshalled their efforts for the pursuit of materialism, not only ignoring God, but manipulating His revelation to serve their own purposes. The only way to recapture ascendancy and victory is by a total renunciation of man-made ideologies and a reorientation toward an unwavering commitment to the realization of Islam in the world. Israel did not get the victory because it represented a better system or a truer religion or a more perfect response to God's revelation; rather God used Israel to punish His errant nation and allowed the forces of evil to conquer the Muslims because they had strayed from the Straight Path. The defeat was thorough because they had deviated so greatly.

Other Muslims, less conservative yet just as painfully feeling the defeat, ascribed it to lack of preparation and planning. The causes of the defeat, they felt, were in the inability to mobilize the masses and bring them into the twentieth century. Still others felt that the defeat was a failure of the Arabs to modernize. Ascendancy in the modern world comes only through creative inventiveness and technological know-how. Unless the Arabs were willing to discard their worn-out heritage, irrelevant to the modern world, they would never be able to join the ranks of the civilized nations.

Some of the more radical socialists felt that this defeat may have brought an end to the socialist experiment in the Arab world. What they regretted was that socialism had been neither radical enough nor sufficiently influential to bring about its purposes. It had compromised itself by allowing the revolution to be colored with an Islamic aura which rendered it vulnerable in several areas. By maintaining the influence or religion over people's lives, it thus restricted the liberating forces of revolutionism from implementing drastic changes to produce the new Arab person.

Thus after the initial shock of defeat, self-criticism and condemnation became common responses. No one, of course, was satisfied with the state of affairs, but while all advocated some kind of definitive action, there was no unanimity concerning what that course of action should be nor what role the Islamic heritage ought to play. There was again division, in other words, over the constitution of the ideal society for which they were striving as well as what means were to be used to arrive at that goal.

The Arab world descended into a kind of psychological morass while struggling with these questions, from which it did not emerge until the 1973 war with Israel, referred to as the October or Ramadan war. As if the pendulum had again made its swing, Arabs viewed this conflict as a clear victory over Israel. That is, had not the United States intervened so decisively and replaced Israeli armaments, the Arabs would surely have defeated their opponents.

The portrayal of the "Crossing" (*al-ubur*) has acquired Exodus dimensions in the recounting of the war. In the religious literature that is produced by the Sadat propaganda organization there is a definite indication of an Islamic victory. This is supported in the first place by the Sadat maneuver of ridding himself of the socialists in 1971, referred to as the Rectification (*al-tashih*). Seen from the perspective of political science as a move to the right, this action had a strong religious connotation; President Sadat in announcing the Rectification program made it clear that the nation would henceforward be built in *iman* (faith) and *ilm* (knowledge, science). *Ilm*, being validly open to interpretation as religious knowledge, has been seen as a clear support of the role of religion in the state. Even Sufi orders that had gone underground during the Nasser regime now operate in the open and hold their Mawlid services in season.

The religious significance of the October 1973 War was obvious since it occurred during the Islamic holy month of Ramadan. The code name for the war was Badr, a reminder of the first Islamic victory under Muhammad in A.D. 623 over the forces of apostasy which, like its twentieth-century counterpart, was fought against seemingly overwhelming odds. In the 1967 war the battle cry of the Arabs was "Land, Sea, Sky," implying faith in equipment and the tactics of military engagement. In 1973 the cry was more explicitly Muslim, the call of "God is great" (*Al-lahu Akbar*), with which Islam has spread the message of God through major portions of the world.

It is not unusual to find Muslim writers who specifically ascribe the 1973 victory to God and His forces. One even wrote that "white beings" were seen aiding in the fighting on the side of the Egyptian army, an obvious reference to the angelic assistance rendered according to the Quran to the early Muslims in their battles against against apostasy. The 1973 war is also seen as an Islamic victory because it was the result of the oil boycott by Saudi Arabia. God thus has favored Saudi Arabia because it is the only nation among Arab/Muslim countries that declares itself to be truly Muslim in that is the only place where religious law and the tenets of Quran are literally implemented.

Enhancing the newly emerging image of Islamic identity is the evident failure of the Western experiment as perceived not only in the Arab world but also in the West itself. The West that in the last century Arabs idealized as ethical, honest, and enthusiastic is flawed by racism, by corruption, by a degenerate "pornographic" society in which every person seems to strive for his own interests rather than for the collective good. The disenchantment with the West is due not only to its treatment of Arab hopes and goals *vis-à-vis* Israel, but also to the apparent inconsistency of Western ideals and what is perceived as the imminent collapse of the West. Such an image frees Islam, purified and committed, to resume its sacred role of spreading the faith to all corners of the world.

The events of Lebanon during the last few years, which have pitted Christian against Muslim and revealed a collusion between the Maronites of Lebanon and the Israelis, has led to the disenchantment of some of those who believed in Arab nationalism as a unity that transcends religious identities. These events, especially recently in Syria and Jordan, have led to an increasing stress placed by many on religious identity as the identity *par excellence*, over against regionalism, nationalism, or socialism.

In February of 1970 the Supreme Islamic Research Council in its Fifth Conference addressed itself to the question of Palestine and occupied territories. In its published findings it says, "The Palestine Question is not a national issue nor is it a political issue. It is first and foremost an Islamic question." This is clearly true if one realizes that the military fortunes of the Arab people in relation to Israel are directly involved in the ways in which Muslims perceive themselves, the world, and history, and that that perception is intricately involved in the question of how they marshal their efforts in order to formulate the goals they seek and the methods they use to achieve these goals.

ISLAM AND NATIONALISM: THE PROBLEM OF SECULARISM[4]

Back in the mid-1960s, some of us argued against the tendency of Western students to give an ideological interpretation of

[4]By P. J. Vatikiotis, political scientist, from his book *Islam and the State*, pp. 72-83. Copyright © 1987 P. J. Vatikiotis. Reprinted by permission.

politics in the Arab states. We were accused of cynicism, and
these students went on describing and interpreting Arab nationalism, Arab socialism and military *coups d'état* in ideological terms.
They constructed a whole new political vocabulary in dealing
with that part of the world, including terms like revolution, reaction, progressive and conservative, militant and moderate. Unfortunately, neither the new vocabulary nor the ideological
interpretation of events and developments in the Arab states
helped us understand the reality of politics and political behaviour in those societies. Nor did the enthusiasm for new trends
and ideas that Western students assumed had seized the Arab
"political mind" explain the tremendous difficulties all of these
states have faced since independence. In our plea that we temper
our ideological interpretation with an historical-social examina-
tion of the environment, the context of politics in these states was
emphasized. In other words, some of us had suggested that we ask
the question, "What kind of political experience did these societies have so far?" By doing this, some of us argued, we could identify and enumerate the social basis of and the economic and other
constraints on their political behaviour that seemed often to ignore—at times transcend and transgress—their expressed ideology and their proclaimed political objectives. But no one listened
to these pleas and suggestions. The Foundations were pouring
money into what they were doing.

Leaving the methodological argument aside, the problem of,
say, Arab nationalism and its decline in the last decade or two, is
directly related to the obstacles and constraints it met in Arab societies. It is elementary to suggest that the first obstacle was the
fact that nationalism as an ideology came from outside the Middle
East, a region in which the majority of its inhabitants already possessed a political ideology of their own, Islam. Nationalism, an
alien political ideology, was adopted by some indigenous political
elites in order to avoid domestic tension and civil strife and to
withstand the pressure of external threats and influence. [See
Yousef al-Hakim, Suriyya wa'l 'ahd al-fayasali (Syria in Feisal's
Era), Beirut, 1966, pp. 96–7]. But in order to survive at all, this
new imported ideology had to be wedded to the indigenous, or
native, political ideology of Islam. Thus its adoption and spread
were not uniform. It was, for instance, more widespread among
the Arabs of the Fertile Crescent and/or the Levant, less so in the
Nile Valley, rather slow and late in the Maghreb where foreign

European control was tight and more direct, and non-existent in the Arabian Peninsula where it was hardly needed as a basis or a prop for political identity. But where it was needed most (as in the Fertile Crescent) it had to be radical for at least two reasons. One was the need to cope with fragmented ethnic and sectarian societies and the desire to integrate them into nation-states; the other was the need to overcome the territorial fragmentation imposed by outside powers over a people that considered itself Arab and, in the majority, Muslim.

By 1920 the concept of the nation-state came to define the state in terms of territory, language, descent, common national identity and political loyalty. In the Fertile Crescent (Iraq and Syria) the new state had to be radically nationalist, i.e. pan-Arab, because the states created by foreign powers there were not co-terminous with the nation.

Another shattering illusion came with the nation-state. According to the ideology of nationalism, a nation governs itself. The Arabs acquired several nation-states but did not govern themselves for a long time (e.g. during the mandates). An early aim of radical nationalism, therefore, was the attainment of self-rule ("complete independence" in populist parlance). Soon the assumption that nationalism does away with depotism (alien or native), flowing from the premise that nation-states are self-governing, was proved false. Finally, there was the intellectual fiction created by nationalism. In the pre-nationalist past, one was a Muslim, a Cairene, a Damascene, a Beiruti, or a Baghdadi; with state nationalism one soon became an Egyptian, a Syrian, a Lebanese, an Iraqi.

But when nationalism was linked to Islam, it failed to accommodate the different, or other, the non-Muslims, and thus accelerated the inappropriateness and the decline of non-Islamic nationalism as an acceptable political ideology.

In the case of Arab nationalism there was an even greater obstacle to its being accepted, or imposed, as the only, or uniform, political ideology for Arabs. Not only was it alien and secular in origin, but it required a personal and societal commitment to political philosophy with a secular political culture, one that abandoned dogma in favour of toleration of opposing views, one that accepted experimentation, and one that removed authority, power and the law from their divine provenance and/or link. Furthermore, it required the generation of a "public ethic" to which most members of society subscribed—a new kind of civil consensus. This, in turn, meant closing the gap between the most durable organization for power in Middle Eastern history and Islamic annals, the state and society, or the state and public order. And for that, one needed a basically corporate society, a people organized as a public. It is difficult historically to overlook these problems, which came home to roost, so to speak, in this century. When in 1969–70 I complained about the political aridity of Arab nationalism, radical or otherwise, I suggested that,

Radical change has occurred largely in the area of the economic activities and aspirations of Middle Eastern states: it is the result of a fantastic oil industry, improved communications, the massive infusion of arms into the region by external powers, and the extensive economic and technical aid received from them. Yet the ambivalence of the Middle Easterners regarding an organizing principle of political and social life essentially continues as one between an ethos inherited from the cultural and political experience under varieties of Islamic domination on the one hand, and several imported varieties on the other.

Now, nearly 20 years later, every member of the so-called Arab intelligentsia echoes this sentiment, or borrows this assessment; although at the time it was made, Englishmen accused its author of being anti-Arab!

In assessing Arab nationalism one cannot avoid a consideration of the concept of the state and its nature in the Arab world. It is linked to the conception of nationhood that each of these states adopts in order to legitimize its existence. It is also linked to the concept of nation and nationalism as referring to both individual states and the wider pan-Arab framework. Similarly, it is related to the concept of national and regional integration on the basis of the limited Arab experience. It is for this reason that I submit one must refer to the Islamic historical antecedents of the state, and their concepts of law and authority. I have already alluded to the difficulty the concept of nation-state encountered in the region because of the procrustean cultural bed created by the marriage of religion and politics, and where authority and law derive from other than a human source, so that abstract conceptions of a Law of Nature or Reason from which can flow such notions as individual human rights do not exist. Nor do those of corporate personalities, with some qualifications and rare exceptions. In short, the nation in the historical experience of the Arabs, and wider afield, the Muslims, at least till the nineteenth century, was not consciously territorial, but ideological.

The fact remains that in recent history, all the above-mentioned states used nationalism in order to do two things. Firstly, they tried to create a consensus of sorts within their respective boundaries based on nationalism (in varying degrees). Secondly, they tried to create a consensus among a number of Arab states for the formation of a wider Arab nation-state (essence and practical expression of pan-Arabism).

One could argue in this connection that in the Arabian Peninsula and the Gulf at its eastern extremity, the oil-wealth that allows for industrialization is also supporting a process which will theoretically at least, transform traditional, tribal states into nation-states through a genuine allegiance to new institutional structures. Yet in view of lingering irredentist claims and counter-claims between these states, firm and final boundaries between them have yet to be agreed upon. Then the question of who is a citizen of these states remains to be properly defined.

Nevertheless (at least until a decade or two ago), the process everywhere in the Islamic world was one of the consolidation of nation-states. In several of them, religion had been in retreat; in one of them, Egypt, for a good 150 years from 1820 to 1970; and in Turkey from 1830 to 1955.

Arab nationalism served as the catalyst, if not standard-bearer in a process of regularizing the state and society in parts of the Islamic world. It was even tried as an ideology for development. In retrospect though, one must concede that it failed as a credible, creative political ideology in Islamic societies; that is why one cannot use it to explain political processes and political behaviour in those states. Furthermore, whatever nationalism may or may not have achieved, it is now being challenged by militant religious movements. As the supreme manifestation of political secularism, nationalism is at bay as a result of the forceful challenge that militant or radical Islam presents. In fact it is under attack from both sectarian and mainstream Islam.

The failure of radical, secular Arab nationalism in 1967, and the emergence of a wealthy constellation of oil-exporting Muslim states, suggested to many that Arab nationalism could be better served and promoted without its secular component. Rather they favoured the religious conception of the nation, the *umma*, as being more efficacious. Recent events, however, suggest that these too are inadequate, not up to the task, although Lebanon is not a good example, since it comprises a sizable population that does not belong to the *umma*, the nation of Islam. One observes, more-over, that both Arab and religious nationalism and political Islam have remained spectators in the Gulf War between two Islamic states. Recently, a presumably Arab country destroyed itself in a brutal civil war and Arab nationalism had precious little to say about it. Forty years ago, a militant and militarily powerful non-Arab state, *Israel*, proceeded with impunity to decimate and dis-perse an indigenous Arab community (Muslim in the main) and pacify its Arab neighbours by force, and neither secular Arab na-tionalism nor the more traditional variant of ideology (militant Islam) was able to stop [it].

Secularism, and the difficulties it has faced in the world of Is-lam, lies at the centre of the problem of Islam and the nation-state. In his recently published monograph on the debate regard-ing the application of the *sharia*, Husein Ahmad Amin introduces a detailed discussion of the issue into the debate. He considers briefly a survey of the rise of secularism in Christian Europe, ar-guing that secularism represents an attempt to free human knowledge from the constraints of metaphysics and the unknown or occult, and that to that extent the famous tract *Fasl al-maqál fí má bayna'l-hikma wa'l-shari'a min al-ittisāl* by Averroes greatly in-fluenced the thought of Thomas Aquinas, followed by Duns Sco-tus and William of Ockham, which helped separate and distinguish rational knowledge from faith or belief, and science from faith or revelation. Cartesian rationalism and the new age of seventeenth-century science marked the end of the Middle Ages and church monopoly over human endeavour. Machiavelli in the Renaissance established the right of the prince to govern independently of the Church. Luther and Calvin of the Protes-tant and Reformation movements, and the European Enlighten-ment that followed, gave a new important role to human science and the new middle classes against the Church, so that the nine-teenth and twentieth centuries worked for the triumph of secu-larism and "secular Christianity."

Husein Amin contrasts this long-term development and struggle between modern or post-medieval European man with his new science and technology on the one hand, and the heavy restraining hand of a powerful Church defending a changing, dying order on the other, with the absence of such a conflict in Islam. After all, there was and is no Church in Islam, nor a clerical hierarchy provided for by the faith. Consequently, there could be no monopoly of knowledge by a non-existent group, class or institution. Nor was there a distinction made in the scripture (the Koran) between temporal and spiritual affairs. Islam has one *imam*, who is leader of both prayer and war. Nothing in the Koran is opposed to earthly or temporal good. And there is no religious authority set up in order to subjugate temporal institutions in Islam. Rather it is a simple faith: it has no need for a clergy specialized in interpreting a complex creed, or in interceding with God on behalf of the believers. And yet Islam acquired an elaborate, powerful class or caste of interpreters of the religious law, the *sharia*, as powerful in their desire to control the community of the faithful and as opposed to change brought about by human science as any Christian clergy in medieval Europe ever was. They developed a vast corpus of religious sciences, especially about the Sacred Law, and their special relation to rulers afforded them a privileged social and economic status and position, wielding great influence over the judicial, educational and social affairs of society.

As such it was in the interest of the religious establishment to promote and defend religious orthodoxy, educational formalism and rigid traditionalism on the pretext of protecting the Islamicity of the community. They put themselves forward as the interpreters and defenders of the faith, and the Islamic consciences of the *imams*. One of the most crucial factors in maintaining their position was their idealization of the past against the encroachment of modernity; their constant escape into the past; the veneration of the "fathers." A wider impact of this example offered by the bastion of tradition was the widespread romantic view held by Muslims in general of their past, past men and events. This is not a mere idle interpretation of how the men of religion sustained their key position as defenders of tradition, as good or bad as any other interpreter. On the contrary, it is crucial in understanding its use by Radical (militant) Islam today. It is through this romantic version of the past and the fathers that militant Islamic movements today try to appeal to and attract recruits, especially when the idealized past contrasts so favourably with the rotten and corrupt present condition of the *umma*, the Islamic nation. Husein Amin suspects that such an approach by someone who means to seek and provide solutions for the problems of his society; in fact, it is the position of someone who wishes to stupefy a people that have failed to solve their problems in order to attract them to these militant organizations.

On a broader front, this process is assisted further by contemporary Islamic historians who also indulge in anachronistic interpretations of the past—Marxist or otherwise. That is, historians who distort the facts to fit their ideological preferences or predilections.

The question, indeed challenge, which Husein Amin poses to both the official religious establishment, the guardian of tradition, and the radical Islamic militant is: Why be like the fathers at all? And what is so great about the past? He is not suggesting that the past be execrated, only that it not be misrepresented and misinterpreted anachronistically or romantically.

The thrust of Husein Amin's argument which merits attention is that there is nothing in the Islamic faith, its religious doctrine, or scripturally prescribed organization that opposes and forbids secularism or a secularist approach to the affairs of state and society. Rather, historical experience, events, developments and deliberate choices by Muslims have given rise to a particular elite in the community which has set itself up as the guardian of religious tradition and the enemy of any innovation or change based on human knowledge or science. But this is not an integral part of the Muslim creed. Husein Amin is also implying that if this nexus were removed, the appeal of militant Islamic movements would diminish accordingly. Stretched to its logical conclusion, Husein's argument postulates that (1) there is no need for something Muslims call the Islamic state, and (2) there is no such institution anyway, primarily because Islam and Muslims do not need it in order to survive and live or conduct Muslim lives. For Husein Amin, there is no contradiction between Islam and the nation-state. The only other contemporary Egyptian Islamic writers who could be placed in Husein Amin's corner are the judge, Said Ashmawi, and the other leading secularists already mentioned in passing.

If Husein Amin's position, acceptable or not, were applied, it would not eliminate the state's or the ruler's periodic leaning on the Islamic crutch. They will still involve the religion for their own political purposes, and solicit the support of the religious establishment. This for domestic purposes. On the international level, they may even find greater and more frequent excuse (or cause) to appeal to the Islamic dimension.

The difficulty may not be one of public secularism at the level of the state. It may well be one of individual secular attitudes at the level of the individual Muslim. The amphasis in Islam has been mostly on certain notions of justice and morality, of Muslim conduct in public, and less on individual or personal morality. This is a matter for Muslim philosophers and deontologists to sort out for themselves.

For 1,400 years now the separation between the religious ideal and the historical reality of the Islamic nation, so avidly pursued and maintained by the doctors of law and the religious teachers, especially since the Abbasid period, has prevailed. The guardians of religious tradition remained victorious over the historians, so much so that the corruption of Muslim historiography was represented by the persistently romantic view of Islamic history held by most Muslims. The Ottoman hegemony over the Islamic realm led to the death of thought, and intellectual inertia and stagnation. Muslims were overwhelmed by highly organized formal religious teaching, controlled by a privileged class of religious teachers who also became the recognized censors of all Islamic thought and action, at a time when the Christian Church in Europe was fast losing this role and function. Even today it is still difficult and hazardous for non-religious scholars to study or inquire into religious matters.

The weakest part of Husein Amin's argument in this discussion of secularism is perhaps the one that tries to ascribe the historical, romantic streak to the nature of the Arab mind or to the Arab's intellectual formation: that it is exaggerative, sharply dichotomous between black and white and allowing for no grey area. Is that the effect of the desert, Husein Amin wonders, and its impact on the Arab's modes of thought where he moves from repose, calm, surrender and dependence (presumably on God, fate, whatever) *suddenly* to an emotional, destructive explosion?

He gives the same explanation for the Arab's lack of precision (imprecise thought) and concludes that exaggeration "is a cultural feature or manifestation of certain social and economic conditions." Hence the escape to idealized images of his past, a kind of wishful thinking to assuage the miserable reality of the present. The Arab or Muslim, in short, is obsessed by his own history. But so are many other non-Muslim peoples and societies.

Despite the formal rejection of secularism by radical Islam and the discrediting of nationalism as an ideology in recent years, the restored ideological primacy of Islam has not reduced either the intensity or level or conflict in the *umma*, the nation of Islam.

In some respects it has, on the contrary, intensified intra-*umma* conflict. Nor has it provided greater cohesion and cooperation among Muslims.

For a decade at least (1956–66) intra-*umma* conflict over secular state interests was dominated in the Arab part of the *umma* by the hostility and rivalry between Egypt and Saudi Arabia. Presented to the Arab public as a contest between two essentially and ostensibly secular political movements, revolution versus reaction, the contest was in fact over the control of an important section of the *umma*, or nation of Islam. A corollary and parallel conflict was the one between Cairo and Amman, Nasser of Egypt and King Hussein of Jordan and the pre-1958 monarchy in Iraq, popularly presented in the search for the allegiance of an ill-defined Arab public as one between two political orders, monarchy and republic. These conflicts spilled over into neighbouring states; in the case of Egypt versus Saudi Arabia, into the Yemen, and in that of Cairo versus Amman and Baghdad, into Syria, Lebanon and Iraq. Yet in both cases, these conflicts were a continuation of earlier rivalries and contests between two Muslim states going back in history at least to the early 1920s, regardless of their common membership in the *umma*, the nation of Islam. Secular state interest, even disparate experience as nation-states, aspirations to leadership and ascendancy in the Muslim Arab world, took precedence over the common religious identity. In short, religion as a political ideology was inadequate, and could be easily overlooked, violated, or ignored, even when the rivalry and hostility were clothed or articulated in religious terms.

Are we witnessing contests between rival ideologies extrapolated from the religion of Islam? Or are we seeing the conflict between rival national-state interests, as these are perceived and formulated by national-state rulers, formulated or expressed in religious terms and put forward as Islamic political ideologies? If this is the case, the position insisted upon by radical Muslim ideologues, that Islam presents the best political order for the Muslim whoever he is and wherever he may be, collapses. At best it can be salvaged by reformulation: as a basis for public morality and public order, Islam is even more problematic than its secular ideological counterparts. As a basis for private morality and a public ethic it has yet to be given a chance. And so the historical and perennial ambivalence and confusion continue.

Considering more recent events of the last few years one can even speak about a recurrence or reappearance of sectarian conflict in the *umma*, the nation of Islam. However one may wish to avoid it, one cannot honestly ignore an underlying Sunni (PLO) versus Shii (Amal and others) conflict in Lebanon, especially Sidon in the south and Tripoli in the north, as well as an heretical Alawite versus strictly orthodox or Sunni conflict within Syria under the regime headed by President Hafiz al-Asad.

There may be no historian, religious polemicist like Baghdadi or Shahrastani of the twentieth century to produce the usual polemical tracts on this intra-*umma* sectarian conflict as yet, but the Iran-Iraq war, originally over a territorial dispute in the Gulf, is the major sectarian conflict in Islam in over half a millennium.

Where Islam was proclaimed as the preferred basis and ideology of the political order, the state, as in the recent case of Iran, does not appear to have reduced, let alone eliminated, either domestic or external conflict. Nor has it engendered the much vaunted economic and social benefits its promised.

Of course conflict between Muslim states is not a recent development. It dates from the earliest period of Islamic history. State interest became a primary consideration of policy from the time the second Caliph, Omar b. al-Khattab (634–44), created the earliest administrative-political institutions of the Islamic state; that is, as a result of his creative structural political reform. At that early stage in the evolution of the political dominion of Islam by conquest, such "state interest" frequently coincided—was even synonymous—with the interest of the nation of Islam, that is, the *umma*. Therefore, it could easily be accommodated, expressed by Islam as political ideology, Islam or religion as the exclusive basis of political order.

It is interesting that Abu al-Hasan al-Nadvi, one of the authors who have greatly influenced the leading ideologues of radical Islam, such as Sayyid Qutb, explains the decline of Islam and the Muslims mainly in terms of loss of earthly power. [See *Madha Khasira'l-'alam binhitat al-muslimin* (What the World has Lost by the decline of the Muslims), 8th printing, Kuwait, 1980.] Himself an *'alim* in Lucknow, India, and Azhar-trained, Nadvi argues in his book that Islam is an uplifting, superior creed. Therefore it cannot be subordinated to other creeds; it must, alone, prevail and be on top. Nor can it cooperate with others in order to reform society or the world. The Muslims have been delegated by

God to lead the world and humanity; they cannot be led by others. Note the insistence by Nadvi on the superiority and exclusiveness of Islam *vis-à-vis* all other faiths and systems. His book represents the clearest statement about the difference between the Islamic and non-Islamic views of the world, and the reasons why Islam must once again become the exclusively dominant perception, creed and world view. To this extent Nadvi's statement is also a firm *rejection* of the non-Islamic perception.

In his book *al-Islam, wa al-uruba, wa al-ilmaniyya* (Islam Arabism and Secularism), Dr. Muhammad 'Imara attacked those who argue in favour of the contradiction between Islam and Arabism (Arab nationalism). Such an argument, he claims, has arisen only in the period of decline, " . . . when Mamlukes attained power in the Arab countries. As they were Muslims and not Arabs, they made the religious bond a substitute—in fact, a negation—of the Arab bond." Ottomans after them followed the same route. When the colonialists marched on the Arab lands and the world of Islam, they played the same game, exploiting the presumed contradiction between the religious and the national bond in order to strike at Arabism and Islam and so conquer and occupy both the Arab countries and the Muslims. At one time these Europeans supported Muhammad Ali's "Arab project," and when he appeared close to succeeding in its implementation, they opposed him in conjunction with Ottoman Islam. Subsequently (e.g. in the Great War), they supported Arabism in the East against the Islam of the Ottomans. At the same time they divided (shared among themselves) the Arab nation that had emerged from the Great War, having managed to abolish the Islamic Caliphate (in Istanbul) and the project of the Arab nation-state. Then, in confronting Islamic thought, they sowed the seeds of secularism and Westernization among the Arabs. More recently, in combating the radical Nasserite Arab nationalist expansionist movement, they sought to set up regional alliances under the banner of Islam.

The thrust of Dr. 'Imara's argument is that non-Arab Muslims who controlled power for several centuries not only caused the decline of the Arabs, but also created the dichotomy between Islam and Arabism. The dichotomy surely dates from an earlier stage in the history of Islam. It was the Prophet Muhammad who offered Islam as the new bond holding the community of the believers together and replacing the older bond of blood characteristic of Arab tribalism which prevailed before Islam. Furthermore, the strict orthodox Muslims, including the interpreters and upholders of the Sacred Law (the *sharia*), as well as the more militant exponents of radical Islam who now clamour for the return of religion to the centre of political life, insist on the incompatibility between Islam and the secular idea of Arab nationalism; for them, Islam is still the exclusive basis of national identity, the *umma*, or community of the faithful, the only nation to which a Muslim belongs. At the same time, such a Muslim does not deny the idea of patriotism, one's loyalty to one's own country: he does not think it undermines or contradicts loyalty to Islam. The fact remains that there has been, so far, no final resolution between all these several levels of loyalty. The matter remains part of the unresolved wider issue of Islam and politics, Islam and the state.

II. KHOMEINI AND THE ISLAMIC REVIVAL: RADICALISM RESURGENT

EDITOR'S INTRODUCTION

After the decline of nationalism as a political ideal acceptable to many in the Muslim world, an era of profound ferment began. The resounding defeat of the semiunited Arab armies by Israel in the 1967 war shocked Muslims everywhere and marked the end of nationalism as an Islamic political force. By the end of the 1960s, in the words of Godfrey Jansen, "Looking for a Luther was the motto of the day, as the Muslim states began to try and bring new order into Dar al Islam, the House of Islam, of which, at long last, they were now the free masters."

A decade passed before the Luther (and the Savonarola) of the Islamic movement finally made his appearance on the world stage. Ruhollah Khomeini had spent much of his adult life in official disfavor or in exile, and he had developed a comprehensive, instinctive understanding of the politics of militancy. He was a grand ayatollah of Iranian Shiism, a strict, conservative form of Islam which tended to mistrust everyone who was not of the faith, of the sect. His grim demeanor, obvious devotion to the cause, high intelligence, unrelenting hostility to foreign imperialism, and above all his rout and expulsion of the luxury-loving Shah and thousands of his close adherents were the elements which made him instantly beloved not only by the people of Iran, who had been waiting for him as for a messiah, but in short order by the awakening militant masses throughout the Islamic world.

"My revolution," said Khomeini about the time of his coming to power, "is about Islam. It is not about the price of melons." Such statements as this—idealistic yet earthy—explain the source of his intense, unshakable sway over militants everywhere. During his ten years of unquestioned power until his death in 1989, he conducted in similar terms an Islamic monologue before his people, hardly reported in the West, by which he outlined the duties of the citizen to the Islamic state and the duties of the soldier of Islam against the enemies of the faith. He built a legacy which will undoubtedly be modified by his successors as world conditions change, but it will be remembered as long as Islam lasts.

This section examines the global rise of Islamic militancy— often in the West incorrectly and misleadingly termed fundamentalism—and its impact on world politics. In particular, we look at the advent of Khomeinism in Iran and its effect on both the Islamic world and on startled and unprepared Western observers. The first article, by Maxime Rodinson, a distinguished French Islamicist, considers the nature of the Islamic revival. Written in the 1970s, it is interesting not so much for prognostications, pretty nearly all of which have come true, as for the trenchancy and accuracy of its analysis. The second article is a careful and illuminating description by an experienced British journalist thoroughly familiar with the Islamic world of the basic outlines of the Islamic state or order in the modern age. The third article, by a U.S. political scientist James Piscatori, presents a historical analysis of the real political nature of the Islamic revival. In "Islamic Revival . . . ", Hrair Dekmejian offers a rundown of the various types of revivalism that have been encountered within the Islamic political world, and of their successes and failures. The fifth article written by the Ayatollah, is a characteristic piece of Khomeinist exposition, a monologue—carefully phrased and not at all rambling—that the Imam delivered in response to a single question from a friendly interrogator about a year after assuming total power in Iran. Here he outlines the essential position of the Muslim clergy both in the making of the revolution and in its maintenance and guidance of the Islamic state. Finally, Marvin Zonis and Daniel Brumberg, two senior scholars long versed in Iranian politics, is an analysis of the practical results of the Khomeinist victory in Iran, in particular of the way militant Islamic political ideas quickly gained influence in other Muslim countries.

ISLAM RESURGENT?[1]

Are we witnessing a rivival of Islamic fundamentalism? This is an interpretation suggested to many people by a host of recent events and developments: the fate of Mr. Bhutto, Pakistan's former prime minister; the applications of Koronic laws, with certain spectacular excesses, in Libya and Saudi Arabia; the leading role played by the Shī'ī ayatollahs in Iran's vast opposition movement; the vigor of the anti-Kemlist reaction in Turkey; anti-Coptic troubles in Egypt, and so on.

A revival of fundamentalism? "It has never lost its sway," sighs one nominal Muslim in exile from the Muslim world, a woman who could not tolerate the dead weight of social constraint imposing religious observance and, above all, conformity with traditional customs, in her own country. There are many others in her position. Does this not seem to confirm the strong reputation for fanaticism which has clung to Islam since the nineteenth century, in European eyes? In the seventeenth and eighteenth centuries Islam was well known for its tolerance. Before that, if Islam as an ideological and political enemy was detested, the piety of its followers was, to a degree, admired. The priests made good use of this to shame the Christians for their halfheartedness.

The facts are there, and they are real enough. But are they part of a trend, whether broken or continuous? Are they linked to the essence of Islam and hence destined to indefinite renewal? Or is this trend perhaps not what is seems? Is it, as the ideologists and apologists of the Third World suggest, just an insidious campaign mounted by "imperalism"—elusive but omnipresent—to bring into disrepute an element in the forefront of the developing world? These are questions that need to be answered. I shall base my argument and my examples on the central domain of Islam: the Arab countries, Turkey, and Iran.

There are many different things at stake. But equally, there are common factors and common trends that link them. What links them for Europeans is the common appeal to religious tradi-

[1]By Maxime Rodinson, emeritus professor of Old Ethiopic and Old South Arabian in the École Pratique des Hautes Études at the Sorbonne and lecturer in Middle Eastern anthropology. From *Marxism and the Muslim World*, pp. 290–306. Copyright © 1981 by Monthly Review Press. Reprinted by permission.

tion and religious regulations, even when by European standards they have nothing to do with that tradition. This is why many people have borrowed the label of *intégrisme* from recent Catholic history. (The French word *intégrisme*, which refers to a tendency in the Roman Catholic church to restore full obedience to dogma and ritual, has in most places been rendered into the rather inadequate term "fundamentalism.") The term is relatively appropriate if we are talking about the desire to use religion to solve all social and political problems and, simultaneously, to restore full obedience to dogma and ritual.

Such an appeal is plausible enough in the House of Islam because Muslim societies still have social foundations of a type characterized as "traditional" (albeit too summarily, but this is not the place for a fuller analysis). This term means, among other things, that religious law remains the supreme authority in the eyes of the masses, even if in practice they neglect or by-pass it. Practices which have other origins are legitimized by being linked, in a derivative and artificial way, to religious law. The weight of social constraint, imposing conformity and punishing transgression, has remained considerable.

From the beginning these Muslim societies have differed from traditional Christian societies. Christianity, at the outset a small, isolated sect within a vast and powerful empire, gradually succeeded in becoming a force to be reckoned with in that empire, and then in becoming adopted by it as the state ideology. But it always had to coexist with the state and its juridical, social, and cultural structures, which plainly had other origins.

In contrast, Islam has never ceased to be in some sense *intégriste*. Born in a society where each elementary group and tribe had political functions and formed a micro-state, the community of the faithful, if it wished to survive and grow, had to assume such functions too. God himself, in the Koran, gave that community not a comprehensive code, it is true, but at least certain precepts of social organization.

These precepts were supplemented with multiple traditions of various origins, borrowed from the different nations and peoples whom the Muslims conquered. But they were all legitimized through being linked, directly or indirectly, with the word of God, in accordance with the fundamental principle that the law of Islam was responsible for the whole shaping of the social order. No such copyright, or even underwriting, has ever been attribut-

ed to Jesus regarding Roman or Germanic law, the Scottish feud
or the Corisican vendetta, or the economic and philosophical
thought of Aristotle. But copyright of this kind has been attributed to the Prophet of Allāh, thanks to the immense body of *ḥadīth*,
or traditions, which became more or less codified in the ninth
century A.D.

The passage of time only accentuated this initial divergence.
Certainly, whatever the extent of its realm, religion remained for
a long time the primary ideological authority and the object of
widespread popular belief, as much in the Christian as in the Muslim world. Both suffered serious erosion as far back as the Middle
Ages because of the multiplicity of schisms and of associated tendencies to challenge the religious leaders—the men of religion
linked to power—sometimes even crossing the boundaries of the
prevailing religion. But this evolution, which continued and grew
in Christian countries, was only brought to a halt within Islam in
the eleventh century by the vigorous Sunnī reaction, whose success was favored by the internal evolution of Islamic societies and
by changes in their situation vis-à-vis the outside world.

Thus loyalty to the faith remained strong. The calm monopoly of truth left little room for doubt. For a long time in the Sunnī
world the few remaining tolerated sects became closed communities, like the other monotheistic religions, with no wish to prosely-
tize and hence tolerable as minorities, as if they were some sort
of established foreign caste. The conversion of Iran to Shīʿī Islam
in the seventh century stabilized the principal heresy, giving it a
state base and dominance in its own domain. As in Europe at this
time, the principle of *cuius regio, eius religio* maintained the established order.

Thus for a long time Islam experienced none of the challenges to its "ecclesiastical" institutions, its dogma and ritual,
which were so marked and so deeply rooted in Europe. The masses were not deeply affected, to the point of abandoning religion,
by the "disenchantment with the world" which industrialization
produces. The Islamic world has not witnessed the death of God
following the death of the angels and demons, and the general
disbelief in miracles, including those which are regularly renewed
in the common rite. Pietist moralism, attributing misfortune and
misrule to the lack of faith and consequent immorality of rulers,
has not on the whole yielded either to this general disbelief or to
an extension of the ideology of moral freedom affecting every level of society.

On the contrary, belief has always been reinforced by an old obsession: the constant dread of a great shift toward a rival religion, existing at the very heart of Muslim society and at the same time finding vital support outside. The Christians, assured of an ideological monopoly in their own world (with the exception of the tiny Jewish minority, which had no external support and presented little risk of spreading its spiritual contagion), have seldom had cause to fear that an infidel army from without would join forces with its accomplices within. This fear, present in Islam early in the Middle Ages and reinforced by the Crusades and the Mongol invasion, could only grow in the face of stronger and stronger aggression by Europe's imperial powers in the nineteenth and twentieth centuries. It reached paroxysms that can only be compared either with Catholic paranoia in the nineteenth century in the face of the increasing decline of religion (supposedly inspired by the Jewish-Protestant-Masonic conspiracy, led by Satan) or with the analogous fears and obsessions felt by the communist world.

As elsewhere, a universalist faith, a particular national identification of the community of believers (in colonial Algeria, as in Poland or Ireland), a supranational identification of Muslims as Muslims—each of these has reinforced the other in varying degrees of emphasis which have assured the permanence of general loyalty to the ancestral belief.

Industrialization and a degree of modernization have had the effect of pushing limited sections of society toward skepticism, religious liberalism, and freedom of behavior, beneath the theoretical umbrella of an Islam reinterpreted in this light, or of a vague deism, or even atheism. But the conversion of these people to such Westernizing trends has reinforced the attachment to Islam, in its most rigidly traditional form, among the larger masses. The poor, driven to the limit of famine or wretched subsistence, direct their anger and recrimination against the privileges of the rich and powerful—their ties with foreigners, their loose morality, and their scorn of Muslim injunctions, the most obvious signs of which are the consumption of alcohol, familiarity between the sexes, and gambling. For them, as Robespierre put it so well, atheism is aristocratic: and so is that "subatheism" which is (supposedly) betrayed by the slightest ungodliness or departure from orthodox morality. These are not, as once was the case here, old-fashioned priests or pious old maids railing against short skirts and kisses on the cinema screen; but angry crowds who indiscriminately attack shops selling luxury goods, hotels where the rich and the foreigners get their drink and debauchery, and (sometimes) the places of worship of "heretics" or non-Muslims.

If there is an apparent revival of fundamentalist Islam, it is because we are witnessing—privisionally perhaps—the end of an epoch in which the crystallization of such attitudes (a process briefly described above) has been partially hidden from view.

Throughout a whole era, beginning in the middle of the nineteenth century, the elites of the Muslim world have been seduced by new ideologies. First, secular nationalism of the type that developed in Europe after a long evolution, and that offered the most suitable answer to the ideological exigencies of the region. Later, to a greater or lesser extent, this nationalism was colored by socialist ideals, and socialism in a universalist form even emerged at certain points.

These Muslim elites succeeded in channeling the feelings and aspirations of the masses into these ideologies, transforming them into support for political mobilization. One must notice, however, that the masses reinterpreted these ideas in their own way. It happened that foreign domination was the work of infidels and that the exploiters were infidels or else one's fellow countrypeople in the pay of infidels. No one in the lowest social strata, where nothing had shaken the faith in Islam, could fail to notice this. Nor could skilled and perceptive leaders fail to add this singularly effective weapon to their arsenal of strictly national and social means of mobilization.

However, the masses, being inundated with propaganda, were little by little conditioned to formulate slogans of the modern sort. Members of the popular classes were moreover genuinely influenced by these ideas. In areas of the Arab East where there were religious minorities, the national and social struggle was often waged jointly by Muslims, Christians, and even (until quite recently) Jews. In Turkey, a prestigious national leader, who scarcely concealed his basic lack of belief, could draw a large following and carry out militantly secular measures.

In Iran, certain elements, even outside the elite, could be seduced by a nationalism which celebrated the glories of Iran in the Zoroastrian era and which considered the conversion to Islam a mere cultural and national regression brought about by barbarous Arab conquerors (and Sunnī, too!). In the Maghreb, emigrants proletarianized in France were exposed in large numbers to the influence of a social climate that linked militancy with (at the very least) indifference toward religion.

None of these modernizing tendencies has been forgotten. But they have all lost part of that power to arouse enthusiasm which gave them supremacy and relegated religion to the status of an auxiliary, everyday morality, and which at the same time could call in question practices and dogmas at variance with modern ideologies and the ideology of modernization.

Marxist-inclined nationalism of the Nasserist variety, identifying the basic enemy not as the foreigner per se, nor as the infidel, but as "imperialism," has not managed to achieve any great success. Its alliance with the supposed coalition between the oppressed of the world and the self-styled socialist states has by no means allowed it to get the better of the Israeli challenge. It has been called into disrepute by the policies of the new class in power, scarcely more seductive than those of its predecessors. This nationalism was, in part, the heir to Westernizing Jacobin liberalism. The mobilization which it preached was to remain secular and multiconfessional. But the struggle against Israel had already made it almost impossible to include Jews in this. The prevailing reactions of the Christians in Lebanon have reinforced the old fears arising from both the Crusades and the historical links with imperalist Europe, to make all Christian Arabs increasingly suspect. The realities of national independence have proved less exhilarating than the slogans that mobilized the masses in the causes of liberation.

Nowhere, moreover, has this type of nationalism resulted in an escape from economic dependence and underdevelopment. The only achievements of the great Arab nation in the field of power politics and national prestige have been the work of the oil potentates—the most fundamentalist and conservative of Muslims—in selling their oil with the haggling of skilled businessmen and technocrats (but whose *kafiyahs*, *agals*, and *abayahs* enable them to be associated with Bedouin tradition). As for the ideal of the united Arab nation, it has grown ever harder in the face of the evident development of regional nationalisms (Egyptian, Algerian, Moroccan, and so on) to maintain that its realization is hampered only by the "plots" of Israel and "imperialism."

In Turkey, as in Iran, it has become difficult to direct the nation's hatred against a Muslim enemy, even if the three main peoples of the Middle East are always ready to denigrate each other. The anti-Arab ideology of part of the Turkish and Iranian nationalist elites does not exert enough leverage—as an irredentist territorial conflict might—to arouse the serious mobilization of populations which are indifferent to the pre-Islamic glory of the celestial Turks of Orkhon, or of Cyrus and Chosroes. The perceived enemies are still non-Muslim: the atheist Russians, who oppress the Turkic and Iranian Muslims of Central Asia, and whose hidden hand is everywhere suspected; Christian Europeans and Americans, who clearly manipulate local leaders, imposing their will through financial and technological supremacy, sapping and corrupting Islam by means of their impious morality, their debauchery and drunkenness. Last but not least, their bad example regarding the equality of the sexes, if not indeed female domination (may my feminist friends forgive me, it is simply that it often looks that way from the outside), gives the indigenous women dangerous ideas.

Thus pure nationalism becomes more and more strongly a Muslim nationalism, a nationalizing Islam. The exceptions are the ethnic minorities that consider themselves oppressed by other Muslims, such as the Kurds, or those Arabs most sensitive to Palestinian irredentism and the Israeli challenge: Syrians, Iraqis, and above all Palestinians; among the latter the significant participation of Christians in the Palestinian movement strengthens the reluctance to give a purely Islamic coloring to the ideology of struggle.

As for socialism, in those states where a regime claiming to be socialist has been established, it has not been slow in making its heavy, oppressive character felt and in demonstrating its deficiencies of all kinds—even if it has also achieved positive results. External models are no more encouraging, as becomes increasingly clear, especially in those countries which have been slow to respond to post-Stalinist demystification. The exceptions are provided by elements of the working class, in places where they are of some importance, and by certain intellectuals or semi-intellectuals who were formerly inspired by the Marxist spirit and who remain under its spell, either through faith, misty vision, ignorance, or hardening of the arteries.

The same disappointments have made themselves felt in Europe. Here, too, the desperate desire to find an outlet for unchanneled fervor has sometimes provoked a return to the old, indigenous, local, national religion. But here Christian belief, for all the mystical or devotional individualism of the quest for salvation, or of organized charity, scarcely offers opportunities for mobilization which is at the same time uplifting and specific. On the one hand are parties and movements which are conservative or boringly gradualist, and reactionary movements whose program of restoring the City of God is hardly convincing when they revere one whose kingdom was not of this world and who rendered unto Caesar what was Caesar's. On the other hand, progressive or revolutionary movements, largely comprising (and in any case initiated by) unbelievers, are tendencies to which Christians can only subscribe when also inspired by other motives.

In the Islamic countries, by contrast, the appeal of the national religion is for many people accessible, stimulating, credible, and alive. Islam, as I have said, has not suffered either internal erosion or the challenge which has gradually sapped Christianity's power of attraction. It has been kept intact among people whose daily culture it has provided and whose aspirations and humble ethics it has sanctified. Throughout the epoch which has witnessed the prestige of nationalism and socialism, the idea has been propagated that Islam defended and incorporated the same values that they did. But it became more persuasive to fight for such ideals under the banner of Islam than to tie oneself ideologically to foreigners whose motives were suspect—as was the case with Marxist-inclined nationalism as well as with socialism.

Even outside the Muslim world, Islam has acquired the prestige of being, now and in the past, unflagging in the forefront of the resistance to a Christian Europe which was expansionist, proselytizing, and imperialist; or simply of being in the vanguard of the anti-European struggle. But henceforth the enemies who direct the greatest hatred against them are the Europeans and the Americans, and the Europeanized strata of the societies at the periphery of the capitalist world. Thus all these enemies can be identified as either non-Muslims, anti-Muslims, or their fellow travelers. It would appear that in the furthest recesses of the House of Islam there may be an awareness of this worldwide polarization, that Islam proudly receives the title of universal champion of good against evil without ever yielding to anyone the banner of the avant-garde.

Muslims make themselves different images of Islam according to the social strata to which they belong, the sort of education they have received, their political affiliation, and even their individual temperaments. But everywhere the dominant, almost unchanging image is of Islam as guardian, guarantor, surety, and protector of traditional morality. Analogous to the image that Christian fundamentalism makes of Christianity—the image of Christianity that it alone (or almost alone) conceives—this image is almost universal in Muslim society. Christian faith is sometimes a fundamentalist faith in a tradition rigidified at a certain period, sometimes a faith which, while rooted in the message of Jesus, is not afraid of the constant revision of tradition. Publicly professed examples of such revisionism are rare in Islam: the message of the founding father is (for the moment) more difficult to extricate from the dead weight of tradition.

Fondness for the advantages of tradition is partly responsible for the male tribe's religious faith, which cuts across political beliefs and classes. As with Latin Catholicism in the past, for example, religious tradition can be exploited in order to dominate the sex which males unquestioningly consider weak and subordinate, even if the vengeance awaiting them in hearth and home, and in the conjugal bed, often deters them from taking full advantage of it. Without needing opinion polls, rulers and would-be rulers were well aware of these inclinations among their people and took good account of them.

Some leaders genuinely want to translate into reality the social and political precepts of Islam, having learned at school that such precepts existed and were alone capable of building a harmonious society. Such were the leaders who established the Saudi state and such, today, it Libya's Qaddafi.

When put to the test by taking office, most of these leaders are (or become) convinced—depending how far their ideological intoxication has conditioned them to reject the lessons of reality—that they cannot achieve very much in this spirit. They end up discovering how right Nasser was when he declared that he failed to see how anyone could govern a state solely with the laws of the Koran. From that moment they realize that they are disappointing those who have come to expect great things from the application of Koranic law. In order to maintain a broad consensus among their subjects they must concentrate essentially on symbolic measures—on what I would call Muslim "gesticulation"—and on the visceral faith in a Muslim identity whose various springs and sources I have in part outlined.

In sum, the problem is not fundamentally different from that faced, for example, by the Soviet leaders. Stalin and Khrushchev, each in his own way, were highly expert in Marxist "gesticulation." But the depth and breadth of belief in the virtues of Marxism were much less great; the Gulag policies have largely discredited it; the symbolism of Marxism is much less rich; the rationalism of its doctrine is far less metaphysically satisfying; and other beliefs, however clandestine and persecuted, have always been available to the Soviet peoples.

Almost alone, Qaddafi ingenuously pursues his project for a Muslim state, by definition free and egalitarian and (also in the name of Islam) opposed to American plutocracy. Persistently he theorizes and refines, straining to specify the right methods in his Green Books and his Libyan policies. Besides the sneers of professional cynics and the cold comfort of those of his countrypeople who have the means to enjoy their pleasures abroad, he earns the frowns of clerics who are shocked by his novel interpretations, his rejection of codified tradition, and his criticism of bigots and hypocrites.

Much more numerous among Muslim leaders are and were those who, whatever the depth of their personal conviction, have known all along that they could carry out only a few of Islam's ideals. They knew that they must govern essentially with nonreligious prescriptions and could hope for, at most, a superficial and limited moral and religious transformation.

They have resigned themselves to achieving little and—for all the world like cynical manipulators only after their own power—have reaped their reward with a more or less clear conscience. They have all realized that they must at least hold Islam and its functionaries in some respect. Or they can go further and get good results through Islamic "gesticulation." The building of a mosque can put a gloss on certain unsavory aspects of reality.

Besides the leaders there are the would-be leaders and, in the sole case of Turkey—where there is at least a recurring, if not peaceful, alternation of power—a third category: those who govern from time to time and, when out of office, can at least stay in business without having to go underground.

Political parties and groups all display a minimum of respect for Islam. Those who are most suspected of being against religion—previously the communists—have shown the most zeal in displaying their respect for performing painful feats of reconciliation (but not, after all, more painful than for the French Communist Party in identifying itself with Joan of Arc). However, in the midst of this chorus of reverence certain groups are prominent by their insistence on the defense of Islam.

The Turkish Democratic Party is one. Its leaders seem on average neither more nor less devout than their Republican counterparts, but they draw on the religious faith of the peasant masses in order to combat the attenuated Kemālism of the Republican Party and the Westernizing modernism which has spread among the military, the technocrats, and elsewhere.

Apart from this type of demagoguery, there exist groups which are authentically religious in the sense that their leaders, whether sincerely or not, declare that they want to construct a Muslim state. One could make fine distinctions about the sincerity of such leaders' faith, the image they project of this Muslim state in relation to their social origins, to their culture and temperament, and to the degree of radicalism in their practical politics—often going to the extreme of terrorism. Here, moreover, these sects can benefit not only from international example, but from a specifically Islamic tradition, that of the medieval sect of Hashīshīyīn—those *fedayeen* who bequeathed to European languages the word "assassin." Some in all sincerity seek power in order to apply Islam, while others choose Islam as an instrument with which to gain power. But in politics such distinctions are only of occasional importance. The results are often the same.

One of these groups is the vast clandestine movement of the Muslim Brotherhood. The extent of its membership is unknown, but the fluctuating numbers of its sympathizers are certainly considerable. It is hard to ascertain the different trends which run through the ranks of this organization. But the dominant trend is certainly a type of archaic fascism. By this I mean a wish to establish an authoritarian totalitarian state whose political police would brutally enforce the moral and social order. It would at the same time impose conformity to religious tradition as interpreted in the most conservative light. So adherents consider this artificial renewal of faith to be the first priority, while others see it as a psychological aid, sweetening the pill of reactionary social reform.

There also exist similar movements, for example in Turkey, to the right of the Democratic Party. But it is in Iran that there is something more akin to a religious party. Its strength has been all too apparent in recent months.

The phenomenon of the political influence of the Iranian 'ulamā (the men of religion), who constitute a sort of religious party, has astonished everyone. The apologists, whether Muslim or pro-Muslim and those who come fresh to the problem in an idealistic frame of mind—as is usual with questions of religion (or even of ideology, to judge from the French "new philosophers")—are quick to attribute this, at least in part, to the nature of Shī'ī doctrine. But it is more complex than this. It is true that the foundations of Shī'ī doctrine, in the first centuries of Islam, were elaborated among opposition groups stubborn in challenging the legitimacy of those in power. The ideology preserved this imprint. But doctrines are always susceptible to interpretation. There is never a shortage of theologians and theoreticians capable of reversing doctrine at the dictates of changing circumstances.

As Nikki Keddie has admirably demonstrated, it was the evolution of the respective strengths of the state and the leading 'ulamā' that shaped the growing power of the latter in Iran and, in contrast, the decline of their power (a power which could also be doctrinally founded) within Sunnī Islam. The Safavid dynasty (1500–1722), which converted Iran to Shī'ī Islam, cooperated with Shī'ī 'ulamā' which it had to import from Arab countries. Their interdependence was given a theoretical base. But, roughly speaking, the state gradually lost its power later on, while the advantages conceded to the 'ulamā' were institutionalized, legitimized, and strengthened. The struggles of the eighteenth century enhanced the flexibility of doctrine and the independence of judgment of each 'ālim (the singular of 'ulamā'), based on foundations which were medieval. Their financial autonomy and security, assured by the Safavids, could not be shaken by weak governments which were afraid of opposition. Their leaders knew how to increase their power by choosing to stay outside the frontiers of the kingdom, near holy sanctuaries.

The apparently paradoxical alliance between the men of religion and the secular reformers or revolutionaries was formed in the nineteenth century, in opposition to the Qajar dynasty's concessions to the West, and cemented during the "constitutional

revolution" of 1905-1911. The two parties were already afraid
of modernization from above, which in their eyes could only aug-
ment the authoritarian power of a dynasty supported by foreign
powers. The religious leaders above all dreaded the consequences for their autonomous power of the secularizing implications of modernization. The secular modernizers within the
opposition feared the strengthening of absolute power. Both
groups directed their struggle against domination by powers
which were both foreign and infidel. The alliance won the vote
for the Constitution of 1906, a compromise between the two tendencies, which greatly limited the power of the Shāh. The religious leaders, shocked by the institution of civil tribunals
alongside religious tribunals, and by the whole idea of intercon-
fessional equality, as well as other measures, were for the moment
appeased by the insertion of an article stipulating that no law
could contradict sacred law—which was to be determined by a
committee of *mujtahids* (the most learned '*ulamā*').

The alliance was broken off in the second phase of the revolution, after most of the '*ulamā*' had discovered its underlying dan-
gers. But some of them continued to participate in the
revolutionary coalition.

The strengthening of authoritarian power under the two
Pahlavi monarchs, since 1925, has resulted in the renewal of the
alliance. The modernizing democratic nationalists, shocked by
the foreign policy of the Shāh, by the degree of repression and
the blatant profiteering, have rediscovered, as they did under the
last of the Qajars, the advantages of alliance with the '*ulamā*'. The
latter, sharing the general dislike of these same policies, and add-
ing to it their fear of modernization and Westernization, are able
to tap this dissatisfaction, enjoying as they do the veneration of
the crowds and the impregnability of the pulpit—rather as the
Polish clergy do.

The events of 1978 are the result of the escalation set in motion by the Ayatollah (literally, "sign"—i.e., proof—"of God," the
honorary title of the most important *mujtahids*) Khomeini as early
as June 1963, when he publicly compared the Shāh to Yazīd, the
Umayyad caliph who ordered the murder of Ĥusayn, grandson
of the Prophet. His imprisonment, with some thirty other '*ulamā*',
caused large-scale demonstrations, from which, this time, the secular nationalists dissociated themselves. The subsequent repression resulted in at least a hundred deaths.

As they had done in the past, the *'ulamā'* could give the word for the establishment of an Islamic state (and it could gain acceptability by virtue of what we have said above). In the restoration of the 1906 Constitution they saw, above all, in addition to the limitation of the Shāh's authoritarianism, that one crucial article, never applied in the past, which could put legislation under their control.

So there came into being a provisional alliance against one form of despotism which usually numbered among its members people dreaming of another from of despotism. Similarly in Egypt, between 1952 and 1954, the Muslim Brothers joined the communists and the liberals, led by Naguib, in calling for the return to parliament. In both cases a hated brand of authoritarianism was to be overthrown in order to set up a regime in which the people could be mobilized in the cause of another brand of authoritarianism. I am not saying that the Iranian *'ulamā'* are all authoritarian. Their political views are probably diverse and in many cases characterized by a notable fluidity and naivety.

Since they have difficulty in applying and defining programs setting out concrete measures, political leaders, as I have said, have recourse to symbols—whether they proclaim them, demand them, or actually put them into effect. The vexing thing for their image in the West is that these symbols are archaic. This is the other side of the coin, the price to be paid for the advantage gained by including in a political program a few precepts taken from the Koran regarding social organization, and many others to be found in the Tradition.

In the Christian world one can call for a minimum (revisionist) fundamentalism by invoking the holy texts only so as to prohibit divorce and contraception. Some Catholic fundamentalists, unwilling to reinterpret their traditions to this extent, want the Latin liturgy and the cassock to be restored. This certainly gives grounds for complaint! But, by contrast, the minimum Muslim fundamentalism, according to the Koran, requires the cutting off of a thief's hand and the halving of a woman's inheritance. In returning to tradition, as the men of religion require, anyone caught drinking wine must be whipped and an adulterer either whipped or stoned. A spectacular piece of archaism indeed—though perhaps a little less spectacular, it is true, than the symbolism of orthodox Judaism. But then, the latter is often impossible to put into effect and, when it is, affects only a tiny community and thus startles fewer observers.

Will the future see sny great change in this situation? It does not look like it. Certainly the panacea of Islamic government may be discredited in future among larger sections of Muslim society. Whatever may be said in Islamic countries or elsewhere, neither Islam itself, nor Muslim tradition, nor the Koran provides any magic guarantee either of fully satisfactory government or of social harmony. Islam is confined to offering precepts regarding only limited sectors of social life, legitimizing certain antiquated types of social and political structure, at best achieving small improvements, and like all universalist, and some other, religions, it encourages people (beneficially moreover) to wield power and wealth with charity and moderation.

Muslim government in itself means nothing. A ruler can declare the state to be Muslim by satisfying certain minimal conditions which are easily fulfilled: the proclamation of adherence to Islam in the constitution; the institution, or reinstitution, of archaic laws; conciliation of the 'ulamā' (which is easy among Sunnīs, more difficult among Shī'īs). But over and above this minimum, the scope is vast. The term can cover different, even diametrically opposed, regimes. Governments can make mutual accusations of the betrayal of the "true" Islam. Nothing is easier or more dangerous than this time-honored custom of dubbing your adversary an "enemy of God." Mutual recriminations, often incorporated in contradictory fatwās (legal consultations) issued by obliging authorities, are hardly designed to strengthen one's confidence in a state's supposedly Islamic character.

At any rate, is it not possible for one of these states to be genuinely Muslim and to inject some spiritual enrichment into the government of human affairs? Some people hope so, or say they do, whether militant revolutionaries because Muslim, or vice-versa, or else Europeans convinced of the vices of Europe and hoping to find elsewhere (why not in Islam?) the means of assuring a more or less radiant future.

It is astonishing, after centuries of common experience, that it is still necessary to recall one of the best attested laws of history. Good moral intentions, whether or not endorsed by the deity, are a weak basis for determining the practical policies of states. The best example is undoubtedly the weak influence of Christ's nonviolent anarchism—however often it may be invoked in writing, and revered and memorized—with regard to the behavior of Christian states (and, for that matter, of the majority of their subjects). Muslim spirituality may exert a beneficial influence on the style of practical politics adopted by certain leaders. It is dangerous to hope for more.

Islam, according to its followers, is still superior to Christanity in demanding less of human virtue, in resigning itself to society's imperfections and prescribing or justifying repressive laws to deal with them. But in so doing, it can be said, it encourages people to expect more from these legal structures. Power can only disappoint. But it will disappoint the more if it promises more, if it pretends to be endowed more than any rival with the power to satisfy. This disappointment can only recoil on the doctrine which made use of it. If the magic potion is ineffective one loses confidence not only in the sorcerer but in sorcery itself.

Waves of disenchantment may thus spread within the Muslim world as they have within Christian society. It is indeed unwise that so many regimes have declared themselves Islamic.

Spiritual malaise of this kind can already be detected among many of the people who have left Muslim societies and are free to express their disenchantment once they are outside. Heavy social constraint resulting from a stifling moral piety is, moreover, an important factor in the (noneconomic) emigration from these countries. The women are especially bitter. In Paris they have recently been declaiming their hatred of Islam—a hatred which owes nothing to "imperialism." One might say they are wrong to link Islam proper—the spiritual force of its gospel—with particular oppressive laws which are only contingent upon it. This is true. But who made the link before they did, and who continues to do so?

This is as pertinent inside Muslim countries as outside, but it is much more difficult to express such feelings from within. Industrialization, as it slowly develops, and the seductive forces of the way of life in secularized countries—as seen on film and television—will probably increase the challenge not only to regimes but to the religion which they have taken up as their banner, as long as this religion is still invoked to justify repression.

Under the pressure of such disaffection it is quite possible that, one day, the men of religion will present a rather more modern, concrete, and persuasive form of Islam. There might then develop a leftist Islamic ideology—and not simply an Islam challenging a particular regime—just as a leftist Christian ideology has developed. This will perhaps be slow in coming. Certainly, loyalty to a community long under attack, communal "patriotism" with its customary paranoia and narcissism, and pride in leading the Third World will still play their part. But this may not always be so.

For the moment this leftist Islam is quite far off. One must make do, at best, with an Islam which retrospectively legitimizes anti-American, anti-Western postures, while exerting pressure to maintain an archaic moral order. One can call this "leftwing" if one wishes. Among their opponents the Shāh and his followers are now (for tactical reasons) discovering "Islamic Marxists." They are not entirely wrong insofar as the implicit ideology of the Third World revolt has let both the people and a wide variety of intellectuals adopt or rediscover militant aspects of Marxism. Some people do so by presenting such tendencies as part of the "essential" Islam. They are wrong, but these are nevertheless universal tendencies which were present in medieval Islam. If they make reference to Islam it is often to enable them to combine the politically progressive with social reaction.

It is this combination of the modern-revolutionary with the social-archaic that characterizes Qaddaffi, who almost alone after coming to power has maintained the vitality of militant rebellion. For their part, the Saudi rulers combine the technologically modern with the politically and socially archaic, and their anxious '*ulamā*' on the Right reproach them for it as Qaddffi does from the Left. Mixtures of this type are unstable, as are alliances between the men of religion and socialists or liberals, at least until the former have brought their outlook up to date. We shall probably see the alliance broken off once again in Iran (and elsewhere), as it was in 1907.

But humankind continually poses problems which it cannot solve, or poses them in terms which make them insoluble. Renewed despair is echoed by renewed hope. One will always find imperfections in existing regimes, whether seen in the light of "true" Islam or of "true" Marxism. For a long time to come, the attempt will still be made to correct "errors" by returning to the lost fundamentalism of hallowed tradition. There is still a future for Muslim fundamentalism—and for the fresh recoveries and fresh challenges that lie ahead of it.

THE NATURE OF THE ISLAMIC REVIVAL[2]

There is no denying that a significant body of Muslim opinion is critical of contemporary international relations. I have a vivid memory of listening to a small group of African and Asian Muslim students in Karachi who bitterly denounced the institution of the nation-state, and also their own governments for being tools of the imperialists in failing to encourage Islamic unity. All the while, their elders, keeping silent, squirmed uncomfortably in their seats. In a sense, these students gave voice to an important strand of thinking in the modern period that completely rejects the very ideas of nationalism and the nation-state and, in some people's opinion, represents the voice of the current revival. In this chapter, I shall examine what the revival means and look at the general effects that it has produced.

The Muslim View of Islam's Decline

Much of the disappointment, even bitterness, which some Muslims express about the nation-state, reflects their view that reality has diverged from what they perceive the ideal to be, that the practice bears no relationship to the theory. There is certainly nothing uniquely Islamic about this divergence: practice rarely conforms to what is thought of as the theory. But the divergence tends to become greater and the disappointment more acute in times of rapid change. That is what is happening now, and in part it explains the much-vaunted Islamic revival: the feeling among many Muslims that Muslim practice has been faulty and that major changes are necessary.

Muslims themselves are certainly conscious that history has brought them to an unhappy state. They differ a great deal in analyzing the causes, but they all seem to agree that Islam has been in decline. There are, roughly speaking, three schools of thought on the subject.

[2]By James Piscatori, political scientist, from his book *Islam in a World of Nation-States*, pp. 22–39. Copyright © Royal Institute of International Affairs 1986. Reprinted by permission.

The first holds that the cause of the decline is the deviation of the believers from the true path. This school has its antecedents, most directly, in the thinking of such people as Muhammad ibn 'Abd al-Wahhab who, in the mid-eighteenth century, believed that because of their ignorance or indolence Muslims failed to follow the precepts of the religion. The school today includes such distinguished figures as the Pakistani jurist Javed Iqbal, son of the great philosopher and poet Muhammad Iqbal. He suggests that as a result of perverting the essence of Islam, Muslims became captive to "autocratic sultanates,'" "sterile mulla-ism,'" and "decadent Sufism." Because of the lust for power, both political and clerical, and the attractions of mystical aloofness, Muslims fell victim to an unproductive and basically irrelevant Islam.

The second school of thought holds that the reason for the decline lies with Islam itself. The proponents of this view would not be surprised at what Mr. Justice Iqbal has to say, but they would maintain that the problems which he points to are part of the very nature of Islam and are not merely the result of distortions by the believers. Most people who feel this way shy away from direct criticisms of Islam, and speak instead of the absence of any analytical tradition and scientific methodology in Arab Islamic society, never quite making it clear whether they see the fault as lying with Arab civilization or Islamic civilization. Isma'il Mazhar, for instance, made the point that traditional beliefs imprisoned the minds of modern believers and therefore that an opening—presumably onto a secular vista—was required. Qustantin Zurayq, a Christian writer long associated with the American University of Beirut, came to a similar conclusion in examining the meaning of the defeats of 1948 and 1967. He said that the Israelis were victorious because their social order is predicated on a modern ideology that encourages the growth of industrialization and values rational inquiry. Arabs must follow suit, separating religion from politics and adopting modern, liberal ideas. Several Muslim writers have accepted this line of reasoning and argued for restricting the public role of Islam.

The third school of thought puts the blame for Islam's decline on the West and, more particularly, on Westernized Muslims for the ease with which unworthy and harmful innovations (*bida'*) have come into practice. The Egyptian Muslim Brother Sayyid Qutb is the best exponent of the argument, claiming that

Islam declined when Muslims coveted the mechanical energy of the West without realizing that spiritual emptiness would follow. The West, to put it simply, is an attractive though false model and, in so far as Muslims follow it, they deviate from "the straight path" (al-sirat al-mustaqim). Reacting against the heavy involvement of Americans in Iran during the Shah's period, the Iranian revolutionaries, religious as well as secular, have taken the argument further by talking about the West poisoning their society. The West thus becomes a pestilence that kills the very heart of Islamic society: 'Westoxification' (gharbzadegi), not simply Westernization, is now the cause of the decline. Muslim student activists throughout the world have enthusiastically taken up this theme and have unrelentingly attacked fellow Muslims for helping to spread the poison, or, to change the metaphor, becoming the "carcass merchants of Western culture." To be Westernized in order to be "progressive" is to be "enslaved."

Background to the Revival

Whatever the causes of decline may have been, there is a widespread assumption among both Muslims and non-Muslims that Islam is experiencing a "revival," or "resurgence," or "reaffirmation." It needs to be said, first, that these are convenient and understandable shorthand expressions. Any one term is as acceptable as any of the others (I will use "revival"), so long as it is understood that all of them would be misleading if their use implied that Muslims have only recently rediscovered their faith and dusted off the Qur'an. The truth, of course, is that Islam has been a constant component of the believers' lives. In addition, the idea of revival would be misleading if it implied that the more pronounced zeal and visibility of Muslims today are novel. This view would ignore that throughout Islamic history many activists have shattered the calm and have thought of themselves as purifiers or 'renewers' (mujaddids) of Islam. Indeed, there have been many other times when an observer could say, as Lady Duff Gordon did in the 1860s, that "a great change is taking place among the Ulema, that Islam is ceasing to be a mere party flag." One thinks of the agitation surrounding the Hashimiyya in the eight century; the Carmathians in the tenth; the Fatimids in the tenth and eleventh centuries; the Naqshbandiyya, particularly Ahmad Sirhindi, in the late sixteenth and early seventeenth centuries; Ibn 'Abd al-Wahhab of Arabia in the eighteenth; Uthman dan Fodio of western Africa in the early nineteenth; the followers of al-Afghani, 'Abduh, and Rida, often referred to as the Salafiyya, in the later nineteenth century; and the Muslim Brotherhood in this century.

Moreover, any one of the various terms for the revival would be misleading if it were taken to imply that a uniform process is at work, or that Muslims share one vision of the future. Muslims differ a great deal on important questions—on account of cultural differences, the teachings of various legal schools, the influence of particular leaders, the ethnic mix, and the degree of exposure to Western or secular ideas. Nevertheless, despite the differences, there is no doubt that a new dynamism has appeared since the late 1960s. Muslims have come to feel that the disparity between what Islam ordains and what people do is intolerable, or to feel that they must reaffirm that Islam is important to their social and political lives. Often they have come to feel both.

John Voll has usefully argued that there are four ways to approach the explanation of the current revival: (1) to emphasize the strengths of Muslim society, especially the oil wealth; (2) to emphasize the weaknesses of Islam in handling modernization; (3) to emphasize particular and changing circumstances rather than general patterns; and (4) to emphasize historical continuity and to see evolving development, not fits and starts. Each of these approaches makes a great deal of sense, and some of them have been followed by Muslims themselves in analysing what is happening today. But they give a part of the picture, and probably no one of them would be sufficient by itself to give the whole picture.

Let us look, for instance, at the approach which emphasizes the strengths of Muslim society. Considerable attention has been given to the connection of the oil price revolution and the Islamic revival. One exponent of this view gives principal credit for the revival of the late 1970s to the oil boom of the mid-1970s. The boom is said to be the cause of the revival because the new wealth gave rise to independent centres of power, notably Saudi Arabia and Libya; because it set in motion the process whereby a charismatic leader, Khomeini, came to dominate the Muslim stage; and because it gave Muslims an opportune infusion of vitality. Other writers put primary emphasis on the self-confidence of Muslims: oil has brought about this new assertiveness, and this accounts in large part for the "international successes of Islam"— institution-building and conferences—which in turn are largely responsible for the revival within individual countries.

These are, nevertheless, really two arguments, which are not equally convincing. First, there is the argument that oil wealth has generated a revolutionary social process, and, second, that oil wealth has provided the means for revolutionary activity. The first deals with underlying causes and is thus different in scope from the second, which deals with the capability to do things. I will return to the first argument later, but the second argument is troubling mainly because it underestimates the importance of other factors.

Indeed, one may well wonder whether this way of arguing, centring on having the resources to act, does not put the cart before the horse. Certainly it is the case that would-be revolutionaries remain unhappy schemers but not doers if they lack the means to act. Ends *are* linked to means. However, the availability of the means (oil) does not in itself account for the pursuit of the ends (revival) in the first place. In fact, to argue otherwise is to flirt with the fallacy in logic, *post hoc, ergo propter hoc*: "after the oil revolution, therefore because of it." Moreover, this view of the genesis of the revival reduces everything to the material dimension and, in essence, simplistically makes the spiritual dimension dependent on the material dimension. As I have argued throughout, religion is probably more often dependent on politics than politics is dependent on religion, but spiritual yearnings are something else. They are not as institutionalized as religion, or as capable of manipulation. Finally, this view gives to the revival a greater uniformity than in fact it possesses; it paints a picture of greater cohesion than is deserved.

Did oil give rise to the revival, or did the revival assure that the oil wealth would be sent in a particular way? The question may strike some as useless, or indeed as irrelevant, as the chicken-and-egg paradox, but it does serve to highlight the basic question: would there have been a revival in the 1970s without the oil revolution? The answer must almost certainly be yes. There have been other revivals in previous centuries without the benefit of oil. And, in our century as well, although the possession of vast amounts of capital may have accelerated the process, and perhaps also helped to coordinate Muslim activities, the revival had begun well before the oil revolution of the 1970s.

Reasons for the Revival

In looking for an explanation of the revival, therefore, we must take a somewhat longer view. Four broad reasons come into sight.

First, the defeat of Egypt, Syria, and Jordan in the 1967 war with Israel shattered the morale not only of the Arabs, who lost in a head-to-head fight with the enemy, but also of most Muslims, who lost the holy city of Jerusalem. This was not just a defeat or a loss; it was *al-nakba*, '*the* disaster'—the culmination of a long series of setbacks and humiliations which stretched back in modern times to the first militarily unsuccessful encounters that the Ottoman Muslims had with the Europeans. These defeats had given rise to a sense of inferiority, which at first was based on an appreciation of technological, though not theological, inadequacy. But now, in the mid-twentieth century, the loss of sacred territory led many Muslims to conclude either one of two things—either that Islam was an inferior religion, or that they were inadequate believers who had not lived up to the ideals of Islam and therefore deserved their fate.

Most Muslims seem to have concluded that they—or at least their governments—had gone astray, although by and large they did not work out the implication of their failure: that the other side, the enemy, had done something right. This inability or unwillingness to grasp the nettle was the despair of many intellectuals, but, probably because of its simplicity, the popular conclusion concentrated the emotions: Muslims needed to be better Muslims, and their governments more Islamic, if God was to spare them further calamity, or if they were ever to have a chance of recapturing Jerusalem. At the very least the Israeli occupation outraged them, and in the common outrage Muslims everywhere found a stronger identification with each other than had existed previously in the modern era. Some Arab Muslims, in particular, came to see a certain hollowness in Nasirism, the ideology that had seemed the panacea for the Arabs' problems, and were prompted to search for an ideology and programme that could be both coherent and effective. Even before the war, some had come to regard 'Abd al-Nasir as an impious and incompetent tyrant, and as such a greater enemy than the Israelis. But, when it came, the catastrophe of 1967 forced many others to reconsider basic principles and to look for an Islamic ideology.

It is all the more ironic, then, that in 1985, less than twenty years after the 1967 war, many Muslim—mainly Shi'i—activists in Lebanon came to see the Palestinians as an obstacle to their own Islamic revolution. They reached this conclusion as a consequence of disputes, over power and territorial control in Lebanon, and these disputes, along with the generally heightened awareness of Islam since the Iranian revolution, led them to de-emphasize the Palestinian struggle *per se* while putting more stress on liberating Jerusalem, the third holiest city of Islam. For whatever reason, then—the defeat of the Arabs by Israel or the conflict between Palestinians and Shi'i groups in Lebanon—a new sense of Islamic commitment has emerged out of the general Arab-Israeli imbroglio.

Second, the process of development has been a contributing factor. It has stimulated the revival in two main ways: (a) it has often strained the social and political fabric, thereby leading people to turn to traditional symbols and rites as a way of comforting and orienting themselves; and (b) it has provided the means of speedy communication and easy dissemination of both domestic and international information.

(a) The most important dimension to the first point is the unsettling and unrelieved exodus of people from the countryside to the cities. For example, between 1960 and 1975 the rate of increase in the urban population exceeded the growth of the industrial labour force in Egypt by 2 per cent, Iran by 3 per cent, Iraq by 8 per cent, Jordan by 18 per cent, Kuwait by 14 per cent, Lebanon by 3 percent, Morocco by 10 percent, Saudi Arabia by 11 per cent, Syria by 3 per cent, and South Yemen by 13 per cent. More recent data would undoubtedly show this trend continuing. Most rural migrants quickly become the urban poor, victims of their own hope, swallowed by the very process which they believed would liberate them. Unscrupulous contractors exploit the members of this seemingly inexhaustible labour pool in order to build as cheaply as possible the new buildings that dot the urban landscape, and government is often unwilling or unable to protect them and to give them basic shelter. In countries such as India and Nigeria, they are also subjected to ethnic or racial discrimination and made to feel that they do not belong and that they probably never will. Many of their children are likely to be forgotten, escaping the educational net and remaining largely unprotected against serious disease.

I must not leave the simplistic impression that these rural migrants have the same destiny or produce the same effect everywhere that they settle. These obviously differ with the culture, the state of the economy, and the size of the city. With regard to the last point, for example, migrants are able to spread rural attitudes more widely in small provincial towns than in the large cities, and not simply because of the difference in size. As Şerif Mardin shows in the case of Turkey, the provincial towns provide fertile ground for Islamic sentiment because the petty-bourgeois merchants and the small-scale farmers feel exploited by the large capitalists and alienated from their Europeanized culture. But there does seem to be a general connection between the sense of not belonging and the turn to religion. In places where Sufi *tariqas*, or brotherhoods, are present, such as Morocco or Senegal, the mystical assimilation of a local saint's grace (*baraka*) is a powerful antidote to the joylessness of everyday life. In some societies, such as Iran, where well-established religious institutions provide some degree of financial assistance, or at least cushion the move from the countryside, migrants naturally come into close contact with the religious officials. In Lebanon the Shi'a who have migrated from the south or the Beqaa Valley to Beirut do not seem to lose their sectarian identification. If anything, they become more aware of it. In the city and suburbs, as outsiders needing the patronage of families to which they do not belong, they feel that they have incurred dishonour and lowered the status that they had in the countryside. In such an alien environment, the political point of reference is no longer family, as it was in the village, but sect. In other societies, such as Nigeria, where extreme economic imbalance and a climate of religious tension prevail, the migrants become natural recruits of millenarian movements. The official report on the Kano disturbances in December 1980, in which the followers of the self-proclaimed prophet known as Maitatsine wreaked horrendous devastation, explained this phenomenon well:

We have earlier made mention of his [Maitatsine's] application for a piece of land to erect temporary structures. His intention, we believe, was to provide accommodation for these men coming from the rural areas since he knew very well that the first problem they would face on arrival at Kano was accommodation. . . . These fanatics who have been brought up in extreme poverty, generally had a grudge against privileged people in the society, whose alleged ostentatious way of living often annoyed them. Because of the very wide gap between the rich and the poor in our society and coupled with the teaching of Muhammad Marwa [Maitatsine], they were more than prepared to rise against the society at the slightest opportunity. After all they did not have much to lose. . . . They did not own more than the clothes they wore. They had nothing to fall back to.

In every case, the migration from the countryside has helped to spread rural attitudes in the cities, particularly a pronounced emphasis on Islamic tradition. It has thus given impetus to the urban Islamic revival.

The effects are less dramatic among the middle classes, but many of these, too, are unhappy with the process of development. As sophisticated education has become increasingly available, technicians, lawyers, engineers, and teachers have become the new "productive" middle class in place of the old bazaaris and landowners. These latter resent the loss of status and influence and are suspicious of the Western advisers, suddenly indiscreetly visible, who are purportedly exemplars of a different lifestyle and set of values, and are supposed to show the local people the way to a more efficient and prosperous future. The former, the members of the "new" middle class, are impatient with the old ideology and anxious to better their position socially and politically.

Poverty and deprivation affect the attitudes of the rural migrants and, equally true, greater wealth and an improved social position affect the attitudes of the middle classes. It is precisely because the middle classes are better off that they are dissatisfied; their appetite has been whetted and they want more. This is particularly true of the lower middle class. According to Saad Eddin Ibrahim's profile of Egyptian Islamic militants, over 70 per cent were from modest, not poor, backgrounds and were first-generation city-dwellers. Nazih Ayubi shows further that there is a difference in social background between those who attend al-Azhar and those who attend the secular universities, and that it is this latter, upwardly mobile and largely non-peasant, group that yields more of the new activists than we might have guessed. In fact, there is nothing new in this pattern: for example, of the 1,950 members of the main assembly of the Egyptian Muslim Brotherhood (al-Ikhwan al-Muslimun) in 1953, only 22 were not of the educated urban middle classes.

For many urban Muslims, however, the sense of not belonging, of being neither fully modern nor suitably traditional, has been the price of success. A 1971 study of middle-class Egyptians indicated that a high proportion did not feel integrated into society and in fact regarded their relations with other people in terms of hostility and even conflict. Religion may not hold the answer for these people, but they are automatically attracted to it because the religious instinct runs deep and because such secular ideologies as Nasirism and Ba'thism have seemed so obviously wanting—both materially and spiritually. Most members of the middle classes will express their religious feeling through the state-controlled religious estalbishment and will oppose a radical challenge to it. Yet some will turn to more radical alternatives as they sense that the religious establishment is indistinguishable from a regime whose policies appear to close doors to them, even as they open doors to foreign political and business elites. (President al-Sadat's economic policy of attracting outside investment was called *infitah*, or 'opening'.) These Muslims will take to radical and often violent activity as they shout "Allahu Akhbar!"' ("God is most great!"), but they have something in common with those others who feel at sea. Islam, not clearly defined but keenly felt, is their mooring. The metaphor is different in a short story by the Egyptian writer Alifa Rifaat, but the point is the same: for the middle-class woman trying to come to terms with her new sexual assertiveness, "the five daily prayers were like punctuation marks that divided up and gave meaning to her life.'"

(*b*) The other way in which the process of development has stimulated a sense of renewal is by advancing the dissemination of information throughout the developing world. Despite the static plight of the sub-proletariat or *lumpenproletariat*, there have been substantial improvements in literacy among the rest of the population; moreover, radios have become a common possession. As a result, people are now more in touch with what is going on in the rest of the world, and are anxious to formulate Islamic positions on current political, economic, and social issues—or, in other words, to think of the world's problems in Islamic terms. At the same time, Muslims come to know how dissatisfaction and protest against injustices can be and have been, in other places, framed by reference to Islam.

The fast and efficient distribution within Iran of Ayatollah Khomeini's sermons, delivered in exile and recorded on cassettes—"revolution-by-cassette"—demonstrates further how modern information technology can help people focus their discontent and build their identity around one set of ideas, even though the exponent of those ideas is far removed. To put it the other way around, it shows how religious leaders can use popular feelings by appealing to traditional values, even when they are not physically present: this projection is the powerful extension of the mosque sermon (*khutba*). Khomeini provides the most celebrated example, but there are others. Cassettes of the sermons of Shaykh 'Abd al-Hamid Kishk, an Egyptian *'alim*, are played throughout the Middle East. Young people are particularly attracted by them, as young people throughout Malaysia are attracted by recordings of the *khutbas* of Haji Hadi Awang, who, from his base in rural Trengganu, rails—impartially—against infidels and healf-hearted Muslims alike. Because of the emphasis on community, the importance of the mosque as a central meeting-place, the gathering together of Muslims from all over the world during the Pilgrimage, and the respect given to such official interpreters as the *'ulama*, Islam constitutes a vigorous communication system of its own and is what Marshal Lyautey called "a sounding board."' Modern technology has dramatically enhanced this capability.

The third general reason for the present revival, in addition to the intellectual and spiritual malaise since the 1967 war and the effects of the development process, is that Muslim societies have been caught up in the universal crisis of modernity. Most Muslims, like virtually everyone else in the developed and developing world, are feeling ill at ease with a way of life that places less and less emphasis on loyalties to the family and seems to find religious institutions increasingly irrelevant. In the past century a discernible shift towards the individual has taken place within societies—i.e., toward lessening the individual's dependence on the extended family (even in such socially conservative Gulf shaykhdoms as Qatar), weakening parental authority, liberating women, and questioning the authority of the clergy. No direct causal relationship exists of course, but this period has also seen an alarming increase in divorce, alcohol and drug addiction, nerve disorders, and crime. It is not surprising, therefore, that "dropping-out,"' or 'evaporation' (*johatsu*) as the Japanese say, has come to seem attractive to many. At the very least, modernism has led to a diminution of belief: "After the dizzying history of the last fifty years, the world has grown strange, and people floated."' Iranian writers, for example, are now beginning to talk about modernity, not modernization, as the problem, and the notion that something is missing in one's life seems to have generated a time of "secular discontents,"' leading many to wonder whether the age has lost its way and to ask, "What is it, after all, to be modern?"'

Modernity gives rise to a basic search for identity, in which many people accept that knowing oneself comes through associating with the crowd rather than seeking to rise above it. This search is in fact an individual act of self-discovery, but because of Islam's intense association of the individual believer with the whole community of believers, it seems as if it is an act of self-abnegation. Muslims in a sense are looking for what Daniel Bell called "new rites of incorporation,"' which link today's deracinated individual to a community and a history. And yet, in another sense, this is wrong: they are looking, rather, for *old* rites of incorporation that appear to be new even as they are familiar. Religion, precisely because in the past it answered questions on life and death and provided its followers with moral links to each other, becomes the means by which individuals hope to answer the new question of what it is to be modern, and, in so doing, to gain perhaps a reassuring, common world-view. In this respect, born-again Christians and veiled-again Muslims are responding to the same broad phenomenon.

Islam supplies a particularly powerful rite of incorporation because it puts great emphasis on the idea of community and on the Prophet's time as the model for the organization of society. Prior to the revelation that Muhammad received, the people of the Arabian peninsula had worshipped several gods and organized themselves according to tribal, blood ties. But it was the radical innovation of Islam to insist that each person is to be subservient to the one true God and to look upon every other person as brother. This community is based on the bonds of morality, not blood or tribal custom or expediency, and involves the acceptance of responsibilities towards God and men. Although the *umma* incorporates all the believers, it will eventually become universal and include all mankind. In the meantime, Muslims are to follow the example of the Prophet and, in the case of the Sunnis, his four immediate successors, "the rightly guided Caliphs,"' or, in the case of the Shi'a, the Imams. It is this perception of fraternity, and of a glorious past, that gives all Muslims—Sunnis and Shi'a—a powerful sense of belonging.

Finally, the fourth general reason for the revival is that the conditions of political development in these societies have tended to heighten the importance of Islam as a political ideology. Because most of these societies are poor in institutions and dominated by unelected rulers, it is natural for those in power to look for a way of legitimating themselves. Legitimation may perhaps be too grand a word to convey what I mean: rulers seek evidence of approval from the ruled or, at least, evidence of acquiescence or the absence of outright opposition. Several monarchies are especially adept at using Islamic symbols for this purpose: the Moroccan king makes much of his traditional title, Commander of the Faithful (*amir al-mu'minin*); the Saudi king finds a naturally sympathetic response when he speaks of his role as protector of Mecca and Medina; and the Jordanian king is careful to emphasize his descent from the Prophet. Monarchs probably always need reassurance, but the need in the case of these leaders has certainly become greater and more definite since the unleashing by the Iranian revolution of a violent ideological storm whose avowed purpose has been to overcome all the remaining shahs of the Muslim world. The fact that development schemes seem to be losing momentum or running into trouble has further contributed to the uneasy climate.

This defensiveness on the part of the existing leaders has been apparent not only in the traditional monarchies, but also in the republics, where such leaders as al-Sadat and Mubarak of Egypt and al-Numayri of the Sudan have faced considerable opposition to their rule and have found it expedient to put Islam to their service. Al-Sadat, for example, found it useful—although it was extremely controversial—to have a *fatwa* from al-Azhar supporting his peace treaty with Israel; Mubarak has created an official Islamic publication, *al-Liwa al-Islami* (*The Islamic Standard*), to rival the popular and often censorious Muslim Brotherhood publication *al-Da'wa* (*The Call*); and al-Numayri courted Sufi leaders and made concessions to the Muslim Brothers, such as the introduction of Islamic law. In Malaysia as well, the government, although keenly aware of the multi-ethnic composition of the population, has increasingly affirmed its Islamic credentials, and the ruling party, the United Malays' National Organization (UMNO), has claimed that it is the largest Islamic party in the country.

In all these countries governments have been able to use Islam with such ease because, as an ideology, it is vague in content yet highly charged: people instinctively respond to it as a general symbol but also as a guide to their loyalties. Its vocabulary, too, is thoroughly familiar to everyone, thereby guaranteeing that the government's message cannot be missed. Napoleon recognized the value—and ease—of using Islamic symbolism at the time of his invasion of Egypt in 1798. His proclamation to the people of Egypt began with the standard Muslim invocation of "God, the Merciful, the Compassionate" (*bismallah*), and went on to say: "I worship God (may He be exalted) far more than the Mamlukes do, and respect His Prophet and Glorious Quran. . . . [T]he French also are sincere Muslims."

Governments have also been able to use Islam to their own ends because it lends itself readily to nationalization: or, to express it differently, they have been able to make it part of the bureaucracy. Even the Malaysian federal government, which is sensitive to states' rights, pre-eminently including the right to regulate religion, has moved to bureaucratize Islam. It has not only created such coordinating bodies as the National Council for Islamic Affairs, the National Fatwa Council, and the Religious Affairs Division of the Prime Minister's office, but has also taken over a number of religious schools in the states. In effect, then, governments have recognized the power of Islam and sought to harness it to their own ends.

But just as Islam can be used to legitimate, so can it be used to express opposition. And there are signs that this use has been increasing too. The increase has come about partly as a reult of the Shah's overthrow, but also because in many countries in which there are no regular outlets for political expression Islam has been found to be an effective and relatively safe way of making a political stand. Governments have been hesitant to suppress groups speaking in the name of Islam because of the need to appear orthodox themselves, in order either to forestall domestic opposition or to attract aid from Muslim "patrons" such as Saudi Arabia. As a result, many Muslim groups have been relatively free to criticize their governments, albeit in a circumspect way. The Muslim Brotherhood has been doing this in Jordan, where it has been tolerated as long as it remains a loyal opposition; this pattern was also true of the Brotherhood in the Sudan for most of the al-Numayri regime. Furthermore, it has happened in Algeria and Tunisia, where Muslim groups have acted as a kind of pressure group that tries to influence policies rather than to replace the regime.

In regimes so repressive that they brook no dissent and regard Muslim criticism of any sort as a threat to their survival, the "Islamic alternative"' almost invariably has become more radical. It has become a kind of party, whose aim is to replace the regime, rather than a pressure group. This radicalization of a political alternative of course happens in any repressive society, as it did in Poland, where Solidarity may be thought of as the opposition party. It even happens in societies perceived by only a small minority to be repressive, such as West Germany, which is totalitarian in the eyes of the Baader-Meinhoff gang. My point is not to demonstrate the uniqueness of Muslim societies but merely to indicate that in the Muslim case, too, ostensibly ideological—or religious—groups may become politically radicalized in certain circumstances.

Islam might acquire an even more contentious political centrality, a revolutionary character, if social and economic conditions were dire. This would be the case if there were a marked division between the haves and have-nots, or, to use the terminology at once Qur'anic and secular of the Iranian revolution, between the oppressors' (*mustakbarun*) (16:22–3) and the 'oppressed' (*mustad'afun*) (4:97). The rural poor and new urban immigrants would constitute the "oppressed" (or the 'disinherited', as is said in Lebanon), and the large landowners and urban middle-class professionals would constitute the "oppressors." In this situation, as was the case in Iran, politics would become increasingly polarized and vicious as all were caught up in a double revolution of expectations: peasants expecting the good life in the dazzling capitals; professionals and intellectuals expecting greater influence, status, and political participation. Both sides would be destined for disappointment, and would inevitably see each other as obstacles. The professionals and intellectuals would come to regard the urban immigrants as a drain on scarce resources; and, more importantly, given the role played by street politics in the increasingly city-dominated developing countries, the 'disinherited' would come to regard members of the new professional middle class as new oppressors, who used Islam as a tactic to gain mass support but who really cared only about advancing their own narrow self-interest. Moreover, those who said they wanted to make Islam relevant to the conditions of the modern world would be seen as having sold out to, or at least compromised with, the Westernized, secularizing leadership. It is in this way that "modernist"' groups, such as the Masyumi party in Indonesia, lose ground to more "traditionalist"' ones, such as the Nahdatul Ulama.

In effect, then, a revolution of *falling* expectations would take place, particularly among the rural poor and urban immigrants. Seeing a prosperous future recede on the horizon, they would naturally cling to the only comfort of the present, the pillar of traditional faith, and, in doing so, would give political expression to the frustration and indignities of living on the margin of the society. It is a phenomenon that Soviet writers have come to regard as inevitable: "It is natural for them, therefore, to express their socio-political aspirations and protest against colonial and imperialist oppression in religious form."'

Interpreting the Revival

The impression that I have left, though, is too stark. There is really nothing inevitable about revolutionary activism among the dispossessed; "the wretched of the earth"' rarely have enough energy left over from the struggle of daily life to mount revolutions. As Farhad Kazemi points out, the Iranian situation was an exception to the general pattern that had been seen in Iran previously and elsewhere, which shows the rural poor to be by and large content with their meagre lot in the cities and politically passive. But there does appear to be a great deal of truth in the point that they turn to religion, even if they do not take to arms. It is hard to generalize further, since the real reasons for political activism will be found in the specific conditions of the various countries.

For example, one cannot explain the importance of Muslim groups in Egypt without explaining the roots of the Muslim Brotherhood in Egyptian soil and the more or less constant struggle between the Brothers and those in power, particularly the Nasirists. In the case of Syria, one would need to refer to the hegemony of the Ba'th Party and the peculiarly hegemonic role that al-Asad's 'Alawi companions play within the party. Opposition to the dominance of the party and to the 'Alawis is the common point of a diffuse opposition that has taken on a quasi-religious guise. With respect to Tunisia, one would have to explain how its Mediterranean culture and the heavy hand of Bourguiba's secularism since independence have restricted the role of Islam. In the case of Nigeria, one would seek to explain the growth of Sufism by reference to the persistence of tribal and regional identities, the growth of Christian proselytizing, and the importance of the traditional *al-majiri* system of Qur'anic education, whereby itinerant teachers disseminate ideas to the young. As regards China, one would have to point not only to the liberalization that issued from the post-Mao change of leadership but to the way in which such ethnic groups as the Uighurs and Kazakhs look to Islam for solidarity against the Han people.

This point—that Islamic politics are not monolithic—is fundamental, but it should not obscure the fact that the current revival is part of broader historical developments. According to one view, it must be seen as part of the revolutionary wave which began with the French Revolution but which has increasingly taken on Marxist form. There is something to this interpretation: one can readily detect evidence in the rhetoric of Iran's revolutionary leaders of what one writer calls "third worldism"'—that is, the belief that the West has controlled and exploited the developing world. Khomeini himself has taken what originally may have been the Marxist theme of attacking imperialism and attached to it the religiously symbolic theme of satanism: America, the arch imperialist, is the Great Satan. One can also see the ease, and utility, of blending Islamic and Marxist categories in the writing of the lay intellectual prophet of the revolution, 'Ali Shariati. Indeed, it is not an exaggeration to say that many of Khomeini's unpalatable ideas became acceptable, or at least that their unpalatability was reduced, by their association with Shariati and his ideas in the popular mind. Shariati reformulated the main Islamic argument against the Shah by explicitly associating political and social revolution—the commitment to overthrowing tyrants and unjust systems—with Shi'i heroism. In the Arab world, Ahmad Ben Bella, first president of Algeria, has recently linked a new Islamic consciousness with "anti-imperialism."

Yet it is one thing to say that Islamic revivalists borrow Marxist language and another to imply, as Elie Kedourie does, that they are advocating a variation on the Communist revolution in which the promise of "a Californian horn of plenty, a Swedish heaven of sexual liberation," spurs on the unhappy proletarian. The reference of course is to the fabled luxuries of paradise that are promised to those who die in a just war. However, even this allusion to a kind of eschatological materialism cannot hide the fact that the Muslim activist wants to create a new *spiritual* order, and that thus in the end his revolution is fundamentally different from that of the Marxist. But I must concede that, though the aims differ, both are ideologies that seek to create political orders, and in this sense they are similar.

There is another general view, held by many Muslims as well as non-Muslims, that the revival must be seen as part of a long historical process that began in the eighteenth century with the direct experience of European imperialism. For example, one writer has argued that the present revival is the third stage in a movement whose first stage was the defensive assertion that Islam is modern and can compete with Europe, and whose second stage was the Muslim elite's wholesale adoption of Western ways. The present stage, unsurprisingly, is a reaction to the preceding one. Whereas most Muslims may not be so analytical, they would endorse this general view. The messianic tradition cuts deeply into Islamic history, but, even when the dramatic appearance of the Mahdi is missing, Muslims understand that the community occasionally needs to undergo renewal (*tajdid*).

This kind of interpretation has obvious merit, since it does what history does: it provides context and *gravitas*. It helps to explain why the present revival is as it is, and it makes the revival seem more than merely superficial. Historical perspective is especially important when it comes, for example, to understanding that "development"' was an upper-class phenomenon until recently, which entailed the elite's adoption of certain characteristics from the West and its material as well as spiritual estrangement from society long before the contemporary period. However, the historical perspective can be taken too far: it might underplay the importance of unexpected and radical events such as the oil revolution of the mid-1970s; and it can be misleading if it makes the revival seem less vibrant or less passionate than it is. There is a danger of forgetting that what Anthony Wallace calls "revitalization movements"' occur because individuals feel themselves to be under severe stress and are dissatisfied with the prevailing social order and identity. It is true, to a large extent, that the revival is the sum of individual unhappiness.

But, to an even larger extent, the revival is the sum of individual contentment. I asked people throughout the Muslim world why they had become more devout than they had previously been. No one mentioned the social, economic, or political dislocations that I have dwelt on, and no one framed an answer in terms of emotional or psychological distress. More often than not, whether an Indonesian woman activist, a Malaysian politician, an Egyptian journalist, a Pakistani engineer, or a Jordanian lawyer, they shrugged and said simply that it had happened almost imperceptibly. If they mentioned any specific influence, it was the example of so many other people like themselves who had obviously become more religious. I imagine that less educated and less urbanized Muslims would have been no better able to explain what had happened.

Their inability to point to the factors that I have mentioned does not mean, of course, that these factors had no place. Clearly, I think that they did. But it does suggest that to many Muslims, the social, economic, and political factors were unimportant or irrelevant; in any event, they say, they would have felt the need to be more devout. There is thus a certain artlessness, almost ingenuousness, in their view of the revival. And this must remind us that, when all is considered, we are dealing with people's hopes and beliefs. These hopes and beliefs may become powerful currents that carry people along—almost, but not entirely, in spite of the social, economic, and political currents.

Conclusion

Several general points emerge from the preceding discussion. First, something that we can call a revival has clearly occurred. Muslims in all parts of the world have become more devout, concerned not only with the faithful observance of ritual but also with the social, economic, and political application of Islamic values. It makes little difference that Islam means many different things to different people. What counts is that all these people believe that Islam, not a secular ideology, increasingly shapes their attitudes and directs their actions.

Second, although revivalist sentiments run broad and deep and are unquestionably genuine, their catalyst is the variety of discontents associated with the development process. Migration from the country to the cities, high inflation, inadequate housing, Western economic penetration, and other factors have brought many people to the point of frustration, even confusion. In this frame of mind, they have taken a fresh look at what they are and want to be, and at what kind of future Islam promises them.

Third, partly because of these discontents and partly because of the example of the Iranian revolution, many Muslims have attempted to make Islam politically relevant. No doubt some Muslims use Islam to achieve their own narrow ambitions, but many others lay blame for the inadequacies of their life at the door of government.

Fourth, no real coordination of activity exists among the revivalists. The appeal to Islamic values, the sense of deprivation and deracination, and the inspiration drawn from the Iranian example are common elements, but the form that the revival takes and the effect that it produces vary according to circumstance and place.

However, the emotional nature of the revival has captured most attention in the West and generated negative, undifferentiated images. "Militant Islam" has become a favourite epithet, although its use is by no means new. In 1853 Palmerston had written that the Ottomans were not "reawakening the dormant fanaticism of the Musulman race." But what sympathy there was in this comment was prompted by specific Russian designs on the ottoman empire at the time, and not by an unusually enlightened attitude towards the Muslim world. Indeed, in the second half of the nineteenth century, Islam was invariably seen as fanatical. Some Europeans thought that Islam was interfering with the nationalist aspirations of the Christian peoples of the empire. Carlyle, for example, argued in 1877 that "the unspeakable Turk should be immediately struck out of the question" and Bulgaria "left to honest European guidance." Other Europeans—especially in the quarter-century from 1880, when a nationalist movement was stirring in Egypt and Mahdism appeared in the Sudan—thought that Islam was fanatical because it promoted the nationalist aspirations of Muslim peoples.

The general condemnation of Islamic fanaticism for being at once anti-nationalist and pro-nationalist had as its common assumption that Islam was not acting in the interest of the European powers. Whether it was the Ottoman attempt to thwart Christian nationalists or the Muslim attempt to gain independence from the West, Islam was fanatical because it ran counter to imperial interests. But it was the converse formulation that became the standard explanation of Muslim conduct: Islam was hostile to the West because it was fanatical. As might be expected from dealing with such a crude stereotype of Islam, however, the differences among Muslims were obscured. Consequently, Muslims came to be seen as a uniformly emotional and sometimes illogical race that moved as one body and spoke with one voice.

In the twentieth century, many Westerners have continued to think in this way and to assume, implicitly or explicitly, that Islam's emotional militancy belies the idea that Muslims can have differing political or national interests. In 1934, with the agitations in India on his mind, Lord Strabolgi prophesied in the British parliament: "There will be attempts made, the beginnings are visible now, to make a Mahomedan political bloc, not friendly to the British empire, from, at any rate, Cairo to Delhi. This is the kind of unity we may end in seeing if we are not extraordinarily careful." The revival dating from the late 1960s, and particularly the tumultuous upheaval of the Iranian revolution, have given new life to such views, even among generally level-headed observers of international relations. Raymond Aron, for example, warned of the Islamic "revolutionary wave," generated by "the fanaticism of the prophet and the violence of the people," which the Auatollah Khomeini has unleashed. Cyrus Vance has explained that a major reason why, as Secretary of State, he opposed any rescue mission to obtain the release of the American hostages in Iran in 1980 was fear that it would precipitate an "Islamic-Western war": "Khomeini and his followers, with a Shi'ite affinity for martyrdom, actually might welcome American military action as a way of uniting the Moslem world against the West."

The idea that Muslims have variable and often conflicting national interests is absent in these statements, and thus many Westerners seem to assume that national divisions are somehow antithetical to Islam's real nature. This view has perhaps been intensified by the current revival, but in order to assess it we need to explore the relationship between Islam and national pluralism in the longer historical record.

THE RELIGIOUS SCHOLARS LED THE REVOLT[3]

A year to the day after the interview conducted in Neauphle-le-Chateau, Imam Khomeini granted the translator a second interview, which took place at his residence in Qum. The first question posed—concerning the central issue of the position held by the religious leadership in the new political system—was answered in such detail that no time remained for other questions. The Persian text of this interview was published in the Tehran daily newspaper *Jumhuri-yi Islami*, on Day 12, 1358/January 2, 1980.

It is apparent to everyone that the militant religious scholars, led by yourself, have played an important role in the Islamic Revolution. One of the factors enabling them to play this role has no doubt been the independence they have enjoyed vis-a-vis the state, an independence that was often complete. Now that, as a result of the Revolution, an Islamic government has come into being in Iran, will the religious scholars continue to function as a separate institution, or will some form of merger take place between them and the state? The latter possibility is suggested by the fact that certain religious scholars have already assumed executive functions.

You know that under the former regime, and also under the other monarchies that existed throughout Iranian history, not to mention the other forms of government in different parts of the world that contravened divine law and the principle of *tauhid*, the laws enforced were manmade laws, the product of the human mind. Whatever the specific form of government in each case, the laws enforced all had that common characteristic, and they were generally inspired by a desire to dominate the people. Of course, it occasionally happened that laws were put into effect for the sake of assuring order in society and the liberty of the people. But if we are looking for a government that is based on the principle of *tauhid* and follows divine law, it is to Islam that we must turn. If such a government did exist before Islam, examples of it must be extremely rare.

[3]By Ruhollah Khomeini, spiritual leader of the Islamic Republic of Iran, from a book of his collected writings and speeches, *Islam and Revolution: Writing and Declarations of Imam Khomeini*, pp. 329–343. Copyright © 1981 By Mizan Press. Reprinted by permission.

The sole determining principle in a government based on *tauhid* is divine law, law that is the expression of divine will, not the product of the human mind. Now in the first age of Islam—an age nearer to us in time, of course, than that of the earlier prophets—such a government existed. It was at first weak and limited in scope, and then later it ruled over vast areas, but insofar as it was Islamic and did not pursue any aims other than those of Islam, its ruling principle was always divine law, or God Himself. The government was the government of God. The prophets and those who succeeded them did not introduce anything of their own devising; their sole aim was to implement divine law. In certain matters of detail, they naturally had recourse to measures of their own, but as far as fundamental matters were concerned—those aspects of government that have to exist in every country—they followed divine law. The Messenger of God (peace and blessings be upon him), who is of course our exemplar, never enacted a single judgment or executed a single law in opposition to God's decree; on the contrary, he executed God's law.

There is a great difference between all the various manmade forms of government in the world, on the one hand—whatever their precise nature—and a divine government, on the other hand, which follows divine law. Governments that do not base themselves on divine law conceive of justice only in the natural realm; you will find them concerned only with the prevention of disorder and not with the moral refinement of the people. Whatever a person does in his own home is of no importance, so long as he causes no disorder in the street. In other words, people are free to do as they please at home. Divine governments, however, set themselves the task of making man into what he should be. In his unredeemed state man is like an animal, even worse than the other animals. Left to his own devices, he will always be inferior to the animals, for he surpasses them in passion, evil, and rapacity. As originally created, man is superior to all other beings, but at the same time, his capacities for passion, anger, and other forms of evil are virtually boundless. For example, if a person acquires a house, he will begin to desire another house. If a person conquers a country, he will begin plotting to conquer another country. And if a person were to conquer the entire globe, he would begin planning the conquest of the moon or Mars. Men's passions and covetousness, then, are unlimited, and it was in order to limit men, to tame them, that the prophets were sent. If this animal that has broken its bridle is allowed to roam freely outside all recognizable bounds, if it is left to itself and no attempt is made to train it, it will desire everything for itself and be prepared to sacrifice everyone to its desires. The prophets came to tame this unbridled beast and to make it subject to certain restraints. After taming it, they showed it how to achieve the perfections that constitute its true happiness, and here it is not a question of this world and the natural realm only. In the prophets' view, the world is merely a means, a path by which to achieve a noble aim that man is himself unaware of but that is known to the prophets. They know what the final destiny of man will be if he continues in his unfettered state, and they also know how different it will be if man is tamed and follows the path leading to the noble rank of true humanity.

All the concerns that, taken together, form the objective of most governments are but a path or a means in the view of the prophets. For them, the world cannot be an objective or a point of orientation, but only a path of ascent leading to the rank of true humanity. If a person embarks on this path, he will attain true happiness. The happiness he may enjoy in this world will not be confined to it, for his ultimate goal is a world that lies beyond the present one. The prophets have seen that world, which is unknown to us because it is beyond the range of sensory perception.

So the prophets came, first, to tame the forces of anger, passion, and evil that are present in man, and then to guide him on the path of ascent to which those forces are in opposition. Unfortunately, there were many obstacles in their way and they rarely succeeded in attaining their goal. For men are inclined by their very natures to passion, anger, and evil, and even those who do wish to tame those forces within themselves face all kinds of opposition and impediment. But whatever salvation or blessing does exist in the world is the result of the exertions of the prophets. Within the limits that were set for them, and as far as the rays of their teaching extended, they were able to impose certain bounds on the evil forces present in man. Their task was extremely difficult, but whatever good does exist in the world proceeds from them. If we were to exclude the prophets from the world, it would collapse, and everyone would see what chaos would ensue. It was the prophets who were responsible for imposing some limits on man, and whatever good and blessedness exist in this world are their work.

Islam has taken all the dimensions of man into consideration and provided for them. The law of Islam is restricted neither to the unseen realm nor to the manifest dimension, in the same way that man himself is not restricted to a single dimension. Islam came to fashion true and complete human beings, complete in all their dimensions. It did not cultivate exclusively either the spiritual dimension of man, which would have fostered in him an aversion to the natural realm, or the natural dimension, which would have made him satisfied with the natural realm. The natural dimension is the means, and the spiritual, the end. Stated differently, it was the task of the prophets to reform the natural dimension of man in order that it might become the means of his ascent.

Unfortunately, true Islam lasted for only a brief period after its inception. First the Umayyads and then the Abbasids inflicted all kinds of damage on Islam. Later the monarchs ruling Iran continued on the same path; they completely distorted Islam and established something quite different in its place. The process was begun by the Umayyads, who changed the nature of government from divine and spiritual to worldly. Their rule was based on Arabism, the principle of promoting the Arabs over all other peoples, which was an aim fundamentally opposed to Islam and its desire to abolish nationality and unite all mankind in a single community, under the aegis of a state indifferent to the matter of race and color. It was the aim of the Umayyads to distort Islam completely by reviving the Arabism of the pre-Islamic age of ignorance, and the same aim is still pursued by the leaders of certain Arab countries, who declare openly their desire to revive the Arabism of the Umayyads, which is nothing but the Arabism of the Jahiliyya.

The Umayyads and their successors in Islamic history did not allow men to grasp the true nature of Islam, in particular, Islamic government. As we have said, government is a means, a lower state that leads to a higher state, but the Umayyads and their successors prevented people from grasping even this lower state. It must be stated that throughout Islamic history, as a result of various kinds of distortion, Islam remained unknown among men.

This was particularly true during the last fifty years. You may be too young, but I witnessed it all during the past fifty years, from the coming to power of Riza Khan through a coup d'etat down to the state of our country just before the Revolution.

It was the British who put Riza Khan in power, as they later admitted themselves in a broadcast over Radio Delhi, and when he disobeyed them, they carried him off to a place of their own choosing.

In the beginning, he sought to employ Islam as a weapon against Islam by doing things designed to please the Muslims. The martyrdom of the Lord of the Martyrs (peace be upon him) is important in Iran, so Riza Khan used to devote much attention to attending *rauzas*, and it is said that he used to go barefoot to *takiyas* [where *rauzas* were being held. He thus succeeded in gaining popularity, although his true aim was to acquire a weapon to use against the people. Once his government was firmly established, he began to carry out his instructions (of course, his own inclinations may have coincided with his instructions, and some of what he did was in imitation of Ataturk. Now he reached for the weapon of unbelief, and the first thing he planned to do was to root out every trace of Islam in Iran. How was this to be done? One way was to take away the religious assemblies to which the people were so attached and to destroy them—the assemblies where the struggle of the Lord of the Martyrs was commemorated, which had such great moral value for the people. Riza Khan banned *rauzas* throughout Iran; no one could organize a *rauza*, not even if only a few people were to be present. Even in Qum, which was then, as now, the center of the religious institution, there were no *rauza* assemblies, or if there were, they had to be held between dawn and sunrise. Before the first call to prayer, five to ten people would gather for a brief talk and commemoration of Karbala, and when the call to prayer was sounded, or very soon after, they had to disperse. Sometimes informers were present, and when they turned in their reports, all who had attended the meeting were arrested.

Worse than that, and striking a more damaging blow to the foundations of Islam, was Riza Khan's plan to destroy the religious institution completely. He began by removing the religious scholars' turbans from their heads and forbidding turbans to be worn. Some government officials would say that not more than six people in all Iran should be permitted to wear turbans, but they were lying since it was their intention to abolish the turban entirely. The goal was to destroy the religious scholars as a class.

Those instructing Riza Khan in these measures had seen for more than a century that whenever they wished to inflict some loss on the people, the religious scholars had stood in their way. For example, when the British had more or less conquered Iraq, they saw a great religious leader, the late Mirza Muhammad Taqi Shirazi, oppose their aims and rescue the independence of Iraq. Earlier, his teacher, Mirza Hasan Shirazi, had saved Iran from the British by uttering a single sentence. In short, they saw the religious leaders as troublesome elements that prevented them from attaining their goals, which were primarily to gain access to the natural resources and minerals of the East and to turn our cities into markets for their goods, so that we would be reduced to the dependent status of consumers.

They realized that in order to deprive our people of the leadership that made it possible for them to concentrate their forces against foreign domination, religious scholars as a class had to be destroyed. The religious leaders had consistently served as defenders of Islam and the laws of Islam, sometimes with success, as in the case of Mirza Hasan Shirazi, whom all Iran followed, and sometimes with failure.

In more recent times, when Muhammad Riza embarked on his satanic rule, he imitated his father by professing loyalty to Islam initially and using Islam as a weapon. For example, he commissioned a printing of the Qur'an, visited Mashhad once or twice a year, and prayed upon occasion. He wanted to deceive the people, and indeed he did succeed in deceiving some of them. But gradually he came to feel there was no longer any need for deceit, and he began to rule by pure force and, at the same time, to rob the people of all their wealth and resources. As you know, it was impossible to breathe freely in Iran. All the newspapers and magazines, as well as the radio and television, served him and opposed the people. Many people were silenced and imprisoned, and the resources of the nation were plundered.

But at the same time, Muhammad Riza made loud claims about having "A Mission to Serve the Country," even writing a book with that title, and conducted a propaganda campaign about the alleged progress the nation had made. Everyone knew those were lies. Everywhere in Iran there is still poverty and wretchedness; conditions for the common people are so miserable that they do not even have homes. The people that live right on top of our oil deposits are suffering from hunger and thirst, and cannot even clothe themselves adequately. I once passed through the region of Ahvaz and its surrounding villages by train, and I remember seeing barefoot people—adults and children—rushing up to the train to beg for a mouthful of food. Vast oil resources lay beneath them, but the wealth those resources produced went elsewhere—into the pockets of foreigners, particularly the Americans. In return, America gave us the military bases it constructed for itself in our territory. That is, it took back the money it had paid for our oil and used it to build military bases for itself; this is one of the worst adversities it inflicted upon us. In addition, there were the burdensome contracts and agreements they imposed on us: none of them benefited our nation; on the contrary, they increased the domination of Iran by America.

As a result of all this, our people came to feel desperate. Many were forced to spend their lives in prison or banishment, and indeed, in a certain sense, everyone was a prisoner, because government agents were always watching to make sure that no one uttered a word of protest. If you or someone like you had come to Iran, it would have been impossible for him to conduct an interview on these matters, or even say a few words.

The people were feeling desperate and waiting for some voice to be raised in protest so that they could join in.

That voice was raised in Qum on Khurdad 15. During the months just before it, the city's religious scholars were beginning to voice their opposition to the regime, and various events ensued that culminated in the great uprising of Khurdad 15. That uprising was suppressed by a huge massacre. I was in prison at the time and did not know what was happening, and even when I was released from prison, I was under house arrest. Nonetheless, people found ways to inform me that 15,000 were killed and an indefinite number arrested. People were reduced to such a state that life no longer meant much to them. They had to live out their lives in the shadow of evil. Fathers and sons watched each other suffer; so did husbands and wives. In short, the life of the people was harsh and difficult, and they again began to wait for a spark of deliverance.

Khurdad 15 had been such a spark, and although it was put out, the people were not entirely defeated. They continued to await a favorable opportunity for resuming their struggle, until finally there began the series of events that started two years ago.

The people were ready for revolution: they were dissatisfied with their government and discontented with their lives, and— most importantly—God had brought about a spiritual transformation in them. The essence of this transformation, which still persists to some extent, is that people began to yearn for martyrdom, just as they had done in the earliest age of Islam. Look at the demonstrations that are still taking place; you will see people wearing shrouds and proclaiming their readiness for martyrdom. Mothers who have lost children come to me and ask me to pray that one or two more of their children may be martyred. Young people, both men and women, also ask me to pray that they may become martyrs. This, then, is a spiritual transformation being wrought in our people by God's will.

In addition, the whole nation was unanimous in its dissatisfaction. Muhammad Riza had done nothing to satisfy any segment of the population. He cared only for the upper echelons of the army and the security forces; he despised everyone else. He took no account of anyone: not of the civil service, nor the army (its lower ranks, that is), nor the bazaar, nor the mosque, nor the religious institution, nor the university. In fact, that was his greatest mistake: he regarded the people as nothing.

The people, then, were united in their dissatisfaction, and when the demand for an Islamic republic was raised, no one opposed it. The whole country in unison demanded the foundation of an Islamic republic and the abolition of the monarchy, and since the people were strengthened by divine support, they reached their goal despite the support and protection that were being extended to Muhammad Riza by various powers, great and small—particularly America and Britain (unfortunately, the governments of most Muslim countries adopted their attitude).

Once the people had shattered the great barrier of tyranny and driven out Muhammad Riza, the factional interests of certain groups came to light and differences began to appear.

It is possible that many of those differences were created by hidden hands and manipulated in such a way as to undermine the strength of the nation.

The strength of the nation has been concentrated in two particular principles, and it is exactly these that have come under attack. One is unity of purpose, and the other, the demand for an Islamic republic.

Certain elements did all they could to oppose the establishment of the Islamic Republic. For example, they said it would be enough to have a republic; to speak of Islam in this connection is quite unnecessary. Others said, "We want a 'democratic republic,' not an Islamic one," and others—the least offensive of them all—spoke of a "democratic Islamic republic."

Our people would not have any of this. They said, "We understand what Islam is, and we understand what a republic means. But as for 'democratic,' that is a concept that has constantly changed its guise throughout history. In the West it means one thing, and in the East, another. Plato described it one way, and Aristotle another way. We don't understand any of it. And why should something we don't understand appear on the ballot form for us to vote on? We understand Islam and we know what it is—namely, justice. We know how rulers in the first age of Islam like 'Ali ibn Abi Talib exercised rule, and we also know that the word 'republic' means voting, and that we accept. But as for 'democratic,' we won't accept it even if you put it next to 'Islamic.'"

Even apart from this, as I said in an earlier talk, to juxtapose "democratic" and "Islamic" is an insult to Islam. Because when you place the word "democratic" in front of "Islamic," it means that Islam is lacking in the alleged virtues of democracy, although Islam is, in fact, superior to all forms of democracy. To speak of a "democratic Islamic republic" is like speaking of a "justice-oriented Islamic republic." That is an insult to Islam because it suggests that justice is something extrinsic to Islam, whereas it is the very substance of Islam.

So the people did not accept these various alternative formulae. Certain writers and intellectuals still continued to insist that the word "Islam" should not be used in the designation. We decided that their hostility toward Islam must mean that they had been dealt a blow by Islam; we related this, in turn, to the fact that the superpowers had been deprived of their control over our oil by a nation that was crying out, "Islam!" It was in the interest of the superpowers that the word "Islam" be deleted from our form of government, and thus, that the mainstay of our Republic be denied. The mainstay of any government must be its people; if it lacks the support of its people, it cannot be a true government, or enjoy stability and permanence. So, certain elements were insistent that our government be deprived of its main source of support—popular devotion to Islam.

Of course, they are still trying to be insistent, although now in a different way. Now it is said that the Constitution is not a "popular" constitution, and that it has many problems. The fact is that this Constitution was approved by the elected representatives of the people and then submitted to a popular vote in the referendum, and it is only a small minority—whose leadership and aims we know well—that seeks to oppose the desires of the whole nation. The conclusion is inescapable that this minority wants to see the former state restored so that it can regain its former interests. Islam dealt it a blow, so it does not want to see Islamic government take firm hold.

Throughout the different stages of the Revolution, the religious leaders played the primary role. Of course, others also took part—university professors, intellectuals, merchants, students—but it was the religious leaders who mobilized the whole people.

In every region there are three or four mosques, presided over by a religious scholar whom the people believe in. I have always advised the Iranian people not to overlook the impregnable fortress that the religious leaders provide for them, and I have particularly advised the intellectuals who might desire the independence of their country that the religious institution constitutes a great barrier to foreign domination, and its loss would leave them powerless.

If the religious scholars were eliminated from this movement, there would not have been a movement. The people do not listen to the intellectuals. Political parties, unless they are Islamic, cannot gather more than a thousand or so members, and the people will not listen to them. However much the party leaders try to attract their attention, the people say to themselves, "They're talking nonsense."

It is this group alone, the religious leaders, who are capable of arousing the people and inspiring them to self-sacrifice. Your remark that they have played a great role is quite true, although of course individual religious leaders have different degrees of influence according to their status. But in proportion to the scope of his influence, each has his words heeded by those who comprise his audience. People understand that he seeks their wellbeing; if they follow him, they will attain true happiness, and even if they are killed, they will die martyrs.

So it was the religious leaders who mobilized the people all over Iran, and it was from the mosques that the people set out behind their preachers and leaders to participate in demonstrations.

I ask all the factions of the people—including those who regard themselves as nationalists—to protect the religious leaders. God is protecting them; the nationalists should also do so, and be careful not to lose them. You see some people today wanting to drag them into discussions in order to weaken them, but it is not in the wordly or the religious interest of these people to do so.

It is not my intention to proclaim the whole class of religious
scholars free from blemish, or to say that anyone who wears a turban is a virtuous, upright, and pious person. I am not making any
such claim, nor is anyone else. But those who oppose the religious
scholars are not opposing the bad ones who may exist among
them; they are opposing the good ones, those who have influence
on the people. If their opposition were directed against evil elements among the religious scholars, their aim would be justified;
such elements must be purged (I accept this, and the purge will
take place at the appropriate time). But when our nation is in a
state of upheaval in the aftermath of a revolution, when it is beginning successfully to confront the problems that always exist
under such circumstances and that have been especially acute in
our case, when it is facing the enmity of a superpower, indeed of
all superpowers—it is not the time to endanger this great support
of the nation, the element that is capable of mobilizing the people. It may be that we have a grievance against a particular religious leader, or objections to another, but this is not the time to
pursue these matters. The problem must be solved gradually.

I do not know whether you are familiar with this story. Once
a man went into his garden and saw a *sayyid*, an *akhund*, and an
ordinary man busy stealing his fruit. Addressing the ordinary
man, he said, "Well, that gentleman's a *sayyid*, a descendant of the
Prophet, so never mind. And his friend is one of the religious
scholars; he's most welcome to whatever he wants. But what do
you have to say for yourself?" With the assistance of the *Sayyid* and
the *akhund*, the owner of the garden bound the hands and feet of
the ordinary man. Then he sat himself down and said to the
akhund: "The *sayyid* is a descendant of the Prophet, and it's not
proper to quarrel with a descendant of the Prophet, but let me
hear what you have to say. How do you justify your coming here
to steal, despite your turban and beard?" And with the aid of the
sayyid, he tied up the *akhund*. There remained now only the *sayyid*.
He asked the *sayyid*, "Did your ancestor ever tell you to steal?"
seized him, and bound him also, hand and foot.

The strategy the opponents of the religious scholars are following is like that of the owner of the garden. They say, "What
do the *akhunds* think they are doing? What is all this 'akhundism'?
The country must not fall into the hands of the *akhunds*." Do they
imagine that the *akhunds* want to take over the country and do
whatever they like with it? That is not it at all. Those who speak

about "akhundism" really wish to separate the people from the *akhunds* so that the people are deprived of this great resource, just as they were in the time of Riza Shah. Their plan is to begin with the lower-ranking religious scholars, and then to move gradually higher until there is no one left and the whole class is completely destroyed. They want to take away from the people this class that is able to diffuse Islam in the world, to propagate it and give it outward expression. The basic object of their hostility is Islam itself.

As for your question concerning the future role of the religious leaders and scholars, their function is to guide the people in all matters. Attempts were made in the past to separate the religious leaders from the people, which meant, in fact, a separation of religion from politics.

As you know from your studies, Islam is a religion whose divine precepts have a political dimension. Sermons given at Friday prayer and on the occasion of festivals; congregational prayer; the pilgrimage with its vast assemblies at Mecca, Muzdalifa, Mina, and 'Arafat—all these are political matters. Of course, they are acts of worship, but politics and worship are intermingled in them. Attempts were made to separate Islam and religion from politics; people were told, "The emperor has his rightful place, and the *akhund* has his. Why should the *akhund* concern himself with what Riza Shah is doing to the people? Let him go attend to his prayers. What is it to the *akhund* that back-breaking agreements are imposed on the country? Let him draw his cloak about himself and go to the mosque for prayers. After all, he's quite free to pray for anything he wants there; no one is going to stop him."

I do not believe that Jesus held the views on this question of religion and politics that are now attributed to him. Could Jesus ever have taught people to accept oppression? All the prophets, including Jesus, were sent to root out injustice, but later, institutions arose that distorted the nature of religion. This happened also in the case of Islam; in every age, there were attempts to prevent its correct implementation.

So yes, the religious scholar will have a role in government. He does not want to be the ruler, but he does want to have a role. On this question of the presidency, there were proposals made to me, some of which even originated in the universities, that the President ought to be a religious leader, and I realized that that was because no one else would be trusted in the role. But I said,

"No, the religious scholar does not wish to be President himself; he wishes instead to have a role in the presidency, a supervisory role. He will exercise this role on behalf of the people. If the government begins to misbehave, the religious scholar will stand in its way."

Now the Constitution makes some provision for the principle of the governance of the *faqih*. In my opinion, it is deficient in this regard. The religious scholars have more prerogatives in Islam than are specified in the Constitution, and the gentlemen in the Assembly of Experts stopped short of the ideal in their desire not to antagonize the intellectuals! In any event, only part of the principle of the governance of the *faqih* is present in the Constitution, not all of it. Given the contingencies with which Islam has surrounded the operation of this principle, it cannot harm anyone. Particular attributes have been set down as necessary for the "holder of authority" (*vali amr*) and the *faqih*, and they are attributes that prevent him from going astray. If he utters a single lie, or takes a single wrong step, he forfeits his claim to governance. The whole purpose of the clause in the Constitution relating to the governance of the *faqih* is to prevent tyranny and despotism. Those who opposed the Constitution said that it instituted a form of tyranny, but how can that be? Whatever we do, it is always possible that some despot will come along in the future and try to do whatever he wants, but the *faqih* who possesses the attributes mentioned in the Constitution cannot, in the very nature of things, be a tyrant. On the contrary, he is just, not in the limited sense of social justice, but in the more rigorous and comprehensive sense that his quality of being just would be annulled if he were to utter a single lie, or cast a single glance at a woman past the degrees that are forbidden. Such a person will not act wrongly; on the contrary, he will seek to prevent others from acting wrongly. Justice, in the sense, has not been made an essential qualification for the President; it is possible that he might wish to do something wrong, in which case the *faqih* will prevent him. If the head of the army tries one day to go beyond his functions, the *faqih* has the legal right to dismiss him. The most valuable part of the entire Constitution is that which relates to the governance of the *faqih*; those who oppose it are acting out of either ignorance or self-interest.

The religious scholars do not wish to become Prime Minister or President, and indeed it is not in their interest to do so. They do, however, have a role to play, a role that has always existed, even though they were pushed aside. Now God has given them the opportunity to fulfill this role as a result of the deeds wrought by our people: they rose up in revolt, and the religious scholars assumed their role. The role that they have is one of supervision, not of assuming executive positions without the proper expertise. It would make no sense, for example, for a religous leader to become the commander of a battalion if he is ignorant of military science. The expertise of the religious scholar lies in the area of Islamic law, that law which, if properly executed, secures us all our goals; and if he sees any mistake being made or any deviation from Islamic law occurring, he will move to prevent it.

This supervisory role is subject to particular conditions and principles to which we are bound. In addition, we are bound to follow the expressed wishes of the people. Once a religious leader has a role in government, he will not permit the President or the Prime Minister to practice oppression. Any power center that wishes to go beyond its bounds he will prevent from doing so. Any act tending toward dictatorship or the curbing of freedom he will also prevent. If the government wishes to conclude an agreement with a foreign power that brings about a relationship of dependence, the religious scholar will prevent it.

In summary, the religous leaders do not wish to be the government, but neither are they separate from the government. They do not wish to sit in the Prime Minister's residence and fulfill the duties of premiership, but at the same time, they will intervene to stop the Prime Minister if he takes a false step. The principle of the governance of the *faqih*, then, is a noble one, conducive to the welfare of the country. Once implemented, it will lead to the fulfillment of the hopes of the people.

EXPORTING THE ISLAMIC REVOLUTION[4]

As the new Islamic regime in Tehran consolidated its power and ideological hegemony during the early 1980s, it turned its attention to the task of exporting its Islamic message to the Arab world. Initially, the ruling clerics invested considerable energy in exporting the universal version of Khomeini's ideology as well as the Arab antagonism to Iran engendered by the Iran-Iraq war lessened the appeal of Khomeini's call. The Iranian clerics then began to devote far more of their energies to exporting the Shi'ite version of their ideology.

To export its universal message, the IRI [Islamic Revolution in Iran] established broadcasting facilities to beam Islamic programs to the Sunni and the Shi'ite worlds. It also held yearly conferences, beginning in 1983, attended by both Sunni and Shi'ite activists. To export its Shi'ite neo-fundamentalist ideology, the regime made use of several clerical networks, primarily composed of individuals who had studied with two leading Iraqi clerics and with Khomeini during his exile from 1965 to 1978 in the holy shrine city of Najaf in Iraq. Several of these men played a key role in Islamic activist groups such as al-Da'wah, the Call, and the Munazzamat al-'Amal al-Islami, the Islamic Action Organization. In turn, these groups participated in the indoctrination and training of Islamic activists at training camps in Iran. Finally, Iran used its strategic alliance with Syria to buttress its efforts at promoting neofundamentalist Shi'ite revolutions in the Arab world.

But the IRI has devoted its major resources for the export of its Shi'ite ideology to the steadfast pursuit of its war with Iraq. Despite pleas from virtually all the leaders of the Islamic states and the clear signals frequently emanating from Baghdad, Khomeini has insisted on "war, war until victory." Victory has been defined by the Ayatollah as the overthrow of President Saddam Hussein, the agent of the Great Satan—the United States—and of the lesser Satan—Israel—and along with him, his entire Ba'athist system. While the regime which would follow this cataclysm in

[4]By Marvin Zonis and Daniel Brumberg, political scientists, from their book *Khomeini, the Islamic Republic of Iran, and the Arab World*, pp. 3–40. Copyright © 1987 President and Fellows of Harvard College Center for Middle Eastern Studies. Reprinted by permission.

Baghdad has been left undefined, it is reasonable to conclude that the IRI would install an Islamic Republic of Iraq on the territory of its neighbor. The structure of that regime, based on the Iraqi Shi'ite group, al-Da'wah, is already in place in Tehran, as will be discussed below. An Iranian victory in the war would virtually guarantee the establishment of the world's second regime, which in the mind of Khomeini, could legitimately claim to be Islamic.

The Export of Iran's Universal Vision

The broadcasting of Iran's Islamic ideology takes place at three radio stations: one in the Chah Bahar region, one in the Bandar Torkaman area, and in the most recently established station on Kish Island. The latter began broadcasting in January 1984. Its 800 kw transmitter covers the Persian Gulf, Saudi Arabia, Jordan, the Sudan, and parts of Egypt, as well as Iran, Afghanistan, Pakistan, and the southern USSR. According to press reports, the station operates nineteen hours a day.

During the last four years, in its bid to unify the Islamic world and to establish itself as the leading Islamic power, Iran has held conferences attended by ulema and Islamic activists from around the world. The first such conference, the Congress of Friday Imams and Prayer Leaders, was held in Tehran in January 1983 and was attended by ulema from over forty countries. The congress voted to establish a permanent secretariat in Tehran to coordinate the activities of the Islamic world's prayer leaders. In February 1984, in response to the holding of the Pan-Islamic Conference in Casablanca, Iran held its first meeting of the Revolutionary Islamic International. Present at this conference was a number of Shi'ite and Sunni radical activist groups from Jordan, Morocco, Egypt, the Gulf, Senegal, Nigeria, and Mali, as well as from countries in the Far East, Western Europe, and even the United States. Subsequent conferences of Islamic activists have been held in Iran, and an international network of activist clerics linked to Tehran has been established. Those clerics, in turn, have returned to their homes to establish other networks linked to themselves.

The Export of Iran's Shi'ite Vision

The export of Iran's universal vision was hindered by the fact that Iran's clerical leaders had not established close ties with Sunni activist groups previous to the revolution. Following the revolution, given Iran's increasing Shi'ite emphasis, the minimalist efforts described above hardly served to create solid organizational ties between the clerical elite and Sunni groups in the Arab world. However, in the case of the export of Iran's Shi'ite ideology, the clerical relations which had been established during the 1960s and 1970s linked leading Shi'ite ayatollahs to one another and to their loyal students. They formed powerful networks based on intense personal loyalties and shared ideological commitments. These networks provided a conduit for the export of Iran's Islamic Shi'ite ideology during the early 1980s.

At the center of those networks are clerics who studied in the Iraqi city of Najaf. It was in the Najaf that a more radical neofundamentalist ideology was developed, first by Ayatollah Muhsin al-Hakim, the leading ayatollah of the time, and Ayatollah Muhammad Baqir al-Sadr. These two scholars were joined by Ayatollah Khomeini in 1965, following his expulsion from Iran. Muhammad Baqir al-Sadr's ideas helped give birth during the late 1960s to a radical Shi'ite fundamentalist group, al-Da'wah, which was in turn led by Ayatollah Muhammad Baqir al-Hakim (son of Ayatollah Muhsin al-Hakim), who is also leader of the Supreme assembly of the Islamic Revolution of Iraq, by his brother Shaikh Mahdi al-Hakim, and by Shaikh Muhammad Madhi al-Asifi, a disciple of Ayatollah Muhsin al-Hakim. Following the execution by the Iraqi regime of Ayatollah Muhammad Baqir al-Sadr in 1980, the sons of Ayatollah Muhsin al-Hakim fled to Tehran, where they based their organization. Since then al-Da'wah has played a key role in exporting Iran's revolution. Arab members of al-Da'wah, for example, apparently participated in the bombings of the Marine headquarters and the U.S. embassy in Beirut in October 1983, in the bombings which followed in Kuwait in December 1983, and in the attempted assassination of the emir of Kuwait in May 1985. Outside the Arab world, al-Da'wah has established party organizations in England, West Germany, and other West European countries.

The Najaf network is also closely related to radical Shi'ite fundamentalist groups in Lebanon, and in particular to the organization known as Hizbollah, the Party of God. This organization is led by Sayyid Hussein Fadlallah, who was born in Najaf and who studied with Ayatollah Muhammad Baqir al-Sadr during the early 1960s. Fadlallah had been assisted by two other shaikhs who studied in Najaf, Shaikah Subhi al-Tufayli and Sahikh Raghib Harb, who was assassinated in February 1984. Hizbollah has also been linked to a number of terrorist bombings in Beirut, including that of the U.S. embassy in May 1983 and January 1984 and of the Marine headquarters and the French military headquarters in October 1983. It has also been associated with the campaign of suicide bombings that helped prompt the Israeli withdrawal from Lebanon in 1985. Other Shi'ite leaders in Lebanon with close connections with the Najaf-Tehran axis are Shaikh Muhammad Mahdi Shams al-Din, son of a leading Najaf scholar, Muhammad Rida Shams al-Din, and Musa al-Sadr, Lebanon's leading Shi'ite activist, who disappeared on a trip to Libya in 1978. Al-Sadr, it should be pointed out, had close ties to the modern-reformist Islamic movement in Iran, although it is likely that he also had some connections with Khomeini, as he came from a leading Qom family of Shi'ite scholars.

Closely aligned with Khomeini is a third Shi'ite group, the Islamic Action Organization, based in Tehran. This group was originally led by Sayyid Hassan Shirazi, who died in 1980. He was succeeded by a close disciple and former student of Khomeini, Hujjat al-Islam Sayyid Muhammad Taqi al-Mudarrisi, who was born and trained in the Iraqi shrine city of Karbala. Their activities have been limited mostly to Iraq. They were reportedly responsible for bombings in Baghdad in November 1983 and July 1984. However, they also are reported to have close ties with activists in Lebanon and the Persian Gulf. Muhammad Taqi's brother, Sayyid Hadi al-Mudarrisi, for example, heads the Tehran-based Islamic Front for the Liberation of Bahrain.

The above activists, along with others, are indoctrinated in the ideology of radical Shi'ite neo-fundamentalism in at least two training camps in Iran. One is located south of Qom, under the direction of Ayatollah Najafabadi, and is reported to have some 2,000 "students" in residence at any one time. The second school, located in the Manzariyeh Gardens north of Tehran, was run by the brother of the son-in-law of Ayatollah Montazeri, Sayyid Mihdi Hashemi, until his arrest in late 1986. Sentenced to life imprisonment under the Shah for having strangled to death, with his bare hands, Ayatollah Shamsabadi, then seen as the chief rival of Ayatollah Montazeri, Hashemi was designated to head the Manzariyeh school by Ayatollah Montazeri to replace Hujjat al-Islam Muhammad Montazeri, the ayatollah's son. Muhammad Montazeri had come to be known in Tehran as Ayatollah Ringo, on account of his brash activism and his predilections for the use of guns and armed retainers in the pursuit of his goals in the IRI. He was assassinated shortly after he stepped down as director of the Manzariyeh school.

Hashemi's "school" trained some 1,000 youths at a time, from as many as two dozen countries, selected by Iranian embassy officials throughout the world, who use their diplomatic immunity to play a vital role in extending the influence of Khomeini's revolution.

Some reports, whose accuracy is unsubstantiated, have suggested that a measure of centralized control over these networks has emerged in Tehran. It is reported that an Islamic Revolutionary Council was established in March 1983 under the leadership of Muhammad Taqi al-Mudarrisi, the leader of the Islamic Action Organization. This organization, it is believed, submits its proposals to a higher authority, the Supreme Coordination Council for the Islamic Revolution in Iran and Revolutionary Islamic Movements in the World. Ayatollah Montazeri leads this group and was supported by Sayyid Mihdi Hashemi.

The extent of such centralized control is dependent on the degree to which the revolution has been consolidated under the leadership of a single, unified clerical hierarchy in Tehran. Although much progress has been made toward centralizing power, the process of revolutionary consolidation still continues. A totally centralized, bureaucratic system of exporting the revolution may not as yet exist. It is also beneficial to Iran to maintain the uninstitutionalized, decentralized, and fluid system of exporting its revolution in a network of personal, teacher-disciple, and family relationships whose structure remains elusive and thus difficult to pin down. The outline of this network, based on available sources, is provided here. The chart highlights the importance of the Najaf clerics and the close ties between those clerics most importantly Khomeini, and a wide network of Shi'ite activist groups whose leaders are tied to the Iraqi ayatollahs, Muhsin al-Hakim and Muhammad Baqir al-Sadr, or Khomeini himself.

The Syrian-IRI Alliance

The effectiveness of these networks as conduits for the export of Islamic ideology was substantially reinforced beginning in the early 1980s by Iran's alliance with Syria. This relationship was not based upon common religious or ideological beliefs but rather emerged as a result of a number of political and strategic concerns. Syria's attempts to control Lebanon were facilitated by a relationship with Iran, since the clerics in Tehran had substantial influence in Lebanon. Syria could count on the Shi'ites in Lebanon, following the Israeli invasion of 1982, to cooperate in a coordinated campaign to expel the Israelis and the Americans. Outside Lebanon, Syria's alliance with Iran provided Syria another means of combatting its traditional rival, Iraq, as well as a means of reasserting its regional influence during a period of increasing Syrian isolation in the Middle East. It also brought Syria inexpensive oil and other revenues. For the Iranians, the alliance provided a convenient means of influencing the Shi'ite community in Lebanon. It furnished the Iranians with Syrian experts in the use of explosives and weaponry useful for the export of its revolution, and it also provided Iran a useful ally in its battle with Iraq.

This strategic political-economic alliance could not have flowered so quickly had it not been for the long and complicated relationship which had been developing for over fifty years between the Alawites of Syria and Lebanon and the clerics of Iraq and Iran. These earlier ties were also based primarily on political concerns and not religious affinity. The Alawites were not recognized, either by the Sunnis or by the Twelver Shi'ites, as Muslims. They venerated Ali, as did the Shi'ites, but their veneration, which involved the actual deification of Ali, went beyond legitimate Shi'ite limits. The Alawite belief that Ali was the very incarnation of God resulted in the Shi'ite claim that the Alawites were *ghulat*, those who exceed all proper bounds of venerating Ali. The Sunnis meanwhile considered Alawites to be *kuffars*, disbelievers, and *mushrikun*, idolaters.

These religious controversies did not, however, prevent the Alawites from seeking a fig leaf of Islamic legitimacy, in the early twentieth century, to protect their communal political interests. From 1922 to 1936 the Alawites had their own state in Syria, under French mandate, but they were subordinate to Sunni law and

Sunni courts. Seeking to assert their full communal independence, the Alawites lobbied for and eventually received the right to apply Twelve Shi'ite laws in their own courts. At the same time, they clung to their own Alawite practices.

In 1936, with the advent of Syrian independence, the Alawites hoped to gain autonomy or at least equality with the majority Sunnis in a united Syrian state. What they won instead was recognition as legitimate Muslims, although that recognition never was fully accepted by the Sunni clergy in Syria. They continued to see Alawites as *kuffars* and *mushrikun.*

Eleven years later, a move was made to strengthen their links to Shi'ites. The Shi'ite Ayatollah Muhsin al-Hakim of Najaf sent the Twelver mufti of the Biqa in Lebanon, Shaikh Habib al-Ibrahim, to Syria in order to investigate Alawite traditions and practices. Following this, twelve Alawite students were allowed to study at Najaf, where they were met by a generally hostile reception from the Shi'ite students. Despite this failure to promote Shi'ite-Alawite relations, Shaikh Habib al-Ibrahim did succeed, during the late 1940s, in establishing a Ja'fari Society for the dissemination of Shi'ite doctrine in Syria. He then won official recognition of Twelver Shi'ism for the Syrian government and, in so doing, provided the Alawites with the means to assert some religious-communal autonomy. This was followed in 1956 by the visit to Syria of the Najaf scholar, Muhammad Shams al-Din, a member of one of southern Lebanon's leading clerical families. He met with Alawite leaders and arranged for the visit of several Alawite students to Najaf in 1966. While these links served to legitimate the Alawites, they never induced Alawites to adopt Shi'ite religious practices or beliefs.

The tradition of promoting Alawite-Shi'ite dialogue in order to enhance the position of the Alawites within Syria—a dialogue essential for political reasons—was thus well established when a series of events during the early 1970s helped cement an alliance between the Islamic movement in Iran and the secular Arab nationalist state of Syria. By then, Syria was ruled primarily by Alawites under the leadership of President Hafiz al-Asad and his clan. In early 1973 Sunnis rioted throughout Syria to protest the publication of a new constitution, which failed to affirm Islam as the official religion of the state. President Asad sought to pacify his opposition by demonstrating that at least he, the president of the state, was a full-fledged Muslim. To this end, he curried favor with the Saudis, the defenders of the faith. But in the face of Sunni-led opposition in Syria, the Saudis rebuffed his overtures. Then he turned to the Shi'ite community of Lebanon.

Simultaneously, the charismatic leader of Lebanon's Shi'ites, Musa al-Sadr, from a leading family of Iranian Shi'ite scholars, was hoping to extend his own influence in Lebanon. He was contemplating recognizing the Alawite community in northern Lebanon as Twelver Shi'ites in order to increase the size of his following. Given the coincidence of his interests with those of President Asad, al-Sadr declared the Lebanese Alawites to be full-fledged Twelver Shi'ites in July 1973, a declaration which implicitly conferred Shi'ite legitimacy on the Alawites of Syria.

This incident of the political use of Islam no more led the Alawites to adopt Shi'ite practices than it had in the past. Instead, their largely secret, esoteric religion remained unchanged and closed to the outside world. The Shi'ite scholars of Najaf and Qom refused to endorse Musa al-Sadr's dispensation, but his dispensation provided the basis for the development of an alliance between al-Sadr and Asad and the Islamic left in Iran, who championed a modernist vision of Shi'ism in Lebanon. By the mid-1970s Syria had begun to train and supply members of the Islamic-Iranian opposition to the shah. When Ali Shari'ati, the leading theoretician of the Islamic Iranian left, died in the summer of 1977, he was buried in Damascus at ceremonies over which Musa al-Sadr officiated. Sadr himself had close ties to President Asad.

However, ever the shrewd politician, Asad maintained his links with the Shi'ite neo-fundamentalists. He offered Khomeini refuge after his expulsion from Iraq in 1978. When it became clear that the neo-fundamentalists were emerging victorious in the revolutionary coalition which ousted the shah, Asad was in a good position to switch alliances from the Islamic leftists to the Islamic fundamentalists and so embark on a close alliance with the ruling clerics in Tehran.

The alliance took concrete shape in March 1982, a particularly treacherous moment for Syria to make common cause with Iraq's enemy. For it was then that Iran was about to drive the Iraqi invaders from its territory and begin to assault Iraq. In that month, Syria's foreign minister, Abdul Halim Khaddam, visited Iran to sign a number of military and economic agreements. Syria agreed to provide Iran with a supply of Soviet weaponry as well as security officers, to train Iran's emerging intelligence organization and to prevent Iraq from exporting oil through its pipeline across Syria. Iran, in turn, agreed to supply Syria with 8.8 million tons of oil annually and was permitted to station some 1,500 Revolutionary Guards in the Biqa Valley in Lebanon. Later in 1982 agreements were concluded. These provided for a flow of 1,000 Iranian tourists per week to Syria; for an air-bridge linking Damascus and Tehran; and for the selling of 5 million tons of crude oil to Syria at $10 below the OPEC benchmark price. An additional 1 million tons was to be suppled to Syria annually, free of charge as support for its confrontation with Israel. These agreements were maintained during 1984, when Iran supplied Syria with a total of 8 million tons of oil, including 1.6 million free tons, while the rate of Iranian tourists to Syria was increased from 1,000 to 2,000 a week. The agreements were renewed in 1985 and 1986 as well. [By mid-1986 Syria's financial problems had grown so acute that it stopped paying for Iranian oil. Those revenues, in turn, were crucial to Iran's pursuit of its war with Iraq. Iran began to pressure Syria for the payments. President Asad responded in character. He threatened to make peace with King Hussein of Jordan and even threatened to do the same with Saddam Hussein of Iraq. The Iranians resumed their petroleum deliveries.]

These links have had notable effects. In the bombings of the U.S. embassy in April of 1983, the Marine headquarters, and the French military headquarters in Beirut in October of 1983, as well as in the bombings in Kuwait in December of that year, Syrian agents appear to have cooperated with Iranian terrorists, with members of al-Da'wah, and with members of Hizbollah in a concerted effort to banish American and Western interests from Lebanon and the Middle East and to liberate Kuwait from its illegitmate Sunni ruling family. Iran, meanwhile, has been able to expand its influence substantially in Lebanon by supporting neofundamentalist groups such as Hizbollah, [Iran spent at least $200 million in Lebanon in 1983] while Syria was able to weaken its Ba'thist competitors in Baghdad by supporting Iran in the war with Iraq. Syria has had evident success in using the alliance to reestablish its role as the arbitrator of Lebanon, following the withdrawal of American and then Israeli forces in 1984 and 1985.

Simultaneously, in order to maintain its position as the single most influential actor in Lebanon, Syria has moved to restrict the influence in Lebanon of Khomeini's Shi'ite allies. Syria has sought a balance of forces in Lebanon rather than the victory of any one group. Thus it has supported the modernist Shi'ite Amal movement under the leadership of Nabih Berri as a counterweight to the fundamentalists. By 1985 signs of serious tension between Iran and Syria were already evident. The Syrians were also keenly aware that fundamentalist victory in Lebanon would strengthen the internal Islamic opposition to Asad's Alawite regime. The continued Syrian support of Persian Iran against Arab Iraq has also weakened Syria's Arab nationalist credentials. These factors and the more recent economic strain in the relationship suggest that fundamental national interest preclude a lasting alliance between the two states.

While the basic interests of Islamic Iran and Syria preclude a vital, long-term relationship, the benefits to both countries have thus far been considerable. One particular gain for Iran has been its ability to use Damascus and Syrian-controlled Lebanon as bases for the export of its Shi'ite ideology to the Arab world.

III. THE SALMAN RUSHDIE CASE: AN OPPORTUNITY FOR UNDERSTANDING LOST

EDITOR'S INTRODUCTION

When in early 1989, the last year of his life, the Ayatollah Khomeini condemned to death the British author Salman Rushdie for having committed blasphemy in his novel *The Satanic Verses*, reaction in the West and in Islamic communities around the world followed familiar and mutually exclusionary courses. As the Imam no doubt intended, many in the Islamic world became engulfed in a frenzy of denunciation and righteous indignation. Most of the demonstrators in the streets had not read Rushdie's book, or even heard of him before; nevertheless, he quickly became for them a notorious sinner who had gone one step too far. What the ferocious crowds in the streets of Teheran, Karachi, and Delhi also understood was that the reputation of Islam and the good name of the Prophet had been smeared by a Muslim renegade, and it was up to them to right this terrible wrong. Hundreds of demonstrators clamored to be numbered among the first death squads.

The West was stunned by Khomeini's proclamation of Rushdie's grisly fate. The attitude of those affiliated with the book business—writers, publishers, booksellers, critics, agents, and others—may be taken as typical of Western reaction, but only in its variety and comprehensiveness. Passionate appeals to standards of fairness and free speech and strong arguments against censorship were repeatedly offered, but with little meaning for the average Islamic militant, whose societies are as prone to censorship as any in the twentieth century. In the West, booksellers worried about their employees' safety in the face of imminently expected Islamic terror. The book's publishers expressed concern about the effect of a further offense to Islam which might be caused by the publication of a paperback edition of the book, although the hardcover, available throughout the West, had sold millions of copies.

Rushdie and his savage plight were largely ignored at the center of this murky storm (the author's income, however, did not suffer). Ironically, Rushdie's robust yet complex sense of irony and thoroughgoing political radicalism, both of which found sophisticated expression in *The Satanic Verses*, were seldom appreciated or even remarked upon by reviewers.

Perhaps the most interesting aspect of this tangled affair is the extent to which, in a conflict seemingly offering the chance for far-reaching, cross-cultural analysis, each side followed its own time-honored taboos and shibboleths. Issues of longstanding cultural incomprehension were ignored by most commentators, and another set of opportunities was lost. Indeed, it appeared as if Islam and the West did not want even to make a try at understanding one another.

This section examines the political realities and surrealities of the Rushdie affair. Some of these are pointed out by the author himself in the first article, written shortly after the pronouncement of the death sentence against him and the start of his protective seclusion. The second article, featuring comments by a number of observers, is a conspectus of Western and Islamic reaction, most notable, perhaps, for the sense of crisis conveyed by all the participants, whether sympathetic to Rushdie or not. In "A Twisted History" Hadia Dajani-Shakeel, professor of Islamic studies at the University of Toronto, seeks to explain the reasons why many Muslims find Rushdie's book subversive. Finally Timothy Brenan, a U.S. English professor very much at home with political discourse, presents a literary-political analysis of *The Satanic Verses* scandal; included here is a thorough discussion of the inherent, incessant irony so characteristic of the novel.

A CLASH OF FAITHS:
THE AUTHOR FIGHTS FIRE WITH WORDS[1]

Mohammed ibn Abdallah, one of the great geniuses of world history, a successful businessman, victorious general and sophisti-

[1]By Salman Rushdie, writer, in *Maclean's Magazine*, February 27, 1989, p. 24. Copyright © 1989 by Maclean's Magazine. Reprinted by permission.

cated statesman as well as a prophet, insisted throughout his life on his simple humanity. There are no contemporary portraits of him because he feared that, if any were made, people would worship the portraits. He was only the messenger; it was the message that should be revered.

As to the revelation itself, it caused Mohammed considerable anguish. Sometimes he heard voices; sometimes he saw visions; sometimes, he said, the words were found in his inmost heart, and at such times their production caused him acute physical pain. When the revelations began, he feared for his sanity and only after reassurances from his wife and friends did he accept that he was the recipient of the divine gift of the Word.

The religion which Mohammed established differs from Christianity in several important respects: the Prophet is not granted divine status, but the text is. It's worth pointing out, too, that Islam requires neither a collective act of worship nor an intercessionary caste of priests. The faithful communicate directly with their God.

Nowadays, however, a powerful tribe of clerics has taken over Islam. These are the contemporary Thought Police. They have turned Mohammed into a perfect being, his life into a perfect life, his revelation into the unambiguous, clear event it originally was not. Powerful taboos have been erected. One may not discuss Mohammed as if he were human, with human virtues and weaknesses. One may not discuss the growth of Islam as a historical phenomenon, as an ideology born out of its time. These are the taboos against which *The Satanic Verses* has transgressed (these and one other; I also tried to write about the place of women in Islamic society, and in the Koran). It is for this breach of taboo that the novel is being anathematized, fulminated against and set alight.

Unable to accept the unarguable absolutes of religion, I have tried to fill up the hole with literature. The art of the novel is a thing I cherish as dearly as the book-burners of Bradford value their brand of militant Islam. Literature is where I go to explore the highest and lowest places in human society and in the human spirit, where I hope to find not absolute truth but the truth of the tale, of the imagination and of the heart. So the battle over *The Satanic Verses* is a clash of faiths. Or more precisely, it's a clash of languages. As my fictional character Salman says of my fictional prophet Mahound, "It's his Word against mine."

In this War of the Word, the guardians of religious truth have been telling their followers a number of lies. I am accused, for example, of calling Mohammed the devil. This is because I use the name Mahound which, long ago, was indeed used as a derogatory term. But my novel tries in all sorts of ways to reoccupy negative images, to repossess pejorative language, and on page 93 explains: "To turn insults into strengths, whigs, tories, blacks all chose to wear with pride the names they were given in scorn; likewise, our mountain-climbing, prophet-motivated solitary is to be . . . Mahound."

Even the novel's title has been termed blasphemous; but the phrase is not mine. It comes from al-Tabari, one of the canonic Islamic sources. Tabari writes: "When the Messenger of God saw his people draw away from him . . . he would gladly have seen those things that bore too harshly on them softened a little."

Mohammed then received verses which accepted the three favorite Meccan goddesses as intercessionary agents. Meccans were delighted. Later, the Archangel Gabriel told Mohammed that these had been "Satanic verses," falsely inspired by the devil in disguise, and they were removed from the Koran. Gabriel consoled Mohammed, however; earlier prophets had experienced similar difficulties for similar reasons, he said. To my mind, Mohammed's overcoming of temptation does him no dishonor; quite the reverse. The Archangel Gabriel felt the same way, but the novel's opponents are less tolerant than archangels.

The zealots also attack me by false analogy, comparing my book to pornography and demanding a ban on both. Many Islamic spokesmen have compared my work to anti-Semitism. But intellectual dissent is neither pornographic nor racist. I have tried to give a secular, humanist vision of the birth of a great world religion. For this, apparently, I should be tried under the Race Relations Act, or if not that perhaps the Public Order Act. Any old act will do. The justification is that I have "given offence." But the giving of offence cannot be a basis for censorship, or freedom of expression would perish instantly. And many of us who were revolted by the Bradford flames will feel that the offence done to our principles is at least as great as any offence caused to those who burned my book.

The Moslem world is full of censors these days, and many of its greatest writers have been forced into silence, exile or submission. To find Labour councillors in Bradford and Labour MPs in

Westminster joining forces with the mullahs is hugely depressing. When [they] start asking for censorship to be *extended* and for the blasphemy laws to be expanded rather than abolished, then it's time for the Labour leadership to respond by disowning such initiatives in the clearest possible terms.

The Satanic Verses is not, in my view, an antireligious novel. It is, however, an attempt to write about migration, its stresses and transformations, from the point of view of migrants from the Indian subcontinent to Britain. This is, for me, the saddest irony of all; that after working for five years to give voice and fictional flesh to the immigrant culture of which I am myself a member, I should see my book burned, largely unread, by the people it's about, people who might find some pleasure and much recognition in its pages. I tried to write against stereotypes; the zealot protests serve to confirm, in the Western mind, all the worst stereotypes of the Moslem world.

How fragile civilization is; how easily, how merrily a book burns! Inside my novel, its characters seek to become fully human by facing up to the great facts of love, death and (with or without God) the life of the soul. Outside it, the forces of inhumanity are on the march. "Battle lines are being drawn up in India today," one of my characters remarks. "Secular versus religious, the light versus the dark. Better you choose which side you are on." Now that the battle has spread to Britain, I can only hope it will not be lost by default. It is time for us to choose.

SALMAN RUSHDIE: A COLLAGE OF COMMENT[2]

Our interview with the author of *The Satanic Verses* was set for 3 PM on Sunday afternoon at the Westbury Hotel in New York. The code name used to protect the registered guest from angered Muslims was Ved Saghdev. Then, three days before our scheduled meeting the stakes rose dramatically: Iran's Ayatollah Khomeini issued an assassination order against Salman Rushdie for blaspheming the Prophet Mohammed. Rushdie disappeared and went into hiding.

[2]By Nathan Gardels, Abdullahi Ahmed An-Na'im, Abol Bani-Sadr, Ali Fakhro, Freimut Duve, Jack Miles, and Ryszard Kapuscinski, whose affiliations are given before their comments. From *New Perspectives Quarterly*, Spring 1989, pp. 48–55. Copyright © 1989 by New Perspectives Quarterly. Reprinted by permission.

What follows instead of a talk with Rushdie are comments from around the world, ranging from the former Iranian president to an Islamic jurist, about the Rushdie-Khomeini affair. Our collage of comments begins with some framing remarks by NPO Editor Nathan Gardels based upon the interview he prepared for Salman Rushdie.

The "Word" Against Wording

The Satanic Verses by Salman Rushdie is really a novel about the metamorphosis of the contemporaty world brought about by migration and communication. It is about the conflicts within individuals and between cultures that result from the immediate juxtaposition in time (mass media, telecommunications) and space (migration) of very different worldviews and civilizations. It is a novel about the conflicts and spiritual dislocation of fragmented individuals in a fragmented world wrestling with its plural identities. *The Satanic Verses* is a novel about the frictions of the global collage.

In the opening pages of Rushdie's celebrated work, the traditional world is blown apart by the metamorphosing agent of a 747 jumbo jet. The author writes: "Up there in airspace, in that soft imperceptible field which had been made possible by the century and which, thereafter, made the century possible, becoming one of its defining locations, the place of movement and of war, the planet-shrinker and power-vacuum, most insecure and transitory of zones, illusory, discontinuous, metamorphic—because when you throw everything up in the air anything becomes possible."

Rushdie speaks of migrants who ply the routes between different worlds as "fragments, absurd, debris of the soul . . . |with| broken memories, sloughed-off selves, severed mother tongues, untranslatable jokes, extinguished futures, lost loves, the forgotten meaning of hollow, booming words, *land, belonging, home.*" These migrants from the past long for the certitude of origins, but only "embrace air."

His characters, like immigrants, are split identities, hybrids. The movie star, Gibreel Farishta, plays 11 roles simultaneously; the radio personality, Saladin Chamcha, has 44 different voices.

In his writing, Rushdie talks about himself as well as the 900, 000 Muslims residing in Great Britain. He asks himself, "Am I Indian, Pakistani, British?" Like Dr. Aziz, a character in his earlier novel, *Midnight's Children*, who loses his faith because he is unable to accept the unarguable absolutes of religion, Rushdie is left "with a hole inside, a vacancy in the vital inner chamber." In the way of the Westerner, he turns to literature as the medium of his doubt and reconciliation between worlds, between past and future.

"What I am saying in *The Satanic Verses*," Rushdie has remarked, "is that we have got to come to terms with our plural identities. We are increasingly becoming a world of migrants, made up of bits and fragments from here, there. We are here. And we have not really left anywhere where we have been." Just as migration transplants other pasts into our present, the Information Age carries our present time into the otherworld of Islamabad, Khartoum and Tehran.

The furor over *The Satanic Verses* caused by Khomeini's death sentence of Rushdie mimics the very theme of the novel. Rushdie's life could only be at risk in the very kind of world his novel describes. Only through the "juxtastructure" of global integration, of a world where Khomeini and Rushdie effectively live side by side could the blasphemous battle, engaging in a fatal "war of nomenclatures," a clash of faiths and languages. It's the Word against words. Milan Kundera [Czechoslovakian novelist] has said that the novel is able to exist in the West because it requires ambiguity and relativity, not a unique Truth that must be conformed to. Rushdie the novelist, like the Western novel itself, blasphemes The Absolute. Khomeini blasphemes the only sacred values of the West: skepticism, relativism, pluralism and tolerance.

Not in his most fertile imaginative moments could Rushdie have dreamed up a scene where the ancient religious rivalries that drive Iran's revolutionary politics are played out on the bookshelves of America's chain stores, nor could he have envisioned a united, usually squabbling Europe rising to the defense of the idea of the novel. How very extraordinary, after decades of hardened balance-of-power-*Realpolitik*, that the world be divided between those who defend the possibility of literature and those who don't.

Now that the Cold War has lost its impetus, it seems that our new preoccupation (along with the environment) will be with the Battle of the Novel, or as Rushdie himself prefers to put it, the War of the Word—a drama of struggle between different civilizations that must live in one interdependent world.

For the moment, Rushdie and Khomeini, the main protagonists of this dramatic tale, are tasting the fate of all actors in the paradox of history. Inadvertently, Rushdie's "sacrilege" has resurrected Khomeini's waning fundamentalist fervor: infidel as evangelist. Inadvertently, Khomeini's death sentence, against Rushdie but really against the idea of the novel, has revived the waning importance of literature in the West: Imam as literary agent. Such are the unexpected twists of plot, the play of contraries, we will learn to expect as this grand drama of the closing years of the last modern century unfolds.

—NATHAN GARDELS

Rushdie Is within Islamic Tradition
ABDULLAHI AHMED AN-NA'IM

A professor of law at the University of Khartoum, Abdullahi Ahmed An-Na'im is a leading reformist Islamic jurist. He was imprisoned in 1983–84 by then-President Numiery, who sought to impose a fundamentalist regime on Sudan.

In the current furor over *The Satanic Verses* one thing should be underscored: Salman Rushdie, by following a long tradition of Muslim intellectuals who have pondered their faith, is not exhibiting aberrant behavior. On the contrary, it is the Ayatollah Khomeini who is out of touch with the laws and traditions of Islam.

Khomeini is in clear violation of Islamic law in three respects: First, even assuming that Rushdie's work is heretical, Khomeini has no jurisdiction over him. In the Islamic notion of jurisdiction, the state or the ruler of the state has jurisdiction only over his own subjects.

Secondly, a person who is being charged with heresy must be charged and tried according to the rules of Shari'a (the historic code of Islam). According to Shari'a, no one can be convicted and sentenced in *absentia* for heresy.

Thirdly, repentance is an absolute defense according to Shari'a, even after conviction. If the person repents at any point before the execution of the sentence, they create the basis for a repeal of the sentence. In fact, the notion of repentance is so fundamental in the Koran and in the Sunna [the body of Islamic custom and practice based on Muhammad's words and deeds] That any sin, any offense would be completely forgiven once the person repents.

Islam is not synonymous with Khomeini and has never been a monolithic, concrete entity. In fact, Islam has been adapted and understood, interpreted and lived by Muslims in strikingly different ways around the world.

In the history of Islam, the period in which the Prophet Mohammed was in Mecca set out the fundamentals of religion: tolerance, equality and freedom of religion and choice. This period constitutes the eternal ethic of Islam. The adaptation of Islam to concrete historical conditions came after Mohammed's migration to Medina, around 622 A.D. It is during this period that one finds the emergence of the "Satanic verses," the notion of *jihad*, and the justification for inequality between men and women.

The adaptive quality of Islam is recurrent and has operated during different historical periods to both expand and contract the fumdamentals set down in Mecca.

Between the 8th and 15th centuries in Spain, for example, Muslims, Jews and Christians coexisted and thrived in a glorious period of liberal tolerance. On the Indian subcontinent, the accepted universals of Islam—articles of faith, rituals of prayer and worship etc.—are integrated with elements of Hinduism regarding manner of dress and social institutions. In parts of Islamic Africa, women are denied the rights given them by Shari'a in terms of inheritance. In other words, the context in which Islam has been interpreted and applied in Africa sometimes modifies Shari'a itself. And the Muslims of that region see no contradiction in that.

The soul-searching and reflection which has led to Salman Rushdie's current dilemma is an exercise many Muslim migrants to Britain, North America and other areas of the "modern" world have engaged in for decades. People may agree or disagree with the manner in which Rushdie tackled the issues or the language he used, but there should be no question about his right to doubt, to reflect and to express himself artistically.

The pnenomena of doubt and skepticism about religion have been experienced by Muslim philosophers and writers throughout history. Some were persecuted and some were executed for heresy. Mahmoud Mohammed Taha, author of *The Second Message of Islam*, was publicly hanged for apostasy in 1985 by Sudanese President Numiery. Others survived the persecution and left us the fruits of their work: Al-Ghazali, a scholar of Sufi mysticism writing in the 12th century, experenced profound periods of doubt throughout his life; scholar Abd Al'Razaq was threatened with death in the 1920s, stripped of his university degree and finally forced to completely withdraw from public life after he wrote *Islam—*The *Foundation of Government*, a book which argued that the Prophet did not intend to create a religious state. Taha Husseni, the Egyptian writer and educator, was denounced and attacked for his views on Islam, though he later became one of the major figures of Arabic literature and was named Egypt's education minister in 1950. Others, like Egyptian Nobel laureate Najib Mahfuz, have also questioned their Islamic faith.

In the past, the persecution of such figures and even their execution was taken as normal practice under Islamic law. Today, however, in a world unified by advanced communications, transportation and international law, the traditional response is seen by the outside world as untenable.

The rapid global transformation brought about by communication and travel make it imperative that we in the Islamic world alter our institutions and our legal systems accordingly, as long as we remain committed to the fundamentals of the faith set down in Mecca. No one can afford to live in isolation anymore. Even those who claim to maintain a very closed society, like Saudi Arabia or Iran, are, in fact, interacting and benefitting from a new and integrated world order. The leaders of these nations are both inconsistent and intellectually dishonest in claiming the benefits of the new order while denying them at another level.

Finally, one must remember that the phenomenon of Islamic insurgence and resentment toward Western domination has been with us for some time. Rushdie's is not the first incident in which we have had this cycle of Islamic insurgence, resentment, and hostility toward the West, East or whoever else is perceived to be threatening Islamic identity and Islamic religion.

We Muslims need to react to outsiders, whether Westerners or otherwise, by asserting our right to be Muslim, not by rejecting everything just because it comes from outside.

An Islamic Victory
ABOLHASSAN BANI-SADR

Until he was ousted in a coup d'état by radical clerics in July 1981, Abolhassan Bani-Sadr was the first president of revolutionary Iran.

The Satanic Verses is a great victory for Islam. The fact that any writer must resort to crude and blasphemons insults against the Prophet Mohammed and Abraham clearly demonstrates the weakness of the West. In other words, in the absence of any valid critique of Islam, the West must settle for crude insults.

Salman Rushdie's book is in no way detrimental to Islam. After 14 centuries, Islam's principles, rights, and values and the Words of the Prophet have endured. Insults can in no way diminish this legacy.

In order to sell books, this author of the West has sought to transform the House of Islam, which is pure, spiritual and solid, into a bordello. He speaks of the love life of the Prophet to gain notoriety and personal profit. This is a sad commentary on Western culture and more of an insult to the West than to Islam.

If I were still head of state in Iran, I would certainly permit *The Satanic Verses* to be translated and published. I would also write a preface for the Iranian edition, which would say to Muslims of my country, "Hold firmly to your faith. After 14 centuries the West, with all its philosophers and social scientists, can only marshall crude insults against Islam. Our faith has been reaffirmed."

Finally, I would pose this question to Americans: If an author sought to speak of the President of the United States and his wife as Rushdie speaks of the Prophet and his spouse, would he be allowed to publish? Would he not be roundly condemned, even prosecuted?

Let us all agree that the rights of the Prophet should be respected in the same manner as the rights of any man.

Truth and Tolerance in Islam
Dr. Ali Fakhro

We asked Dr. Fakhro, minister of education for Bahrain—the Gulf state with a majority Shia' population—to comment on the compatibility of Islam and the West.

Islam is a total system. Muslims cannot choose parts of their religion and discard others. In fact, it is not possible for a true practicing Muslim to accept everything Western Culture offers. However, many concepts such as the scientific approach to solving problems, the democratic and constitutional organization of politics, the dynamic utilization of technology, a government of laws, respect for freedom of the individual within the limits of law, and discipline and order in work, among many others, are definitely harmonious with Islamic values.

Such concepts are universal, but the West has to be careful, as well as modest, and not claim that all worthwhile values originate in its culture. Human rights can be taken as an example of such claims. Fifteen centuries ago, Islam advocated and established many aspects of what we know today as "human rights." Man was totally freed the moment he was asked to submit *only* to God. Islam means submission to God.

However, it has to be admitted that throughout the history of Muslim societies, Islamic human rights were violated. A concept like Al-Shura advocated self-governance and democratic rule. Instead, autocratic rule and dictatorship prevailed. Islam ruled that there should be no compulsion to believe, but some Muslim tyrants suppressed freedom of belief and expression. Like the Christian societies of the Middle Ages, the Muslim societies witnessed atrocities committed in the name of religion.

It's true that the separation of religion from the affairs of the state is not acceptable in Islam, which considers itself concerned with both religious matters and worldly affairs. Islam does not only concern itself with organizing the life of the individual; it is also concerned with the way the community is organized. Islam rejects pluralism and insists on one single monolithic power in this universe: God. Islam attaches great importance to Muslims' belief in the Hereafter in Heaven and Hell, in Angels, in the whole system of Messengers and Prophets. Such beliefs are absolutes.

Finally, what can never be compromised in Islam is the belief in One God. It is the basis upon which everything is built. That is one reason why Islam acknowledges other monotheistic religions, such as Christianity and Judaism. On the other hand, atheism is absolutely rejected by Islam. Philosophy, and political and economic theories that were built on atheism can also never be reconciled with Islam.

Islam expects Muslims to believe in prophets of other monotheistic religions and respect their followers and live in peace with them. Islam declares that Reality was taught to all Prophets and Messengers, starting with Adam and ending with Mohammed. There are churches and synagogues throughout the Islamic world which stand as witness to that tolerance. Christians and Jews are called the "People of the Book." Historically, Christians and Jews who declined to join Islam were *never* forced to do so even after their communities were conquered by war. Compare that with what happened in Andalusian Spain: When the Muslims were defeated they were all driven out of a land in which they had lived for over 800 years. All mosques were either destroyed or changed to Christian churches. Islam was simply uprooted together with its followers.

Intellectual interaction and tolerance are, however, deeply rooted in Islam. To quote the Koran:

Every soul draws the meed
Of its acts on none
But itself: no bearer
Of burdens can bend
The burden of another.
Your goal in the end
Is toward Allah: He will tell
You the truth of the things
Wherein ye disputed.

And an equally revealing passage:

To you be your way,
And to me mine.

That said, we have to differentiate between freedom of belief and expression and the imbecile hallucinations of disturbed minds. Name calling [of the sort Salman Rushdie engages in— ed.] is not acceptable if directed at an ordinary person; why should it be acceptable when directed at Prophets, Holy Books and virtuous women? If we are to live as neighbors, we must all be reasonable, not just one of us. Unfortunately, in this particular case, the assassin of sacred figures and values was made the victim.

Khomeini's Declaration of War
FREIMUT DUVE

These comments are excerpted from a parliamentary speech by Freimut Duve, a Bundestag deputy whose Hamburg district includes a large number of Muslims. This speech became the basis for West Germany's official response to Iran on the Rushdie affair.

The word "Islam" means peace. The name "Khomeini" stands for war and violence. A message of peace has always been implicit in the great tradition of Islamic culture. The tradition of the Khomeini Mullahs [Muslim of quasi-clerical class trained in traditional law and doctrine] is the sword.

Anyone who issues an assassination order based on his own laws, supported and reinforced by the political head of state, declares war on us. This applies even more to the high-technology 20th century than to medieval times. Anyone who would use mosques as launching-pads for human cruise missiles, aimed at selected targets in London on New York, Frankfurt or Cologne, is a warmonger who is breaking international laws, trampling on the United Nations Charter and attempting to undermine other countries' constitutions.

War has been declared. The Iranian President has said, "The black arrows are already on their way." According to our criminal code, he is guilty of incitement to murder.

We take the assassination order on Rushdie as seriously as it is meant, Khomeini's arrows have already caused the utmost damage to the thin fabric of peaceful coexistence between Western-oriented and Islamic states. Incitement to murder conflicts with the call for tolerance implicit in our tradition of Enlightenment.

Of course, there are such things as religious feelings that can be wounded. These deserve respect, especially in our country. Respect belongs to the tradition of Enlightenment. As a young man, I myself saw how traders in an Arab market refused to wrap up vegetable, meat or fish in sheets of newspaper, because the letters of the holy scriptures must not be defiled. But wounded religious sensitivities are one thing. The breaching of international law by assassination-commands is another.

Khomeini's arrows have hit other, unintended victims. In Europe, we have millions of fellow citizens of the Islamic faith, many of whom are Shiites. They should be able to live in Europe, in the same way Salman Rushdie should be able to, without fear.

In recent days, many Muslims have asked to make their views known because they remember the Islamic concept of peace and have distanced themselves from Khomeini. However, I must futher call on the Shiite mullahs living here in Germany never to allow your mosques to fall under the suspicion that they could be misused as bases for terrorism. This our legal system will not tolerate.

As Shiite [Shiites-Islamic sect which believe in Ali and the Imans as the only rightful successors of Muhammad and in the concealment and messianic return of the last Imam.] mullahs, you must state, clearly and unequivocally, what you think of the assassination order. You have a political responsibility toward the community in which you and your followers live. We call on you to point out in your sermons the difference between wounded religious sentiments and a cold incitement to murder.

Prople of Islamic faith must be able to love here without fear. Khomeini has presented this faith to the international public in a bad light. We Germans have experienced the ways in which cold power politics, mass fanaticism and naked force discredited our own cultural traditions. We Germans know what we are talking about when we say that all Muslims who have the courage openly to stand up to Khomeini for the sake of their religion deserve our respect and protection.

In this age of vision as well as television, peaceful coexistence between the Occident and the Orient is imperative. Finding a way to live together in this interconnected world where we are all neighbors confronts us with a task more momentous than ending the Cold War conflict between the superpowers.

In these dramatic times, let us recall those words of wisdom from an East-West anthology of verse:

He who knows himself and others,
Will also have decided,
That Orient and Occident,
Shall no more be divided.

That will still hold true tomorrow, in spite of Khomeini.

The Novelist and the Liar
JACK MILES

A former Jesuit, Jack Miles holds a doctorate from Harvard in Near Eastern languages and is editor of the *Los Angeles Times* book review.

Salman Rushdie is both an apostate Muslim and a novelist. Islam, worldwide, understands apostasy; it does not understand fiction.

The result—audible in much of the worldwide protest against *The Satanic Verses*—is an apples-for-oranges category mistake alongside the legitimate outrage of a religious community at its mocking repudiation by a former member.

Rushdie has described the part of his book that has most offended Muslims as "a secular, humanist vision of the birth of a great world religion." In this he offers an offense to Islam of a sort that Christianity and Judaism have long since grown accustomed to receiving from Western writers. Leo Tolstoy, though he was obsessed by Jesus, did not believe in a personal God or in an afterlife. His book *Resurrection*, though unquestionably religious, was profoundly heterodox. The same might be said about Nikos Kazantzakis' *The Last Temptation of Christ*. Kazantzakis, however pious in his own passionate way, offered a wildly idiosyncratic verse of the origins of Christianity. Among many relevant Jewish examples, Bernard Malamud's late novel *God's Grace* might be mentioned as that writer's attempt to imagine himself into the mind of the Creator, perhaps even to improve on it. When Rushdie says that he possesses a "God-shaped hole" inside him which he has attempted to fill up with literature, he describes a Muslim version of just this imaginative rebellion, an event now familiar, not to say almost trite, in the West.

Christians and Jews, I hasten to add, as they take the point of heterodox (or more aggressively anti-religious) novels, may be offended and may give furious voice to their offense. Muslims, when and if they take the point of *The Satanic Verses*, will definitely have much at which to take offense.

But there is this difference: Christians and Jews, in the West, have long experience in taking the point of a novel. Muslims do not, for the novel, as a genre lying somewhere between history and simple falsehood, scarcely exists in the Muslim world.

Najib Mahfux, the Egyptian novelist who recently won the Nobel Prize for Literature, is not only the best novelist in the Arab world, he is for all practical purposes the first. Further east in Pakistan and for the Muslim minority in India the novel is almost equally an alien form of speech. Obviously this is not true for the minority (Salman Rushdie belongs to it) who have been drawn into close cultural contact with Britain. But thereon hangs all the tales of scandal and anger.

During the week that followed the *Los Angeles Times'* review of *The Satanic Verses*, the refrain among the perhaps twenty (only) evidently Muslim callers who objected to the piece was that the book was "full of lies." How is this charge to be refuted? Clearly, not by saying, "Oh no, it's full of truth." The book isn't truth, it's fiction. But fiction—in our highly developed, perhaps highly pecular view—doesn't become falsehood by virtue of not being truth. The strangeness of this lies lightly on us after so many decades of familarity with it, but that strangeness is quite new for many who have been scandalized by *The Satanic Verses*. A reconciliation, if one can be fashioned, between those Rushdie has offended and those, myself included, who want to defend him will require not just an explanation of Western ideas of freedom of speech but also an explanation of Western literary genres.

Meanwhile, those Western commentators who have seen the Rushdie affair as an example of the power a book can still have, even in the age of television, should perhaps think again. It is unlikely that, absent the category mistake that so many Muslims seems to have made, any novel could have this kind of impact. Saul Bellow [American novelist] wryly commented in a recent interview that a scientist with whom he served on a foundation committee considered his novels, like all novels, to be "light entertainment." Our most serious novels are never taken with the same kind of seriousness, even in literary circles, that the Muslim world has directed at *The Satanic Verses*. Ironically, we reserve this kind of seriousness for such forms of documentary truth as the Pentagon Papers.

The more the Communist East and the often fascist Third World, Muslim or not, join the common culture of the West, the more they cease persecuting their imaginative writers—and the more they cease taking them seriously. The liberty of fiction in its fully developed Western form comes at a price: relative trivialization.

The Writer as Combatant
RYSZARD KAPUSCINSKI

The author of *The Emperor* and *Shah of Shahs*, Ryszard Kapuscinski lives in Warsaw.

I know the Ayatollah Khomeini and Salman Rushdie. I saw Khomeini for the first time in Tehran, when he returned to Iran from exile. Several years later, in London, I met Salman Rushdie. The fact that I have met both the characters in this drama that the world has been talking about, since the moment on February 14 when Khomeini pronounced the death sentence on the author of *The Satanic Verses*, has given me an additional reason to follow attentively the press reports, commentaries, and opinions on the whole affair.

Most such statements present this drama as a conflict (even as a historic conflict) between Islam and the West. Various Koran experts have spoken out on the side of Islam, and defenders of free speech on the side of the West. It can, of course, be called a conflict between Islam and the West, but this makes the controversy narrow and superficial, as well as loading it egregiously with emotional content. For me, it comes down to something more: namely, I see in this confrontation a fragment of a much larger struggle, a fragment of the greatest contemporary conflict—the conflict between democracy and dictatorship.

From such a viewpoint on these events, we can see that their is little new in the whole affair. Those who were born and have spent their lives in Central Europe will know this best. Dictators have always fought independent writers, condemned them to death, burned their books at the stake or, simply, kept them out of print. Hitler sentenced the Nobel Prize–winning writer Carl von Ossietzky to death and bears the responsibility for the suicides of several other German writers (Walter Benjamin, Joseph Roth, etc.) He sentenced dozens of other writers and scientists (Einstein, Mann, Arendt, Brecht) to exile. Stalin murdered scores of fine writers (including Babel, Pilnyak, and Mandelstam). Moreover, he promulgated death sentences (carried out, unfortunately) upon writers of other lands and nationalities (the Polish writer Bruno Jasienski, for instance, died at his hands). And the Peruvian poet Javier Heraud, murdered by the military dictatorship in the 60s? And the Spanish poet Garcia Lorca, exterminated by Franco? And the writers persecuted by Ceausescu? And the writer Vaclav Havel, thrown into prison this year by the Czechoslovakian regime?

A permanent conflict has existed (since the times of Galileo and Cervantes) and still exists between dictators and independent writers, since each of the sides represents divergent, mutually opposed interests. Dictators, with the help of terror and blood if need be, want everyone to believe in what they believe in, while writers are people who try to express the most elementary human desires—the desire for freedom, the desire to be a person who can think, who can speak, who can have a personal opinion—to be oneself.

In the last weeks many friends have called me from the United States, from England, from Holland, to tell me the latest news in the Khomeini-Rushdie affair. I could feel excitement and bewilderment in their voices. Why? Of course, the affair smacks of the grim and brutally grotesque, like a bad dream. But has the twentieth century ever spared us the climate of the brutally grotesque and the bad dream—or often, the grimmer reality?

It seems that the affair of *The Satanic Verses* has been a shock to many people because they took it for granted that literature was a petty diversion, an antidote for boredom, or at the most, a little acre of experimental forms, language games, and tricks of the trade. Literature, in the meantime—real, great literature—is an instrument of the battle over the fate of man, it is a cry of protest and a voice of hope; it is responsibility.

When I spent time on the fronts of contemporary wars—in Iran, in Africa, in Central America—it always amazed me that there were no writers present (or that they appeared infinitely seldom). Afterwards, no less amazed, I would read that the latest French prize had gone to a man who had written a novel about a bordello, or a woman who had written a novel about a *menage à trois*. How far it all was from the great, tragic matters of our time!

In his latest book, Rushdie returns to literature its seriousness; he returns its pride and dignity. The Rushdie affair ought to awaken the consciousness of writers who have regarded literature only as a matter of signing a favorable contract or seeing their books on the best-seller list. It ought to remind them that a writer is a conscience and a combatant.

Rushdie was born in Asia, on the continent where fanaticism has claimed millions of victims in the middle of our century, across which religious frenzy, insanity, and doctrinal fury have visited misfortune and tragedy on an endless number of families, whole masses of people, whole nations. As a child, the author of *The Satanic Verses* witnessed all this. Already then, perhaps, the question that permeates his latest book was born in him: the question of the price of fanaticism, of the price that people must pay for purity of doctrine, for its freshness and inviolability, which is often the highest price, the price of life. For me, Rushdie's book is a mutiny against a world order in which the rights of doctrine prevail over the rights to liberty and well-being, and in which the word, even if it is the word of God, can condemn a man to death.

A TWISTED HISTORY:
A SCHOLAR EXAMINES THE TEXT[3]

The uproar in the Moslem world created by *The Satanic Verses* is hardly surprising. For the book has been seen—and perhaps not without justice—as an attack on the lifestyle and message of the Prophet Mohammed. It has been severely criticized as ridiculing the Prophet's wives and also Abraham, the archetype of all prophets, and its author has been declared an apostate deserving execution.

Here in the West, people may wonder, "Why all the fuss?" The answer is that, in the past few centuries, perhaps nobody has written so bluntly, so openly, about Islam and its messenger. And so nobody is prepared to hear it. Also, a strong Islamic identity is now emerging. People in many parts of the Moslem world are identifying with Islam rather than merely with their nation and they consider this book an attack on their religion. In the Western world, many Christians accept attacks on the Bible because it has long been subject to literary criticism; there was an uproar when it was first criticized, but now that is a part of Western tradition. It is not a tradition in Islam.

Ambiguous: *The Satanic Verses* is an intricate novel. At times, it is purposely ambiguous, blurring the line between reality and fantasy. It consists of many tales, some rooted in seventh-century Arabia, in modern India and in England.

There is no doubt that the novel portrays the birth of Islam, often referring to names well known in Islamic history and to places connected with the emergence of the Faith. It also deals with the changes that Islam has undergone throughout the centuries—the way it has adapted itself to different cultures, such as the Indian culture that forms the background of the author, and, in modern times, to the English environment in which large numbers of Indian and Pakistani immigrants find themselves. The author's target is not Islam as such, but what he conceives to be the "fundamentalism" that has afflicted many Moslems.

[3]By Hadia Dajani-Shakeel, Islamicist, in *Maclean's Magazine*, February 27, 1989, p. 21. Copyright © 1989 by Maclean's Magazine. Reprinted by permission.

While the novel refers to specific historical periods and lo-
cales, it transcends time and space and strives to pursue the long
journey of man, who, having fallen from Paradise, continues to
seek his roots, questioning his origin, deities and creation. Those
philosophical questions are at the core of the novel. However, the
author's references to pre-Islamic deities and Islamic beliefs are
apt to cause misunderstanding of the novel's central themes.

The narrative, including several dreams, introduces two characters—Gibreel Farishta, an Indian actor who is reincarnated as
a namesake of the Archangel Gabriel, and Saladin Chamcha, who
is both an artist and a prototype of the religious believer who never questions his tradition. Gibreel, after his plane explodes in
flight, tumbles from Heaven and sings: "To be born again, first
you have to die. . . . To land upon the bosomy earth, first one
needs to fly." These oppositions in Gibreel's song become reflected in Rushdie's novel, which combines the sacred and the pro-
fane, the celestial and the earthly, fact and fiction.

Triumphant: Gibreel and Saladin land in England, initiating
a saga of the Moslem immigrant in England. The notion of the
immigrant is pivotal to the novel because it refers to the migration of the Prophet Mohammed—Mahound in the novel—
between Mecca and Medina; to the political exile in London of
an Imam, who probably symbolizes Ayatollah Ruhollah
Khomeini; and to the author himself. All have one thing in common: a yearning for the land of their birth, and their youth. The
immigrant and the exile eventually return to their homelands tri-
umphantly.

Gibreel, the novel's main character, also symbolizes Ishmael,
the father of the Arabs. Ishmael's place in Islamic history is connected with the Ka'ba, a house of many deities in pre-Islamic Arabia and directly related to the Satanic verses. By Moslem
tradition, Mohammed in those verses at first acknowledged three
female deities other than God. This recognition was seen as a
compromise with pagans, and the Prophet quickly recanted, de-
claring that the verses were not inspired by God but by Satan. In
retelling that episode, Rushdie seems to twist history for the sake
of artistic creativity. He overdramatizes that issue, which is not
basic to Islam.

In addition, Moslems are bound to be offended by the use of
the name Mahound—a Satanic figure in medieval times—for the
Prophet Mohammed, as well as the unsavory portrayal of his

wives and the power-hungry character of the exiled Imam. In all fairness, however, the author explains that Mahound is a repulsive name applied in the medieval West to the Prophet of Islam. As Rushdie says, Mahound is only "the demon tag that the farangis [Westerners] hang around his neck."

Those are some of the main reasons why Moslems have felt the book to be offensive, particularly because it was written by a lapsed Moslem. This is not to denigrate the artistic achievement of the novel. It does have literary merits. And, at times, it demonstrates a touching humanity. But that is another matter, one that has been drowned in the uproar.

PITTING LEVITY AGAINST GRAVITY[4]

We are finished with it, struggling against exile. Our duties today are those of integration. No longer the prodigious generality of clamor, but the disagreeable recording of the country's detail.

EDOUARD GLISSANT
Le discours antillais, 1981

In the poem *"Shikwah"* ("Complaint") from a collection published in 1908, the great Urdu poet Muhammad Iqbal once accused God of infidelity. That fact is interesting to consider in the aftermath of *The Satanic Verses* scandal. The rage of Islam against the book, and the consequent rage against Islam fuelled by the scandal itself, make it hard to understand how a poet generally taken to be the spiritual founder of Pakistan could say this and live. For he catalogues in that poem all that Muslims have done for God over the centuries, and points out that God has nevertheless neglected them, and allowed the Muslim world to be destroyed. In one of its more startling passages, Iqbal exlaims: "At times You have pleased us, at other times / (it is not to be said), You are a whore."

The line of most Western commentators, unaware of examples like these, has been that "intolerance" is the written law of the undifferentiated Muslim heart. But that is a position that does

[4]By Timothy Brennan, professor of English literature, from his book *Salman Rushdie and the Third World*, pp. 143–66 Copyright © Timothy Brennan 1989. Reprinted by permission.

not appreciate the diversity with which Islam (like most religions) is actually assimilated and expressed. Writers as sensitive to the colonial question as Eqbal Ahmad, Ibrahim Abu-Lughod and Edward Said have condemned the "bigoted violence" against Rushdie and his book, and pointed out that the violence was "antithetical to Islamic traditions." But it was a practical, and not merely a theological, matter that brought tens of thousands of British Asians into the streets to protest about the novel, and made thousands more risk (and in some cases lose) their lives in rioting in India and Pakistan. They were tired of seeing one more orgy of vilification in the Western press.

As very few pointed out in the frenzy of late February 1989, this extreme response had everything to do with Rushdie's special position as an "insider/outsider—a position this study has tried to examine at some length. If Rushdie had not already been known throughout the subcontinent and Middle East as a bestselling novelist who had managed to popularise real Indian history and customs for a mass Western reading public, his opinions would not have mattered as much. His revisions of the historical and mythical narratives of Islam, in other words, were the work of one who knew all the pressure points and who went about pressing them. In the end, *The Satanic Verses* is not simply blasphemous but a systematic attempt to unravel the religion from within.

Rushdie could certainly control (if not predict) the way the novel would scandalise orthodox Muslims. Unlike *Midnight's Children* with its suggestion that the inspirational founder of Pakistan should not be Muhammad but rather Buddah, sitting glassy-eyed and stupid under a tree in Gaya; or *Shame*, with its suggestion that Pakistan's *Quranic* "recital" was indistinguishable from the rantings of the military, the similar irreverences of *The Satanic Verses* are flagged in the title itself, and therefore much more obvious. Anyone reading the table of contents alone, with chapter headings such as "Ayesha" and "Mahound," could see that the novel was a 500-page parody of Muhammad's life. But it is probably not true that Rushdie foresaw the way *The Satanic Verses* would be manipulated by the Western press. Given Rushdie's adherence to the principle of satiric "equal time," it must have been dismaying to him to see the novel made into a fable of Western freedom vs. Oriental fanaticism.

At some level, the issue for the protestors had not only been the novel's trangressions of the *Quran* and the Prophet, but a recognition that the banner of "secularism" has for more than a century been the standard of a Westernised elite eager to "vend [its] Islam wares in the West." Rushdie was not simply ridiculing the mimic men and mimic women of empire who happened to be hiding behind Islamic garb, but also the programmes of change encoded within the contradictory fears, hatreds and aspirations of the oppressed as they actually exist. Syed Shahabuddin, the Indian minister responsible for having the novel banned in India, had a point when he spoke of *The Satanic Verses* as "literary colonialism." The West has, he argued, not yet "laid the ghost of the Crusaders to rest," and although Rushdie had not joined its ranks, he was sufficiently unaware of its existence to avoid being used by it. Literary colonialism had become a campaign carried out "in the name of freedom and democracy. . . . under the deafening and superb orchestration of [the] liberal band."

It is good to remember, at any rate, that ordinary lower-class Muslims in India and Pakistan—as well as in the English cities of Bradford, Birmingham and London—had attacked *The Satanic Verses* long before the Ayatollah Khomeini entered the scene to capture the headlines, and palce the entire affair in the framework of an easier and more convenient demonology. While the conflict soon became the familiar morality play featuring high-level confrontations between Iranian "terrorism" and English respect for law, there had been from the start a much more popular component among the protesting faithful, who had nothing material to gain from demonstrating their outrage (unlike the Ayatollah or Shahabuddin, for example), and who had nothing to lose but their faith. It is important not to forget that. Aziz Al-Azmeh, in a somewhat different response to the book, explained that "in many third-world countries, *The Satanic Verses* is characterised as the work of a self-hater eager to ingratiate himself with the coloniser simply because the novel challenges the most conservative instincts of those groups claiming Muslim 'nativism.'" This characterisation of Rushdie is unfair, I think. But it comes close to locating the class resentments that are simmering beneath the surface of an affair that has persistently been seen in religious terms alone.

To betray a religion one has first to be a real part of it. As an "England-returned" student during brief stints in Pakistan where his family had moved from Bombay in 1964, Rushdie was living (like his character Gibreel) a "childhood of blasphemy." Opposed to his family 's move, and resentful of the new surroundings on his extended visits home, Rushdie early on got a reputation for troublemaking. Rumour had it that he liked to draw the Arabic script for "Allah" so that it resembled the figure of a naked woman. Rushdie did not just pick up the outward gestures and moods of Islam passively while growing up in Bombay, but conducted a full-scale study of its history while at Cambridge. The hold of Islmaic thinking on his work is deeper than might be suggested by a scattering of allusions.

His very first unfinished novel, after all, was about a Muslim holy man (the novel that later became *Midnight's Children*), and from that point his career progressed through the Sufi mysticism of *Grimus* and the textual apostasy of *Shame*. Much of the plotting of the earlier novels depends on key events in the life of Muhammad, who like Saleem Sinai was an orphan, who like Raza Hyder had a daughter but no sons to survive him, and who like Flapping Eagle escaped repression by fleeing to Abyssinia. Despite all the attention given *The Satanic Verses*, it has not been seen how deeply it takes the central subjects of Rushdie's fiction (cultural hybridity, migrant consciousness) and finds their essence in Islam itself—as, for example, in his fictional Mecca "(Jahilia")" which is said to be inhabited by those who "have miraculously made permanance out of mutability," for whom "journeying itself was home," and who live "at the intersection of the caravan routes."

Rushdie, then, is a renegade only in the sense that Muhammad was to the pagan Meccans and the Jews of Medina. *The Satanic Verses* poses as a revelation of a refurbished Islam based on the flawed humanity of the Prophet. In an interview with the Indian magazine *Sunday*, Rushdie called Muhammad the "only prophet who exists even remotely inside history." In response to the protests against the novel in England, he later developed this point:

Muhammad ibn Abdallah, one of the great geniuses of world history, a successful businessman, victorious general, and sophisticated statesman as well as a prophet, insisted throughout his life on his simple humanity. There are no contemporary portraits of him because he feared that, if any were made, people would worship the portraits. He was only the messenger; it was the message that should be revered. ("The Book Burning," *New York Review of Books*, March 2, 1989, p. 26)

Rushdie takes the chance of portraying the Prophet here (knowing it is taboo), and of placing him back into history, because the letter of the law is today being observed without reverence for the original message. To challenge the "handful of extremists [who] are defining Islam," he therefore needs to break the law. As the reference to the Iqbal poem above shows, there has traditionally been less tolerance towards attempts to humanise Muhammad or historicise the *Quran* than to attack God himself. The way Rushdie destroys this idol-worship is by assuming the gall to place himself at the Prophet's level. Thus, as history records, Muhammad was about forty years when his revelations began; so now is Rushdie, and so is his character, Gibreel Farishta. Like Rushdie, Muhammad was not only a seer, but a social agitator, substituting religious brotherhood for the tribal identities of the Arab peoples, and his attack on pagan worship was a direct threat to the commercial enterprise set up around the pilgrimage to the pagan Kaaba, just as Rushdie in the novel continues the critique developed in *Midnight's Children* where religion was portrayed as "a good business arrangement."

In the end, though, the novel cannot be seen through the distorting images of the protests or what the media made of them since they overestimate the Islamic themes of a novel that is, after all, primarily about a very secular England. The book has to be seen against the background of Rushdie's career.

Rushdie and the Black Communities of Britain

Among Rushdie's novels, only *The Satanic Verses* does not end in oblivion. The countries of the earlier work had been countries "of the mind" ; they could be thought of in terms of apocalypse because they were the ones left behind. But forced to take a stand abroad in the England of *The Satanic Verses*, the immigrant is left with nothing but survival.

At first sight, then, the novel looks more oppositional—more a product of that art of communal resistance suppressed in the earlier work—simply because its survival is won at the expense of English insitutions: the British bobby, the BBC newscaster, and the government of a Prime Minister congenially referred to as "Mrs. Torture" and "Maggie the Bitch." If the black communities [Asians, Indians, Pakistanis and Africans] are given the same savage scrutiny—if Asian middle-class hostel owners bilk their West Indian tenants, complain of being stuck in a country "full of Jews and strangers who lump [them] in with the negroes," or who can think of the English only in the bigoted terms of the mad barber of Fleet Street, with a stiff upper lip on the outside but a secret obsession for kinky sex and death—a mood of specifically anti-institutional anger remains, and one that is not altogether cancelled by the ironies of the earlier work. Following Fanon's criteria, we are not surprised to see this slightly new perspective produce subtle shifts in the narrative. Although "translating" just as heavily from a borrowed Islamic tradition, the novel no longer simply targets that tradition for rebuke; as a part of what makes the new immigrant different from the English, it is something that can be learned from, even emulated, at the cultural level. Because here Rushdie is dealing with a life not only remembered and longed-for but experienced first-hand. England is where Rushdie lives (not India or Pakistan), and so the immediacy of the account takes us away from those snapshots of emotion, and those distanced descriptions of lives actually lived, that fill the pages of the earlier novels. Those works were essentially pieces whose only really vivid human interactions took place where the personal narrator spoke directly to the reader; the plotting of the characters was essentially an orchestration of parodic vignettes that collectively made up an argument. By contrast, the metafictional strategies of *The Satanic Verses* are not nearly so pronounced; the characters are for the first time people living in the world, acting out their lives in a story of their own. The story is not *about* events, but in them.

A good part of the intellectual background of the novel had been sketched out in an essay Rushdie wrote in 1984, a year of saturation Orwell coverage in the British press. In "Outside the Whale" he had taken Orwell to task for failing to account in theory for what Orwell himself had done so well in practice—namely, take on the politicians in fiction. The "logic of retreat" of Orwell's late work was, however, cast against the background of a much larger contemporary drama. Recent British television and film had allowed "The British Raj, after three and half decades in retirement, [to make] a sort of comeback." Singling out films such as *Gandhi, Octopussy* and *A Passage to India*, and television serials like *The Far Pavilions* and *Jewel in the Crown*, he concluded that "Raj revisionism, exemplified by the huge success of these fictions, is the artistic counterpart to the rise of conservative ideologies in modern Britain," among them the government's increasingly hostile and restrictive anti-immigration laws, the growth of the National Front, and the "feel-good" ideology of empire in the speeches of Margret Thatcher, depressingly demonstrated in the war with Argentina over the Falklands (Malvinas) Islands.

In another essay written a year earlier for *New Society*, Rushdie had taken on the question of racism itself: "Britain is undergoing the critical phase of its post-colonial period. This crisis is not simply economic or political. It is a crisis of the whole culture. of the society's entire sense of itself." It was the postwar immigrations that had given the imperial pose new life:

The British authorities, being no longer capable of exporting governments, have chosen instead to import a new empire, a new community of subject peoples of whom they can think, and with whom they can deal, in very much the same way as their predecessors thought of and dealt with "the fluttered folk and wild," the "new-caught sullen peoples, half-devil and half-child." (The Empire Writes Back With a Vengeance," *The Times*, July 3, 1982, P.8)

Noting "the huge, undiminished appetite of white Britons for . . . the Great Pink age," he went on to consider the unusually varied "vocabulary of abuse" in the English language itself (wog, frog, kraut, paky), the way the word "immigrant" in England's public debate invariably means "black immigrant", and Margaret Thatcher's use of "we" in a speech recalling days when England ruled one quarter of the world—a "we" that naturally excluded England's two million formerly colonised peoples.

The novel, however, does not devleop these polemical observations. It sets out instead to capture the immigrants' dream-like disorientation, their multiform, plural "union-by-hydridization." *The Satanic Verses* is the most ambitious novel yet published to deal with the immigrant experience in Britain, but it is not by any means the first. Both its originality and its departures are visible only in terms of the enormously varied work that came before it, especially in the postwar period. These include the novels of the West Indian diaspora of the 1940s and 1950s —Samuel Selvon's *The Lonely Londoners*, Edward Braithwaite's *To Sir with Love*, George Lamming's *The Emigrants* and many others. G.V. Desani's *All about H. Hatterr* had been published as early as 1948. Even in the first postwar generation, novels such as these were operating within a larger milieu of activism, community organising and the founding of the first black publishing houses, all of which were to lead in the 1970s and 1980s to an ever more vocal and visible movement exemplified today by the novels of Caryl Phillips, the poetry of Grace Nichols and Linton Kwesi Johnson, the plays of Mustapha Matura and the films of Menelik Shabazz. "Blacks" had, after all, been a presence in Britain for centuries as African musicians in the court of Henry VII, as Indian servants or *ayahs* accompanying returning colonial nabobs, or as sea-going *lascars* settling in the port towns of Cardiff, Bristol and Liverpool. The sudden increase in the numbers of blacks coming to a labour-starved England following the Second World War—from the West Indies, the Punjab, Pakistan, Africa and elsewhere—made a self-consciously "British" community of the 1970s and 1980s possible. As *Race and Class* editor A. Sivanandan put it, they became "a people for a class" with a "legacy of holism [that] made our politics black."

Although intellectually and politically, Rushdie does not share these views of Sivanandan, he remains sympathetic to many of them, and has in fact lent his support through jacket blurbs and introductions to some of the books that document the emergent black communities. He is, however, simply not a part of that movement which in a military metaphor, has called itself the artistic "frontline." The circles in which he travels are much closer those of playwright and screenwriter Hanif Kureishi, whose *My Beautiful Laundrette* and *Sammy and Rosie Get Laid* have enjoyed the same international acclaim as Rushdie's novels, and which typically concern themselves with middle-class Asians who own small businesses and have influential relatives from the home country visting an England that has come to look, as Kureishi once put it, "very much like a Third World country." The contrast between this kind of focus and that, say, of Bombay-born British author Farrukh Dhondy, is startling. A member of the British Black Panthers in his teens, a former teacher in the East end, and currently director of programming for Channel 4, the alternative television station, Dhondy is only one of several current writers (and perhaps the best) to look at the very different world of Southhall streetlife and the working-class Asian youths of the housing estates. In other words, as we have been saying, the differences are not the result of simple place or privilege—the fact, for example, that the Asian communities themselves tend to be more middle-class than the West Indian—it is a difference expressed in a larger political aesthetic.

"Pitting levity against gravity" is a phrase that helps explain this difference. Taken from the novel's opening pages (in a procedure that is typical of Rushdie's methods), the phrase embeds within a passing comment important clues to his narrative strategy. Staring in the face of misery, and with serious doubts about the future of the human race, Rushdie insists on the comic. The first thing to strike any reader of Rushdie is that, while engaged and pedagogical, his novels are simply funny. At the same time, the phrase echoes the idea that the "weightlessness" of the migrant sensibility is universal—both in the sociological sense of the effects postwar immigrations and mass media have had on our collective thinking, and in another sense. He is in other words, attacking the creation of a racial or ethnic "other" by suggesting that we are all, in a way, migrants because we have all migrated to earth from our home "out there." These religious imaginings, not entirely metaphorical, are an important component of what he means by "defying gravity," and are borne out by the mystical overtones of the word "levity" which he later confuses intentionally with "levitation." As we learn almost from the very first page, *The Satanic Verses* is not (like the earlier novels) a rational critique of religious charlatanism by a Westernised Bombay Muslim. Now set in the West itself, it is rather a novel whose questions are essentially religious, and which takes its imagery from Islam in a much more positive sense than previously. Cast into an alien territory that very often seems like hell, the immigrant is thrust into a mental framework of questioning at all levels. *The Satanic Verses* is an immigrant theodicy.

IV. THE FUTURE OF ISLAMIC POLITICS: NO DEARTH OF CAUSES TO ESPOUSE

EDITOR'S INTRODUCTION

Predicting the political future is not a pastime much favored by Muslims. There is so much to be corrected in the injustices and shortcoming of the present, so much change which must come about before Dar al Islam is a clean and fully inhabitable place, that reflecting on a rosy or even dismal future holds little sense or appeal. Looking at the future of the Islamic World must therefore be the province of moderate Muslim commentators or of Western observers, whether sympathetic academics whose audience is tiny, or media figures whose professional reflections seldom develop into a sympathetic response.

Readers of international Islamic journalism will be well aware of the immense waves of concern occasioned by important events within one or another of the national Islamic states, such as the secularization moves by the government of Indonesia in the late 1980s. Although very little remarked upon in the Western media, these moves were a source of voluminous commentary in the Islamic press. It expressed intense dismay that the move away from Islamic fundamentals by the world's most populous Muslim state was a giant step in the wrong direction, a failure to comprehend and accept the direction the rest of the Islamic political world was taking in common. Similarly, the successive failures in Sudan of both the quasi-Islamism of Jaafar al-Nimeiry and the truer faith of Sadiq al-Mahdi were widely ignored in the West—at least in their Islamic contexts—while they have received a great deal of comment and reflection in the Islamic world. The triumph of the Islamic party in Algerian municipal elections in mid–1990 with 65 percent of the vote was treated as an event of overwhelming importance to world Islam everywhere except in the West, where it was in the main reported as just another political occurrence of limited interest and significance.

Thus, there seems little hope at the beginning of the 1990s for a significant change of attitude either in the West or in the

Islamic world which would result in a move toward rapprochement or even warily respectful understanding. The Arabs view themselves (and not without good reason) as victims of Western imperialism and aggression, and militant Islam's hostility towards the West and in particular the United States show no signs of abating. The popular Western media are almost entirely bereft of commentators on Islam who are either themselves Muslim or are sufficiently knowledgeable about Islam to render informed and unbiased judgments on the ongoing political situation and its impact on countries where Islam is a force. Moreover, whatever hope existed for mutual accomodation between Westerners and Muslims was dashed by the events surrounding and following the Iraqi invasion of Kuwait.

This section looks at the future of Islamic politics. These predictions were made well before—in some cases long before the August 1990 invasion. Nevertheless, a close reading of the pieces that follow will afford the reader some highly informed background material which is likely to be helpful in making sense of the unfolding events in the Middle East. First, Alan Taylor, a U.S. political scientist presents a highly critical theoretical analysis of the Islamic political future, from a historical perspective. The second article, by French Islamicist Maxime Robinson, is a short survey of the social, political and economic prospects for Arabs and Arab unity. The third article, part of a summary of proceedings of a conference on Islamic unity held in Karachi in 1983, is an idealistic view of how the *unmah*, the community of believers, "can restore to man the dignity and excellence to which he is entitled." The fourth article is an account from Muslim journalist Amir Taheri of what he predicts will be the coming disintegration of the Islamic revival, caused by fanaticism and terrorism. The final selection, "Islamic Fundamentalism is Winning Votes," written by Youssef M. Ibrahim, seeks to explain some of the reasons why Islamic fundamentalism is gaining political ground in many Middle eastern countries. It is reprinted here for the insight of a Muslim reporter writing for a major Western publication about the increasing power of Islamic militants.

ISLAM AND THE FUTURE[1]

Interpretive Issues

The attempt to sort out the character and implications of the various political experiments tried in the post-Ottoman Middle East raises substantive questions regarding the validity of different interpretive approaches. Any analysis of the doctrines seeking the establishment of a secular nationalist order or an Islamic reform program or an Islamic state necessarily involves some position on the ideal model of secular nationalism or the attributes of genuine Islam. Theories differ on the true nature of each as a sociopolitical system and on the endeavors to use them as guidelines in the task of reconstruction. Some are polemical and opinionated; others are scholarly and profound, with a variety of shades between the two extremes. An effort will be made here to formulate an analytical framework that combines a comparative evaluation of conflicting interpretations with a realistic consideration of the actual circumstances prevailing in Middle Eastern society at the end of the twentieth century.

Secularization and nationalism, and the concomitant subordination of Islam as a guiding sociopolitical principle, became the dominant themes in the public life of much of the Middle East after World War I. As interrelated doctrines in the popularized nationalist ideologies designed to mobilize and reshape many of the countries in the area, they created new behavioral models and loyalties. Certainly they represented a sharp break with the past and generated new hopes and aspirations. In time, however, their use as platforms for ambitious development programs proved disappointing. The political malpractices and monopolization of power by the regimes that upheld them as a preferred alternative to Islam made them disenchanting as well.

The shortcomings of the nationalist experiment led to a climate of reevaluation and stock-taking, sometimes revolutionary in orientation, that has had a profound impact on the entire area. But as yet almost no attempt has been made to find out exactly

[1]By Alan R. Taylor, from his book *The Islamic Question in Middle East Politics*, pp. 113–127. Copyright © 1988 by Westview Press, Inc. Reprinted by permission.

why secular nationalism has lost some of its appeal and in certain cases become more disruptive than creative and beneficial. A major reason is that the kind of nationalism that took root in the Middle East was a limited reproduction of the Western original. Though committed to liberation from foreign control and fostering a sense of responsibility to common aspirations, its political philosophy provided no safeguards against the misuse of power.

The most durable forms of nationalism in the West are related to broader movements seeking liberalization, carefully defined limits of authority, and protection of the rights of citizens. Though imperfect in many instances, this liberal nationalism at least had the theoretical basis that guaranteed the continuity and progressive revision of itself as a viable institution. John Pocock has developed a convincing interpretation of the American revolutionary movement as the culmination of English opposition thought and Renaissance political theory. His analysis of the contribution made by the founders of the United States to the concept of just and mature government reveals an intellecutal depth, drawn from European sources and later perfected in the New World, that became an inseparable part of contemporary Western democracy.

The absence of such a tradition in the formulation of nationalism in the Middle East suggests a direct relationship between a weakly developed political doctrine and governmental systems that have difficulty integrating their constituents in an open and equitable system. The problem with nationalism in the Middle East may not be the institution itself but the superficial way it was formulated from only partially understood Western models. There is also the argument that the peoples of the area were not ready for European-style liberal nationalism because of limited educational resources and an incompatible sociopolitical orientation. Although this may be an aspect of the problem, the capacity of Middle Easterners to change their attitudes and outlook radically in a short space of time has been demonstrated in some cases, notably in Turkey. Misinterpretation of borrowed concepts was therefore a more important factor in the limitations of nationalism in this area.

Developing a reliable assessment of the Islamic tradition and an evaluation of the divergent contemporary approaches to it is a difficult task. The position taken [here] and accepted by most scholars is that Islam evolved from a religious doctrine into a multifaceted civilization representing a composite of diverse cultural elements brought within an Islamic framework. Islam has also grown with time, expanding its perspectives and elaborating its world view. It has never been static or rigid but rather a legacy that accrued a variety of often highly refined and profound attributes over the centuries. Because of this and its own understanding of man's relationship to God, Islam is historically oriented and attaches great importance to what transpires among people in time. Though Islam acquired a political dimension as a result of this concern, it has had considerable difficulty with problems of power and order. Its humanistic aspects therefore became more durable and ultimately more fulfilling parts of the heritage.

Another observation about Islam, one almost universally accepted, is that in recent centuries it has been relatively stagnant and uncreative intellectually, as well as corrupt and degenerate in the sociopolitical sphere. This was a major reason for the decline of the Ottoman Empire and other political entities in the Middle East and the subsequent intrusion of the great powers into the area. It was also the cause of [a] diversified search for reform and reconstruction.

The state of siege that beset Islam in the Middle East during the nineteenth and twentieth centuries led to a debate among Muslims as to what should be done to remedy the situation. There were different opinions among those who did not opt for the secular Westernizing solution. The conservative *ulama*, undoubtedly still the largest single grouping within the clergy, continued in their traditional nonpolitical role preaching a rather uninspiring version of Islam and protecting their interests by avoiding any conflict with the ruling elite. Mohammed Arkoun, admittedly partisan on the subject, has described the limitations of these conservatives in vivid terms:

Intellectually and culturally, the official Islam of the *ulama* in the era which concerns us was marked by an extreme doctrinal poverty. For a long time Islamic thinking had allowed itself to fall into the dogmatic repetition of several handbooks of law, grammar, exegesis and history. . . . Cut off from classical sources as well as from the spiritual influence of the great sufi masters, popular Islam was in its turn victim of the debasement of the social imagination and of the collective sensitivity. ("Positivism and Tradition in an Islamic Perspective: Kemalism," trans. R. Scott Walker, *Diogenes*, Fall 1984, p. 89)

During the latter part of the nineteenth century, there was a sharp break with this inept form of Islam by the Islamic modernists. The interpretive issue in the controversy surrounding Muhammad Abduh and the *salafiyya* thinkers is whether their endeavors represent a revival of genuine Islam or a subtle manipulation of concepts designed to make Western institutions and values acceptable by presenting them as Islamic in origin. Daniel Pipes took the position that the modernists were trying to reconcile Islamic law with Western culture. Nevertheless, he insisted, "Equating Islam with the ideals of liberalism obviously requires a radical reinterpretation of the faith." He also argued that the modernists emphasized the Quran over such other sources of Islam as the *hadith* (traditions of the Prophet), consensus, and analogy, because the Quran is less precise and therefore more adaptable. Their contention was that "Each generation must reread the Qur'an, reach its own consensus, and use its logical facilities to change the law and make it current." Pipes rejected this approach as a way of subordinating Islam to the requirements of change: "The Qur'an in their hands becomes a collection of disjointed quotes and proof texts. Instead of endeavoring to comprehend God's will, they use it to confirm preconceived notions." He concluded that Islamic modernism "is a tired movement, locked in place by the unsoundness of its premises and arguments."

Inasmuch as Pipes also took issue with the neofundamentalists, the thrust of his book is that since modernization requires Westernization, the only real choice open to contemporary Muslims is emulation of the West. This summary relegation of Islam to the category of obsolescence overlooks not only the continuity of a living tradition but also the problems that have attended the Westernization process in the Middle East. Marshall Hodgson asserted: "The [Islamic] heritage does remain as an active cultural force, even as a single whole." At the same time, he recognized that the impact of the West in modern times "ushered in a new period in the world's history, in which the bulk of mankind . . . came to form a global society of closely interacting nations." But this world scope did not pose a problem for Muslims because Islam "had not been isolated even in its origins, since it presupposed the wider historical complex of which the Occident formed a part."

For Hodgson, the challenge confronting contemporary Islam in the Middle East and elsewhere was to find a way of preserving its own heritage in the context of the universal cosmopolitanism that grew out of the encounter between the West and the rest of the world in our own times. Unlike Pipes, therefore, he had a positive attitude toward Muhammad Abduh and the Islamic modernists, whose approach represents the only realistic and satisfactory solution to the problem.

In Hodgson's view, Muhammad Abduh did not reject the Islamic tradition as it existed in the nineteenth century in favor of Westernization but to revive *ijtihad*, "the free exploration within the originally established rules of legal inquiry and the moral norms of Islam, of what was best here and now." Although admitting that Abduh was influenced by modern European thinkers, he noted that the Egyptian reformer was particularly drawn to the ideas of Auguste Comte, who championed science and positivism but affirmed man's need for religion. Abduh felt that Islam was naturally disposed to such a combination of science and religion and devoted much of his life to reviving and blending these compatible dimensions of the Muslim-Arab heritage. If this approach involved a marriage between Islam and certain aspects of modern Western culture, the same result can be expressed in a different way. As Hodgson put it, Abduh's "influence was in part a personally moral one: he fought all superstition and corruption in the name of self-reliant honesty and efficiency . . . he was bent on showing to modernly trained men the validity and relevance of Islam as a faith."

The theory of Islamic modernism was never fully developed or considered for any kind of implementation. Eventually the whole idea of Islamic reform was radically altered to the point that it bore little resemblance to what Muhammad Abduh had in mind. Yet the new neofundamentalist concept of reform became a more controversial issue because of the activist role it came to assume in Middle East politics.

The neofundamentalists seek to obliterate all traces of modernity from Middle Eastern political life and to restore what they see as the original Islam, literally interpreted and forcibly imposed. They have little or no reference to the legacy of Islam as a civilization developed over centuries. As the French scholar, Gilles Kepel, phrased it, "What distinguished the extremist Islamicist movement from the bulk of Muslims as far as the golden age is concerned is that the former blot out history in favour of the reactivation of the founding myth, while the latter accommodate themselves to the history of Muslim societies."

In failing to grasp the content and significance of the medieval Islamic synthesis, the resurgence ideologues developed a unidimensional concept of Islam based principally on its political and legal precepts. Their dogmas were often highly generalized, even simplistic and anti-intellectual, because their primary practical aim was to arouse the masses through emotive metaphors expressed in common colloquial language. They also played on the grievance psychology engendered by the failures and malpractices of the nationalist order.

The inherent problems in the neofundamentalist doctrine and program have been analyzed from a number of perspectives. The comments of two scholars seem particularly apt. Daniel Pipes, whose interpretation of Islamic modernism may seem based on hasty conclusions, made some thoughful observations about the significance of the position of the neofundamentalists. Maintaining that they have, in effect, converted the *sharia* into an ideology, he pointed out that the result is "a vague 'Islamic order,' unrestrained by objective standards, [which] becomes whatever fundamentalists wish it to be." This ambiguity creates a fluid and unpredictable situation in which those who have power, whether in an organization or an Islamic state, can impose their interpretation of Islam on others, even if it is patently heretical. Another problem is that "when fundamentalists codify the Shari'a, they petrify an evolving rule and make it restrictive. The law had always adapted to time and place in small but key ways, but fundamentalists make it a fixed doctrine, leaving no room for individual responses." In the end, Pipes believed, the Islam of the neofundamentalists "begins to usurp the role of God."

Since the Islamic resurgence movement actively sought the overthrow of existing regimes deemed corrupt and contaminated, it was axiomatically revolutionary. Yet though Shiism is receptive to the idea of revolt, there is discinct resistance to it in Sunni theory. For this reason Sayyid Qutb and other neofundamentalist ideologues revived the political philosophy of Ibn Taymiyya (1268–1328) in an attempt to legitimize revolution from a Sunni point of view. More specifically, Qutb was trying to use Ibn Taymiyya to justify his doctrine of insurrection against *jahili* regimes, derived largely from the Pakistani theologian, Sayyid Abul Ala Mawdudi. Nevertheless, as Emmanuel Sivan has correctly observed with regard to Ibn Taymiyya:

A firebrand he surely was, but hardly a revolutionary. . . . His whole endeavor was to cleanse Islam of the dross accumulated during centuries of decline . . . and not even hostile sultans and emirs accused him of sedition. . . . Never did Ibn Taymiyya challenge the legitimacy of any particular sultan. . . . He was indicted as a . . . "deviant" from theological norms, but never as a harbinger of insurgency. (*Radical Islam: Medieval Theology and Modern Politics* [New Haven, Conn.: Yale University Press, 1985], pp. 95–96)

Despite the liberties taken by Sayyid Qutb in creating a new image of the late medieval thinker, "The Ibn Taymiyya message, as reinterpreted by Sayyid Qutb, . . . continued to transmit in cultural code the frustrations and animosities vis-á-vis modernity, and to legitimize in Sunni terms the deeply felt protest against the [Egyptian] regime, which upholds its values." Qutb and his mentor, Mawdudi, thus converted Islamic neofundamentalism into a challenging opposition to the status quo, equating modernity with *jahiliyya,* calling for a remedy through rebellion, and prescribing a solution to the problem of making the resurgence movement a countersociety and a vanguard of radical re-Islamization. Khomeini, who was influenced by Qutb and Mawdudi, accomplished a similar and more successful result in Iran. What remains very questionable, however, is whether the militant movement that these personalities helped galvanize draws on the entirety of the Islamic tradition or a limited segment.

All these interpretive issues must be carefully weighed as we probe for answers to the Islamic question in Middle East politics. In final analysis, however, each investigator has to develop a particular theory, based on the individual's own appraisal of the circumstances, motivations, value systems, and sociocultural dynamics that determine commitment and behavior. All these considerations should relate, however, to an analysis of actual needs and the limitations and possibilities that exist with regard to their fulfillment.

Islam and the West in Middle East Political Thought

Secular nationalism and Islamic resurgence represent diametrically opposed approaches to the sociopolitical reconstruction of the Middle East. Their encounter over the years as competing ideologies has been openly hostile and often bitter. One of the paradoxes of contemporary politics in the area, however, is that both the secularists and the Islamic revolutionaries have derived their doctrinal systems from Islamic and Western sources. The irreversible combination of these two traditions is reflected in this incongruous phenomenon.

The Islamic components in each political creed include the utopianism of the early Muslim world view, the unresolved issues of power and authority, and a pattern of interaction involving myth and resignation. The visionary picture of the ideal *umma* was inspired by the model of Muhammad's rule in Medina. It was based on the concept of a dedicated and united community seeking to fulfill its historic mission under the direction of a pious and enlightened caliph. The patent idealism of this image understandably encountered difficulties in the real world of history. In the medieval period, the problem was resolved by adjustments in the conceptual framework and practical measures taken by the *ulama*. Most contemporary neofundamentalists, however, take the premises of the myth at face value, leaving them far less capable of dealing with the contradictions between theory and reality.

Dedication and unity were often thwarted by circumstances, but this deficiency was concealed by a leadership tradition that preserved executive power for centuries. Though frequently of questionable legitimacy, Islamic government survived from one age to the next because there was a general consensus that a facade of harmony and unity was more important than equity and the right of opposition.

In the modern context, this concentration of authority in an exalted leader is evident in both secular and Islamic neofundamentalist political structures. The only difference is that charisma has become more important because the citizenship concept made mass appeal necessary. Mustafa Kemal Atatürk and Gamal Abdul Nasser became the prototypes of the populist national hero, leading their people out of a despotic and superstitious past into a new and just age filled with hope and opportunity. Khomeini exercised a similar kind of charismatic appeal, galvanizing the antishah movement with his uncompromising condemnation of the regime and projecting an image of himself as a "deliverer." In all these cases, there were opposition elements, but these were either suppressed by force and cunning or prevented from assuming an effective role by the popularity of the leader and his platform.

The leadership syndrome, which pervades much of the Middle East, is really a recapitulation of the political tradition that developed in Islam during its earlier centuries. This syndrome in turn engendered issues of power and authority, partly resolved in the formative period but perpetuated with most of the component problems in the contemporary era. With a harnessed judiciary and the absence of a representative legislative function, the political supremacy of premodern Islamic rulers was relatively unchecked, though some administrative autonomy existed in a number of cases. Sovereignty resided with the wielder of power, and this power was hardly ever challenged for the sake of preserving the stability and cohesion of whatever Muslim community was involved.

Contemporary Middle East governments, with a few exceptions, operate in the same fashion but with greater control over their constituencies. Many of the secular nationalist regimes have monopolized power and wealth to an incredible extent and deal repressively with all forms of opposition. Most of the Islamic resurgence organizations are also authoritarian and regimented, while the Islamic government in Iran is absolutist in forcing conformity to its program. Unapologetic about its disinterest in democratic practices, it insists that only an Islamic dictatorship can exterminate Western culture and revive the sociopolitical principles of Islam.

Related to this kind of political orientation is a pattern of behavior in which myth and resignation are prominent ingredients. Here again, the contemporary manifestation is a partial recapitulation of the Islamic past. In former centuries, the ruling institution generally enlisted the support of the religious establishment to reinforce its legitimacy while leaving the *ulama* free to preside over many administrative functions. Since there was no way the society could challenge this kind of status quo, the constituents accommodated themselves to it. In modern times, the ruling elites employ more deceptive methods to preserve their power. Most regimes in the area engage in an elaborate myth-making process designed to gloss over various forms of malpractice and repression or the inability to keep promises and achieve designated goals.

The secular nationalist ideologies are based on generalized and often romantic aspirations, and those who forward them are pictured as virtually faultless heroes of the national cause. Neofundamentalist doctrines are equally sweeping in what they claim to represent, and the organizations that propagate them pose as the vanguard of a divinely ordained historical event of ultimate importance. In both cases, the cult of the personality forms an integral part of the myth's mystique. Leaders such as Atatürk, Nasser, Asad, Saddam Hussein, and Ayatollah Khomeini are portrayed everywhere on posters and lapel buttons. This publicity is designed to give the leader the appearance of being superhuman, a way of exalting the ideology he champions and covering up any weaknesses or contradictions in its position. The general public, often overawed by such histrionics, as well as terrified by the brutal suppression of opposition, has to acquiesce unless some viable avenue of revolt opens for it.

Those aspects of Middle East political thought derived from Islam, whether in secular or neofundamentalist ideology, represent the very dimensions of the religion most problematical historically. Discarding the determinist theory that societies are locked in a repetition syndrome from which they cannot escape, it is possible to look at this situation as subject to change. If, as has been suggested, the humanist traditions of Islam could be revived, some of the political problems carried over from the past could at least be ameliorated, if not removed. Without such a development, however, the despotism passed down through the centuries and identified as a source of decline when the idea of reform was first introduced will almost certainly continue indefinitely in different forms. Nevertheless, as this continuance would mean a lack of progress or regression, the mood of the people seems not to be receptive to that kind of stagnation.

There are also Western components in both the secular and neofundamentalist ideologies of the Middle East. The Western origin of the secular nationalist doctrines is fairly obvious except for the often overlooked fact that the borrowed concept was transposed to the Middle East with some defects in the development of political principles. This raises some question as to how "Western" the various Middle Eastern nationalisms really are. Though secular and utilitarian in orientation, their lack of safeguards against the monopolization of power links them more to Islamic than to European political tradition.

The Islamic resurgence leaders and organizations consciously spurned most aspects of Western culture. They were, nevertheless, influenced by certain modes of European political behavior.

Daniel Pipes maintained: "Ironically, in an effort to stave off Western ideologies, fundamentalists radically change their religion and direct it along Western lines." Acting on the citizenship concept, itself Western in origin, the neofundamentalists inadvertently imitated European models in their revolutionary style and their methods of galvanizing the commonality through populist activism. They may also have taken something from examples of demagogic leadership and mass manipulation found in some forms of European political practice, such as fascism and communism.

Daniel Pipes summed up this paradoxical aspect of militant Islamic neofundamentalism succinctly by observing that "self-conscious rejection of the West changes a Muslim as much as adopting its ways. Maududi and Khomeini are thoroughly modern men." In the final analysis, then, while the Islamic modernists were trying to use the best of the Western legacy in an Islamic context, the neofundamentalists were unconsciously borrowing the more questionable aspects of that same tradition in their quest for power and influence. The differences between the two approaches to Islamic reform are therefore considerable.

The existence of Islamic and Western conceptualism in both kinds of contemporary ideology points to the inescapable reality that Middle Eastern sociopolitical orientation is the product of a cultural composite. If such a combination is inevitable, then the major task of the future is to find ways of making the most constructive and valid components of each tradition compatible parts of a modern synthesis. This was done in the past, and there is no reason it cannot be done in the present.

The Quest for a Viable Ethos

The disruption of traditional culture and the introduction of Western attitudes and institutions have confronted Middle Eastern societies with the challenge of developing a conceptual-behavioral framework that preserves their own historical legacy and identity while adapting to the universal cosmopolitanism of the modern global system. In Hodgson's view, this situation has created a need for a new moral vision to fill the void left by the disintegration of former allegiances and cultural patterns. This need is made all the more imperative by the prevalence of rigid and simplistic interpretations of Islam and by the breakdown of the secular nationalist order because of ideological deficiencies.

One of the greatest barriers to the construction of a synthesis capable of addressing the demands of modernity is the utopianism apparent in most Middle Eastern political doctrines. Though originally generated by the Islamic concept of the *umma* and its historic mission, which was considerably revised in the medieval period, it was reinforced by nineteenth-century European positivism, which became an important part of nationalist ideologies. The problem inherent in utopianism is that by injecting the idea of perfectability into a political philosophy, it increases the risk of exaggerated interpretations and minimizes flexibility in the theoretical and practical approach to politics. The formulation of finite goals and an acceptance of human imperfection would facilitate the emergence of more realistic and less rigid programs of sociopolitical development. Such an orientation would also stimulate a climate in which the underlying issues can be defined and analyzed.

The most important requirement in constructing a synthesis of Islamic and modern Western culture is a rediscovery of the historical Islam and a redefinition of Islamic values appropriate to the contemporary situation. As Wilfred Cantwell Smith put it, "The fundamental *malaise* of modern Islam is a sense that something has gone wrong with Islamic history. The fundamental problem of modern Muslims is how to rehabilitate that history." It is not a matter of trying to resuscitate the past but of using an accurate reexamination of the Islamic heritage as a principal guideline in the reconstruction of culture and sociopolitical institutions in the present. Hodgson pointed out that

all cultural action takes place within a setting of tradition, even when in sharpest revolt against particular creative events of the past. As we have seen, tradition is not contrary to progress but a vehicle of it, and one of the problems of Muslims is that on the level of historical action their ties with relevant traditions are so tenuous. (*The Venture of Islam: Conscience and History in a World Civilization*, 3 vols. [Chicago: University of Chicago Press, 1974], vol. 3, p. 167)

The inability of most contemporary Muslims to correctly interpret the Islamic legacy is a problem of devastating proportions. It is the major obstacle to the evolution of a sound and appropriate cultural composite that could provide the basis of sociopolitical viability in the future. Emmanuel Sivan noted that present-day "Muslims made use of the past—for apologetics, for window dressing—rather than a case in which the past had a creative impact upon the present." Mohammed Arkoun maintained that those representing the secular and Islamic frames of reference in the Middle East are involved in "the manipulation of the symbolic heritage by social performers dominated by a false consciousness of their real historical and cultural situation. . . . Both attitudes reveal the radical inadequacy of the mental equipment applied to analysing Muslim societies and to the definition of a historic action appropriate to their situation."

Arkoun believed that important decisions have to be made about the degree to which Muslims can and should be cut off from their symbolic heritage, on the one hand, and insulated from every foreign influence to the point of enclosing themselves in a single phase of their own history, on the other. He insisted that the secular nationalist and militant neofundamentalist approaches to reform are incapable of dealing with decisions of this kind. What is required is the historian's way of thinking, the methods developed by the school of "applied Islamology," of which Arkoun himself is a leading representative. This approach involves a rediscovery of what the Islamic tradition actually was in history and a reinterpretation of the Quran with specific reference to contemporary issues and challenges.

Marshall Hodgson felt that the general orientation of Islam, contemporary aberrations notwithstanding, is well suited to the related tasks of cultural synthesis and historical reexamination:

The Islamic heritage was built in a relatively cosmopolitan milieu and its traditionally world-wide outlook should make it possible for Muslims to come to terms with Modern cosmopolitanism. . . .
. . . [P]erhaps the greatest potential asset of Islam is the frank sense of history that from the beginning has had so large a place in its dialogue. For a willingness to admit seriously that the religious tradition was formed in time and has always had a historical dimension makes it possible to assimilate whatever new insights, into the reality of the heritage and of its creative point of origin, may come through either scholarly research or new spiritual experience. (op. cit., vol. 3, pp. 436–437)

If the Islamic tradition is based on this kind of cultural and historical vision, as indeed it is, the noticeable lack of such orientation in the present situation is the most tragic reality confronting the Middle East. As Daniel Pipes noted, "By rejecting the medieval synthesis, fundamentalists commit themselves to apply every facet of the Shari'a; they choose to ignore human foibles and a thousand years of experience. . . . If the umma found Islamic precepts unattainable when they were devised a thousand years ago, how could they be applied in the twentieth century?"

The neofundamentalists are not alone in the inability to use Islam constructively. The Islamic conservatives and the secularists who are at least nominal Muslims are equally inept. Islamic modernism, which could have provided many helpful guidelines, is a virtually forgotten movement. Though some of its ideas are being revived by such thinkers as Mohammed Arkoun, their impact is very limited and they maintain an extremely low profile because of the sensitive nature of their undertaking.

John Voll distinguished several pairs of contrasting predispositions in Islamic history, opposite sides of which have been emphasized in different contexts. Among these are the tendencies to affirm the diversity of Islamdom and the Islamicate, and the openness of both to acceptance of the achievements of other cultures, as opposed to the conformist and insular position, which seeks to preserve a monolithic and pristine form of Islam. In the contemporary situation, the attitude toward these two alternatives is crucial. The open approach of the Islamic modernists is the only viable option, but the revivalist movement is dominated in the immediate present by the closed and narrow neofundamentalist interpretation. The major challenge of the late twentieth century, therefore, is how to achieve a reorientation of the endeavors to make Islam a vital part of contemporary Muslim life.

As Muslims in the Middle East and elsewhere search for an interpretation of Islam appropriate to contemporary circumstances, they may take increasing interest in the work of the Sudanese Islamic thinker Mahmoud Mohamed Taha (1909 or 1911–1985). The leader of a group known as the Republicans, Taha elaborated a highly original theology in his book, *The Second Message of Islam*. He distinguished between the concept of Islam developed during the Meccan period of the Prophet's ministry and that formulated after the first *umma* was established in Medina. The original Islam was completely egalitarian and democratic, and it stands as a model of the perfect religious community that will come into being toward the end of time. Medinese Islam, however, was forced by circumstances to abrogate this early manifestation of an ideal to be realized at a much later stage and to institute a sociopolitical system based on *jihad* as the normal approach to the non-Muslim world and a restrictive code of the *sharia* as the only way to preserve the unity and viability of the *umma*. This "first message of Islam," which has determined the institutional basis of Islamdom ever since, represents a postponement rather than a repeal of the Meccan version, which constitutes the "second message of Islam" to be reinstated at a later date.

Taha's notion of a higher humankind of the future, endowed with absolute freedom and a perfected humanity, may appear to some as an example of metaphysical utopianism. Yet its strongly humanistic orientation and open rejection of repressive forms of Islamic practice could, if his theories are accepted as valid, stimulate extensive revision of traditional Islamic jurisprudence and facilitate the cultural synthesis that seems essential for Muslims to accomplish in the modern age.

Both the Islamic and Western traditions contain important elements that can be combined and used in the reconstruction of the cultural, social, and political life of the Middle East. A central theme of this book has been that the highly refined world view that was developed in the early Abbasid period represents a humanistic dimension of Islam that could be instrumental in addressing the current decline of political order in the area. The concept of the unity and harmony of nature and of humankind, developed in Islamic philosophy and portrayed in Islamic art and architecture, can serve as the basis of a fresh approach to the human condition. Recovery of some of the sufi tradition has the potential of stimulating a new sense of spirituality. A reinterpretation of the Friday prayer service and the pilgrimage as the inspirational basis of a doctrine of equality and equity could lead to radical changes in Islamic political thought. The most significant impact of a revived Islamic humanism, however, would be the elimination of a literalistic and largely political understanding of Islam.

The transposition of Western political institutions into the Middle East has permanently changed the area's public orientation. The problem is not that an alien tradition has been introduced but that it has been understood in an imperfect way. Middle Eastern political theorists and practitioners need to reexamine the liberal nationalist idea in its entirety, as it was developed in Europe and the United States. This would help them develop a constitutional framework for their own national movements and minimize the malpractices and instability that have characterized these systems for three generations.

The combination of Islamic and Western traditions in the Middle East has already been undertaken, and this process cannot be reversed. What is subject to change is the way both are interpreted. With proper understanding and implementation of the nobler aspects of each heritage, the cross-fertilization will be relatively free of problems, for these very dimensions are most compatible. What the peoples of the Middle East are groping for is a sociopolitical-intellectual culture of their own, drawn from Islam and parts of other complete traditions and systems but uniquely theirs nevertheless.

The argument that Islam is not Islam unless it conforms to what it was at some particular time and in some particular place should be seriously challenged, since it is demonstrably false. Equally fallacious is the notion that liberal democracy and nationalism can only function in the West. They can operate and have operated elsewhere. They are not the exclusive property of special people. The only requirement is that the necessary institutional structures be in place, and even when they are, they have to be constantly reviewed and reinforced. There is consequently no reason to believe that a satisfactory synthesis cannot be achieved in the Middle East.

Given the now widespread belief in the citizenship principle throughout the area, there will be a growing impatience among the increasingly active and influential populace with misuse of power, whether in the name of nationalism or of Islam. A powerful and ultimately decisive tension has been established in the midst of the body politic. Despite the machinations of political leaders and elites, the demands of the people will eventually prevail. If a ruling class ceases to represent the dominant forces in a society, it will in one way or another be replaced by another elite that is representative in this respect. The same is true for cultural symbols and values.

The Middle East is in transition. Its people have been through painful experiences in the process, and they will encounter more as the quest for a viable ethos moves on to its natural resting place. The end result is difficult to predict, but what does seem reasonably certain is that Islamic humanism and Western liberalism should and will constitute equally important parts of a new tradition that has a distinct Middle Eastern identity. The unidimensional interpretations of Islam and the West produced regimes that frequently violated human rights and dignity to an incredible extent. At some point, the connection between ideology and practice will become clear, and this will be the moment of decision for a troubled area. It is hard to believe that people may make the worong choices all over again, and it is hoped they will not.

PROSPECTS AND PITFALLS FOR THE ARAB WORLD[2]

What role can the Arabs play in today's world?. What are their prospects for tomorrow? Obviously, the answer to these questions depends in large part on the answer to another question: To what extent will they unite or remain divided?

Unifying and Differentiating Factors

As we have seen, Arabist ideology has pressed for unity. On the other hand, there have always been deep political divisions. What accounts for this twofold tendency?

There are, of course, deep reasons for the fact that the ideology of of Arabism has taken Arab unity as its goal and that this choice has received such enthusiastic support. The most obvious unifying factor is written language, the only language of culture, classical Arabic. The Arab countries also share a common history, particularly in its beginnings. The chivalric tales of the pre-Islamic Arabs, the rise of Islam in Arabia, shrouded in sacred aura, the heroic deeds of the conquerors, the glory and sumptuousness of the Damascus and Baghdad empires are riches in a treasure-house of memories that all Arabs have cherished through the ages. Broadly speaking, the Arabs have always faced the same enemies—the crusaders and Mongols in the Middle Ages, European imperialism in the modern era—and they have always had the same ambiguous relations with the Turks. To some extent they share a common culture. This culture has continued the medieval Muslim cultural tradition, which was based on the Arabic tongue (in its intellectual aspects, at least) and so was often conceived of as an extension of pre-Islamic Arab cul-

[2]By Maxime Rodinson, director of studies at the Ecole Pratique des Hantes Eiudes at the Savbonne, from his book *The Arabs*, pp. 129–42. Copyright © 1981 by the University of Chicago and Croom Helm Ltd. Reprinted by permission.

ture and early Islam, enriched by many later contributions, most notably Iranian.

Many elements of this common culture are still alive, immediate, and active. Classical Arabic literature of the Middle Ages, though studied in school, no longer offers much to attract the modern reader. It is more respected than read but remains nonetheless a model of style and a vehicle of fundamental cultural values: moral, aesthetic, etc. Its most readily comprehensible elements, the innumerable anecdotes and maxims with which it is adorned, provide a frame of reference. The popular literature of the Middle Ages (chivalric stories and tales along the lines of the *Thousand and One Nights*), which the litterati held in deep contempt then as now, is still accessible and more eagerly read than the classics. Modern Arab literature, a product of the nineteenth century, is more readable. It has helped give wide currency to the ideas of the leading cultural circles.

Classical Arabic is not only a common literary language. It makes mutual communication and comprehension possible (through simplification and, frequently, compromise with the various dialects). Arabs who speak different dialects can understand one another perfectly in this tongue and can write so as to be understood anywhere in the Arab world. It is the language of political speeches, radio, and to some extent of the cinema and theater.

There are, moreover, important aspects of social life and many elments of daily culture (this time in the anthropological sense), customs, and collective mentalities that are to some degree shared. This is a vast area, very difficult to explore; to understand it, we would need a searching, detailed scientific study that would attempt to establish objective criteria. For the moment such studies are virtually nonexistent, and we must make do with literary surveys, both Arab and non-Arab, which sometimes reveal many interesting intuitions and much perspicacity and psychology understanding, but which fail to meet scientific criteria of verifiability. Here we shall refrain (we have no space in any case) from venturing too far onto this slippery ground. We shall merely point out that some of the elements in question, which derive from medieval Muslim civilization or its common roots, are also found among non-Arab Muslim peoples, and on occasion even among non-Muslims. (Concerning familial customs, see, for example, Germaine Tillion, *Le harem et les cousins* [Paris: Seuil,

1966], with which I cannot agree entirely, particularly where the explanatory hypotheses are concerned, but which provides excellent descriptive material that clarifies a good many points.) Thus they cannot be regarded as specifically Arab.

Compared with these unifying factors, the factors of regional differentiation are no less striking. The various Arabized countries constitute economic regions, with all that that entails. In some cases a political unit corresponds roughly to at least a potential geographic and economic unit (Morocco, Tunisia, Egypt). In others the political unit does not correspond to a clearly defined geographic unit and has difficulty achieving economic unity. In any case, political boundaries have by now been successful in marking off zones within which networks of economic relations ensure that there will be a certain inherent unity and that common responses, aspirations, and interests will be able to form.

The language spoken in daily life varies from place to place. Infinite variations distinguish speech of each village, each tribe, each city, and often each neighborhood. These variations are small, but their cumulative effect is large and gives rise to a group of related dialects in each region. Under modern conditions there is a tendency for these to coalesce. (The term 'accent' which has been used by some to minimize this phenomenom, is linguistically misleading; it refers to precisely this normal fragmentation of a language into different dialects.) Often the difference is greater between sedentary and Bedouin or urban and rural dialects in a given region than between dialects of different regions. Broadly speaking, the difficulties of comprehension increase with geographical or social distance. Modern life, however, as we shall show momentarily, has tended to bring these different linguistic forms closer together.

The mental outlook and daily customs and activities differ from region to region, as they differ according to way of life, social class, and religious affiliation. Each type of activity has its own boundaries, with some overlapping of different traits. Each region also has its own history, before and after Islam, before and after Arabization. Life in the various regions is built on different substrates: Berber and Latin in the Maghrib, Pharaonic and Coptic in Egypt, Aramaic in the Fertile Crescent, etc. These substrates often produce noticeable differences in the forms of life erected upon them.

Modern conditions sometimes seem to weigh in favor of unity. Wide circulation of books and newspapers, radio, television, movies, and increased ease of travel have made it possible for Arabs living in widely separated areas to become more familiar with one another. Mass education has increased familiarity with the common classical language in its modernized form. Even knowledge of dialects other than one's own has been on the rise. Everyone, for instance, knows at least the main distinctive features of the urban Egyptian dialect, thanks to the popularity of Egyptian films and songs.

Weighing on the opposite side of the balance, perhaps, are bureaucracy and other trappings of the modern state.

If the bases of Arab unity do exist, the question whether that potential is to be realized or the present division perpetuated will be decided less by the underlying factors than by the balance of power among existing states and political movements and by possible external challenges calling for a more or less unified response—in short, by historical circumstances. The same statement also applies to other politically divided but more or less culturally unified areas such as Europe, Black Africa, and Latin America; it was formerly true of the Greek cities of antiquity.

The most likely outcome is some degree of unification in certain areas. At present the order of the day is to overcome political divisions, at least in part; there are likely to be a good many ups and downs along the way to achieving this goal, including attempts at unification and, in their wake, separatist movements leading to secession, which may prove temporary and then again may not.

Resources

The Arab world is in possession of considerable resources. The member countries of the Arab league cover nearly 14 million square kilometers, or nearly twice the area of the United States (excluding Alaska and Hawaii). Counting only countries whose population is primarily Arab, when looked at from either a political or ethnic point of view, we should be obliged to exclude Somalia and Djibouti (666,000 sq. km.), which would leave around 13,350,000 square kilometers.

The region boasts an impressive array of natural resources. "With only 3.1% of the world's population [the Arabs overall] possess a third of the world's proven reserves of phosphates and a large portion of world petroleum reserves, not to mention enormous resources in natural gas, copper, zinc, and coal, copper-bearing and potassium ores. (Abdelkader Sid-Ahmed, *Léconomie arabe a l'heure des surplus petroliers* [Paris, 1975], p. 299 *[Economies et Sociétés* 9, no. 3 (March 1975);- *Cahiers de l'ISMEA*, series F. no 26, paginated 279–522]. Much use has been made here of this remarkable synthesis.) Iron in Mauritania and Algeria and manganese and lead in Morocco should also be counted. So much for underground resources. As for agricultural production, there are (long fiber) cotton in Egypt, Syria, and the Sudan, wood in the Sudan, and flax in Egypt. Human resources are abundant, of course, even overabundant under present conditions. But if mobilized in a well designed development plan, this plentiful population could provide an adequate and useful supply of labor. There are skilled workers, though not in very large numbers; a program of professional training could increase the number of middle-level personnel, at present in particularly short supply. The potential internal market is sufficiently large to allow development of a self-contained economy.

The major weakness is in the area of food production. Only 20% of the land in the fifteen Arab countries can be cultivated, as compared with 47% in the United States. There is a crying lack of water. Despite some growth in agricultural production through expansion of the land area under cultivation and improvements in yield, agriculture in many Arab countries is still far from satisfying the rapidly increasing demand of a steadily growing population. These countries have had to resort to massive imports. Owing to the climate and the nature of the soil, considerable investment is necessary in order to create additional arable land and increase yields. The result is an alarmingly precarious food supply and sporadic but undeniable malnutrition, with deficiencies particularly of animal protein.

It might be possible to remedy the inadequacy of the agricultural sector by carrying on with efforts to expand the area under cultivation and to increase yields. If scarcity persists, the Arab world has more than adequate finances to pay for the needed importation of foodstuffs. Now that Arab petroleum is being bought by the industrialized nations at a more reasonable price than was the case a few years ago, financing of these imports is no longer a problem, though this will remain true only for a limit-

ed period of time. If one adopts the Arab point of view, it becomes clear that the Arabs must take advantage of this petroleum
rent as long as it lasts in order to eliminate or at least reduce their
dependence on the outside world, to ensure suffecent advances in
agricultural production, and to achieve an industrial development adequate to enable them to pay for their foreign purchases
of food and other goods on a lasting basis.

To this potential in human, mineral, and vegetable resources
we must add a geographical situation that offers numerous advantages. To be sure, it has offered, and no doubt continues to offer,
a good many disadvantages as well. Proximity to industrialized
Europe, a historical factor of great importance, is less important
now than it was, in both positive and negative senses, thanks to
speedier transportation. But the location of the region, between
the advanced countries and Black Africa on the one hand, and
Iran, India, and the Far East on the other—an unavoidable
bridge between these areas—is just as important now as ever,
both for good and for ill. On a whole range of vital problems,
many countries must deal with the Arabs either as neighbors or
as more distant partners. This makes mutual concessions a must,
to say the least, and from this circumstance a modicum of unified
leadership should be able to draw considerable advantage. In today's bipolar world, the Arab region has been like a turntable—
able to hook itself on to a track leading to either of the great superpowers, whether their relations happened to be in a phase of
conflict, competition, or "détente"; this has brought the Arabs
much trouble, but they have also been able to make it pay, at
times handsomely.

That natural handicaps have hampered the progress of the
Arab world is undeniable. Mention has been made of those that
have interfered with agricultural production. There is less variety
in the mineral resources of the region than in other major regions
or leading states. Systematic exploration of this potential is far
from complete, however. A portion of the land that is barren today was once fertile but was abandoned to the desert, mainly for
political or social reasons. But modern technology, providing it
is backed by adequate financing, should be able to make up the
ground lost and conquer new territory.

Prospects for Development

For the moment, only a small part of this potential has gone into development of a kind likely to bring a decent way of life, along with the full advantages, profits, and responsibilities of power, to all the inhabitants of the region.

This state of affairs is reflected in the still far from adequate progress of industrialization. While regular increases in the rate of growth (which has been quite high, moreover) have been registered during the last two decades, this overall progress has been the result of development of the extractive sector in a relatively small number of Arab countries.

Taken as a whole, the manufacturing sector is very weak. It proudces few exportable goods. It requires little labor (like petroleum production). It contributes little to the modernization of other sectors. Its growth has been slow and has run up against a variety of obstacles. It consists mainly of light industries that transform agricultural raw materials for internal consumption: foodstuffs, textiles, construction, etc. Apart from producing necessary items of consumption, it has catered mainly to the tastes of the privileged upper classes.

Industry is unable to provide work for the enormous rural, or originally rural, population, which is dramatically underemployed. The percentage of the adult population included in the active work force is low. Underdeveloped agriculture absorbs far too high a proportion of the population. Illiteracy is widespread, and there are not enough skilled workers. Underdevelopment of higher education and research is a great handicap. It (along with other factors) is responsible for the "brain drain." According to UNESCO statistics, one-quarter of the "displaced brains" in the world are Arab. Thus thousands upon thousands of qualified invdividuals who, if properly utilized, could contribute greatly to the prosperity and progress of their own countries have left to add their talents to the riches of the developed countries. Similarly, some Arab countries lack an adequate labor supply and have even gone so far as to import workers from the non-Arab world (Turkey, Pakistan, etc.), while others have seen hundreds of thousands of their citizens emigrate to Europe.

It is legitimate to reject the European, American, and Soviet model of development through industralization and to emphasize the kinds of distortion, alienation, and pernicious and disastrous consequences to which it leads. But underdevelopment gives rise to hunger, misery, catastrophe and suffering without limit. The peoples that endure these scourges only hope for a kind of development that will afford them material well-being. No model is available to them but that of the industrial societies. the examples they see before them demonstrate that industrialization yields both greater prosperity and increased strength. They know that a nation unwilling to submit to the law laid down by more powerful nations must itself become powerful.

All the Arab countries have therefore chosen to proceed with industrialization, subject to the limitations imposed by the amount of available resources. But the degree of effort put into industrialization and the choice of sectors to be developed depend both on natural and social constraints and on governmental decision. These choices are contingent upon political options, both internal and external. The petroleum kingdoms of Arabia and the states in which the market economy predominates have chosen to develop their economies within the framework of the world capitalist economy. Structurally, this entails dependence on economic decisions made at the center of the system, within the most developed countries, and on the consequences therof. This dependence is disguised and partially counterbalanced by spectacular results: the pressure that enormous petroleum revenues have made it possible to exert and the power thereby acquired to influence the system.

Such a choice can, of course, result in considerable growth, but it tends to give undue advantage to certain classes while doing nothing to remedy the wretchedness of the majority. Only in the tiny Gulf petroleum states have small populations made possible a broader distribution of the wealth. The alternative, to develop under a state capitalist system, makes it possible (in theory) to allocate resources more coherently, to plan investments more rationally, and to avoid the more glaring inequalities. But the smallness of the economic zone and the low initial level of development also enforce a high degree of foreign dependence. For the most part the aid of communist powers has been sought. This has made it easier for the states involved to exert some control over their dependence by maneuvering and manipulating coercive pressures from several "benefactor" countries, rather than deal with an uncoordinated variety of private interests. The "socialist" countries have discovered the possiblity of making supervised and limited use of the services of capitalist firms. On the whole, however, dependence continues to exist.

At least at the present stage, genuine self-contained development and rational planning for the future would seem to require states to exert extensive control over their economies and to rule relatively extensive geographic areas. No Arab state is sufficiently large in this respect. Most of them are dramatically lacking in basic resources, while a few are choking on a glut of them. Here, economic necessities and pressures for increased prosperity converge with Arabist ideology. The best way to meet these requirements would be for the "poor" countries the join with the "rich". A widespread myth among the Arabs maintains that this union is hampered mainly by the maneuvers of the "imperialists." This is false, despite the involvement of the European powers in the division of the Fertile Crescent in 1920. It is in fact illusory to think that union can be achieved by joyful, willing sacrifice of what has been won on the altar of Arab fraternity (or even socialist internationalism), by voluntary renunciation of the potential for exerting political control over the unification process on the part of present governments, and by spontaneous dissolution of ties of interest and local demands arising out of regional aspirations. At best ideology can produce limited forms of "aid." Most likely, deeper needs will make their force felt through inter-Arab struggles, which are likely to promote one or more Arab countries to a position of at least relative hegemony. Depending on what policies are adopted, the resulting political unit may achieve gradual consolidation of its constituent elements, or separatist demands may arise to impede such consolidation.

THE POST-COLONIAL PHASE
OF THE WORLD OF ISLAM[3]

This seminar views the contemporary historical situation of the world of Islam with grave concern. The Islamic Revolution

[3]Part of a summary of proceedings of a conference on Islamic unity held in Karachi in 1983; pp. 354–360 of Kalim Siddiqui, ed., *Issues in the Islamic Movement 1983–84*. Copyright© 1985 Open Press Ltd. Reprinted by permission.

in Iran has clearly halted the onward march of *kufr* as the supreme and arrogant determinant of history. We are deeply concerned, however, by the universally hostile attitude of all established political systems in the world of Islam towards the Islamic Revolution and the Islamic State that has been established in Iran.

It appears to us that the colonial period caused greater and deeper damage to the world of Islam than was realized in the era of decolonization and the emergence of nation-states. It was thought at the time that the new States emerging in the world of Islam would gradually shed their colonial past and move towards the emergence of truly Islamic States. It was also hoped that greater freedom and the participation of the Muslim masses through new Islamic movements and parties would lead to the transformation of the post-colonial political order into Islamic systems of government. Similarly, it was widely expected that the capitalist and feudal economic systems would be transformed into economic systems based on the principles of *'adl* defined by the Qur'an and the Sunnah of the Prophet, upon whom be peace. Similar hopes were entertained for the transformation of the educational systems and all other parts of the social order. Finally, it was hoped that the deep inroads made by the emotions of nationalism stirred by the colonial period and western influence would die away and a more global Islamic consciousness towards the unity of the *Ummah* would emerge.

It is clear to us that, more than a generation after decolonization was completed, none of these hopes has been fulfilled. The States that replaced the colonial authorities have become more secular rather than less, and more oppressive of the Muslim masses rather than less. The capitalistic and feudal base of Muslim societies has become more deeply entrenched and exploitative than at any time before. So far none of the Islamic movements or parties has succeeded in making any perceptible impact on the post-colonial secular order. State education in all Muslim countries remains western and secular. Culturally and socially the influence of the western civilization has increased rather than decreased in the years since Muslim nation-States secured "independence."

In the meantime the power of *kufr* in the world has become even better organized. The political, economic, social and cultural hold of *kufr* over societies has greatly increased. So much so that virtually every Muslim State today is directly or indirectly controlled and manipulated by one or another of the superpow-

ers. Today all the Muslim States of the Arab world, South Asia,
the Far East and North and West Africa are in effect colonies and
clients of the United States. It is painful to admit, but objectivity
demands that we do, that the rulers and the ruling classes in Muslim nation-States are acting as the political agents of *kufr*. In this
situation the Muslim masses throughout the world are more politically oppressed, culturally invaded and economically exploited
than at any time before. Only in Iran has this situation been totally reversed.

The Superpowers

The two "superpowers," the United States and the Soviet
Union, have their rivalries and areas of conflict over spheres of
influence, balance of power, and control of markets and mineral
resources of the world. They also have a "philosophical" or
"ideological" conflict over their respective "capitalist" and
"communist" preferences. They also define such terms as
"freedom", "liberty", and "democracy" somewhat differently.
These differences, however, are superficial; at root their philosophical axioms are identical. These relate to their common view
of history. They differ only in the semantics, not the substance,
of materialism. Both are equally hostile to religion, though the
US is more tolerant of a subservient form of religious culture
than the Soviet Union.

From the point of view of the Islamic movement, both superpowers are centres of *kufr* and both are open and unashamed enemies of Islam and of Muslims. This is obvious in all the policies
pursued by the superpowers in all parts of the world, but the most
glaring example of their hostility to Islam is their combined support for zionism and the Israeli State. Between them the superpowers represent the global power of *kufr*. We Muslims cannot
afford to make any distinction between them.

Non-Muslim Allies of the Superpowers

Both the superpowers have allies in all parts of the world.
Their major allies are the states of Eastern and Western Europe.
Both superpowers also have other allies, with or without treaty
obligations. Chief among these are India (a major ally of both superpowers), Japan, China, Australia, New Zealand, South Africa,

Israel, Cuba and Kenya. These and other smaller allies of the superpowers are all committed to the secular trend in history. All the allies of the superpowers are fully committed to *kufr* as the dominant force in the history of mankind. None of them can be a friend of Islam or of the Islamic State.

Kufr as a Cultural Unity

The western civilization has acquired cultural dominance throughout the world. It is noticeable that there is no difference between the cultural aspirations of the two superpowers and their respective allies and clients. There are no significant cultural differences between societies as far apart as Israel, South Africa, the Soviet Union and the United States. Each claims a separate "philosophy" for its existence, yet culturally they are identical. This cultural universalism of *kufr* is evident in their arts, sciences, films, theatre, music, architecture, and the increasing promiscuity of sexual behaviour. It is also reflected in social and political instutions, symbols, ideas, literature and other artifacts. Even long-established societies with different cultural histories, such as India, Japan and China, are aspiring to cultural identity with the west. The result is a cultural unity of *kufr* of frightening dimensions.

The most worrying part of this increasing cultural dominance is that most regimes in the Muslim world are also engaged in the wholesale importation of the culture of *kufr* into long-established traditional Muslim societies.

The nation-State structures in the Muslim world are an imposition of the west. They are more than a political imposition; the nation-States can only survive by creating cultural harmony with the west as well. This amounts to the transformation of the Islamic culture of our societies into the culture of *kufr*. This process is now in full swing in all the Muslim nation-States that are ruled over by secular westernized elites.

This cultural domination of *kufr* and the cultural invasion of Muslim societies by *kufr* through local elites is a greater danger to the *Ummah* than political and economic dominance.

This seminar notes with satisfaction the almost total elimination of the culture of *kufr* that the Islamic Revolution has achieved in Iran. The Muslim *Ummah* must now go on and offer an alternative culture of Islam to mankind as a whole.

Science and Technology

The powers of *kufr* have achieved enormous advances in the field of science and technology. Knowledge in any form is a common heritage of mankind. However, scientific knowledge that leads to the greater recognition of Allah's Supremacy and Sovereignty is the knowledge of Islam; knowledge of any kind if pursued or used in defiance of the Creator of the Universe is the work of *kufr*. It is, therefore, all too evident that the west, being the greatest exponent of *kufr* that history has ever known, is using science and technology to arrogate to itself the right to ultimate power over all things.

All human societies throughout the world, and the physical and ecological endowments that the world has received from its Creator, are today threatened by the largely immoral and amoral behaviour of the west. Western science and technology poses a grave danger to man and his physical and spiritual health.

The control of the power of science and technology within the moral paradigm and epistemology of Islam is the only guarantee that man will not destroy himself. In the opinion of this seminar the Islamic State of Iran should give urgent attention to the mobilization of worldwide public opinion against the destructive uses of science and technology.

Hunger, Poverty and Disease

The world's resources are enough to meet the basic needs of all mankind. The widespread prevalence of hunger, poverty and disease in the world today is due largely to man-made barriers that prevent the free movement of the world's material resources. These barriers are not only national frontiers but also trading policies and practices designed to ensure that the poor areas of the world remain poor and that the rich of the world get richer. In many cases the producers of agricultural surpluses, such as those of North America and Western Europe prefer to destroy their produce rather than allow the hungry, poor and sick access to it. Such ideas of "equality" as are found in the west are limited in application to frontiers defined racially, nationally, or by some other criteria of "development" and "progress." Their ideas of "equality" and "justice" exclude the greater part of the world and its population. In pagan Africa and other parts of the world even Christian missionaries are used to secure the black man's compliance with the whim and fancy of the white man's "civilization." The western civilization, which is the chief embodiment of *kufr*, uses wars, conflicts, hunger, poverty, disease and other forms of human suffering as instruments in the pursuit of its global dominance. These functions were formerly performed by colonial administrations. Now the same functions are performed through client-States, dependent regimes, aid, multinational corporations, trading cartels and such international institutions as the UN, the IMF, the World Bank and their various affiliates.

The Islamic Revolution has ended the economic dominance of the west over Iran. The global Islamic movement will have to commit itself to rescue not only the world of Islam but all mankind from the present stranglehold of *kufr* and to the elimination of hunger, poverty and disease in all their forms from all parts of the world.

Conclusion

The world today suffers from an illusion of "development" and "progress." In reality man's behaviour towards other men has never before been more bestial than it is now. The western civilization is leading man towards total self-destruction. The global power of *kufr* is greater today than ever before. The Islamic Revolution in Iran is the first defeat of the global power of *kufr* at the hands of Islam. The Muslim *Ummah* alone has the divinely ordained duty to save mankind from the dominance of *kufr*. Only the *Ummah*, acting as a global Islamic movement, can restore to man the dignity and excellence to which he is entitled as the viceregent (*khalifa*) of Allah on earth.

The committee, after deliberating for two days, came to the conclusion that the most important and clearly defined problems facing the *Ummah* are as follows:

1. Lack of religious as well as general knowledge.

2. Lack of quality as well as number of *ulama* throughout the Muslim world.

3. As a result of the "historical background", the *Ummah* is divided in several ways. This committee is of the view that only discussions, deliberations and draft proposals have so far failed to satisfy us (Muslim brothers and sisters). We therefore decided to

initiate suitable programmes to bring these ideas into fruition at our own levels in different parts of the world.

In order to achieve results, it is necessary immediately to begin the task of canvassing and creating contacts with like-minded, concerned Muslims initially to impart the necessary and important knowledge concerning Islam as well as news of events occurring outside their immediate environs.

This committee further agrees to embrace certain "trunk" issues vis-a-vis necessary steps to be emphasized within our dismembered *Ummah*. "Trunk" issues can be defined as fundamental Islamic principles, including knowledge of Islam, unity, identificaiton of the common enemy, and training for *jihad*.

This may be summed up as "commitment to Allah *Subhanahu wa ta 'ala* and His chosen *deen*." It necessarily requires performances by the committed people appropriate to the Islamic way of life.

It is also suggested that an international Islamic committee be organized to act as the torch-bearer for the entire Muslim *Ummah*.

THE FUTURE OF ISLAM: A CONCLUSION[4]

A Third Spiritual Way. . . . We all believed in it. But it was only an illusion.

DARIUSH SHAYEGAN

At the beginning of 1985 Field Marshal Ja'afar Muhammad al-Numeiri looked like a man convinced of a long and tranquil reign ahead of him in the Sudan, where he had just completed the building of a "truly Islamic state." Numeiri had come to his own version of "hard and pure Islam" after years of flirtation with socialism, Arab Ba'athism, Nasserism, nationalism, and pro-American liberalism. His decision to impose the *shari'ah* as the law

---

[4]By Amir Taheri, journalist, from his book *Holy Terror: Inside the World of Islamic Terrorism*, pp. 223–237. Copyright© 1987 by Amir Taheri. Reprinted by permission.

of the land, and to use his army for enforcing the veil, had been taken under the influence of Hassan Turabi's Muslim Brotherhood. The majority of the Sudan's twenty million inhabitants were Muslims and were therefore expected to welcome the prospect of life under Islamic law.

In March 1985, however, a series of anti-Numeiri demonstrations organized at the University of Khartoum brought together students, lawyers, schoolchildren, office workers, and even housewives. The movement quickly spread into the streets of the capital and its twin city of Omdurman. All the demonstrators were shouting the same slogan: "Down with the *shari'ah!*" For the first time in Islam's contemporary history tens of thousands of Muslims openly rejected life under the law of the Qur'an, preferring Sudan's traditional legal system, largely put together by the British in the nineteenth and early twentieth centuries. The people who marched against Qur'anic law were not members of the westernized economic or social elites, nor could they all be members of the Sudanese communist party, which had never represented a serious force in the country's politics. The vast majority of the demonstrators were poor workers, peasants come to town, students from modest families, and above all women determined not to be forced into *purdah* and all that it represented in loss of social status and legal rights.

The Sudanese had put up with Numeiri's many experiments for nearly twenty years but were in no mood to accept the rigid Islamic republic he wanted to create in the hope of depriving his own Party of Allah adversaries of their central theme. Numeiri was eventually deposed on April 6 while on a state visit to Washington. By August 1986, after a general election, a civilian coalition government was in power in Khartoum and already committed to making the application of the *shari'ah* optional. In practice, Qur'anic law was no longer enforced beyond a ban on the sale of pork and on the serving of alcohol in most restaurants.

The anti-*shari'ah* backlash in the Sudan was by no means the only one, although it deserves special attention because of its roots at the humblest levels of society. In Egypt, where the various groups and parties that constitute the Holy Terror movement were the strongest in the whole of Islam, a countermovement began to assert itself in 1986. A number of intellectuals who had learned by experience that they could not pretend to represent "true Islam" against the mullahs and mili-

tants, as Sadat had once tried to do, decided to risk their careers
and their lives and called on "all those who believe in the future"
to take on the Party of Allah at an ideological level. Early in 1986
a Cairo lawyer, Nur Farwaj, pronounced a sentence no one had
had the courage to utter in the land of Islam for nearly a decade:
"The *shari'ah* is a collection of reactionary tribal rules unsuited to
contemporary societies. Another lawyer, Faraj Fada, a persuasive
speaker as well as a passionate essayist, went even further and
published a pamphlet under the provocative title of *No to Shari'ah*.
He put his argument directly: Islam has no policy suitable for
modern society and should not be mixed with politics. Instead of
entering into lengthy discussions all we have to do as thinking
people is to cry out together: "No to *shari'ah*." Fada's pamphlet,
which he liked to refer to as "the book" became an unexpected
success and certainly sold as many copies as the most popular writings of Shaikh Kashk, Egypt's version of Khomeini. *No to Shari'ah*
was also quickly translated into other Islamic languages and
found a considerable echo in Turkey, Iran, and Pakistan. Banned
in the Islamic Republic, it joined another far more provocative
work, Ali Dashti's *Twenty-three Years*, on the bestseller list of
"illegal and anti-Islamic books."

The record of the Party of Allah in government, both in the
Islamic Republic and in the areas of Lebanon under its control,
was subjected to closer public scrutiny in many Muslim countries
and condemned even by some of the most influential figures in
traditional-style fundamentalism. By 1984 Shaikh Omar al-
Talmassani had concluded that the network of Holy Terror
would only lead Islam to "spiritual suicide." And Zaynab al-
Ghazzali, another "saint" of the Muslim Brotherhood in Egypt,
spoke of her conviction that the movement symbolized by
Khomeini would take the "same path to perdition" that took the
Kharejites of the seventh century into oblivion. She saw as the
main weakness of the Partisans of Allah the fact that "they divide
Muslims into good and bad and thus reject some. . . . Theirs is
a suicidal policy which will lead them to self-destruction."

Right from the beginning, Nasserites and other Arab nationalist groups figured among the principal targets of the revived
fundamentalist movement. In 1981 attempts to organize nation-
wide gatherings to mark the tenth anniversary of the death of the
first *rais* in Egypt were abandoned under direct pressure from
militant fundamentalist groups. Bookshops selling Nasser's pam-

phlets or books on him were set on fire in Cairo, Alexandria, Asyut, and Port Said. Students suspected of Nasserite tendencies were savagely beaten up by Partisans of Allah on the campus of the Ain al-Shams University. By 1986, however, Nasserite and other nationalist groups were very much back in evidence. Nationalism, attacked by the Partisans of Allah as a Western plot aimed at dividing the Muslims, showed signs of regaining some of its lost prestige in Egypt.

The experience of Iran, at first enthusiastically welcomed but not properly analyzed, began to force the political elite in Egypt and other Muslim countries to rethink some of their earlier assumptions. Nationalists, liberals, socialists, communists, and social democrats began to realize that the tremendous force of Khomeini's revolution had been partly due to the Ayatollah's success in harnessing under his command the whole of the nation's political energies. Once it was clear that the Party of Allah in government would in no way consent to any form of power-sharing, the reassertion of one's true political identity became a matter of life and death in many Muslim countries. Westernized intellectuals who—whether out of ignoble opportunism or because they misunderstood the situation—had agreed to conceal their true political identities in order to help the Party of Allah win power paid dearly for their mistake. The tragic fate of Iran's westernized elites, who did not appreciate the bitter fact that the shah was closer to them than the Ayatollah could ever be, was by 1986 recognized in many Muslim countries as an example to avoid. The Iraqi government, at war against the Party of Allah since 1980, used the Iranian tragedy as a central theme in its own propaganda aimed at preventing the creation of a vast coalition of opposition forces under the leadership of Khomeinist mullahs.

Another factor that contributed to the slow but steady buildup of a new form of intellectual resistance to Holy Terror groups throughout the Muslim world was the revelation that Islamic fundamentalism almost inevitably led to violence against both individuals and communities. Under the iron rule of Assad-Allah Lajevardi, one of Khomeini's closest friends and associates, Tehran's Evin Prison was seen as a model of the Party of Allah's rule in practice. Between 1981 and 1985 an average of five people a day were executed at Evin; the majoity of those put to death were students and intellectuals, mostly from left-wing parties, who had previously concealed their true political colors in order to help the mullahs overthrow the Shah.

From 1986 the term *ebraz howyaat* or "announcing one's [ideological] identity" represented an important concept among Muslim intellectuals, once they realized that the future tyranny implicit in the program of the Party of Allah could be far more violent and degrading than that of any current dictatorship. The idea was that westernized intellectuals opposing dictatorships in Muslim countries should fight them openly and remain constantly on guard against the domination of any popular movement by the Partisans of Allah.

In Egypt, revelations in the media by the widow of Major Abboud al-Zammor, a member of the commando raid that murdered Sadat, sent tremors through the country. She related how Zammor, "originally a man like any other, one who smoked and even allowed me to attend university unveiled," suddenly changed into "a different creature" after joining the Islamic Holy War organization. "First he told me and his mother that we ought not to eat cucumbers, as this could awaken in us instincts that are hard to control," she went on. "Then he forced both of us to wear the veil and forbade us to watch television. He also ordered us not to serve stuffed vine leaves any more as this would—according to his organization—heat our blood and lead to deviations." Zammor's widow, a simple, straightforward woman from a peasant background, was not the only one to share her experience with the public. Other women, including nurses who had had acid thrown at them because of their "immodest behavior," began to talk in 1985. They spoke of the incredible pressure put on them by Party of Allah militants, including many Western-educated doctors, to end their careers, wear the veil, and become "good wives."

The Party of Allah's attitude toward women, founded on a mixture of fascination, fear, and hatred, had at the start of the 1980s been kept as well guarded as a family secret. Some sections of the party even tried to pretend that the full emancipation of women could not be achieved except through their version of Islam. In Tunisia in 1984, the disciples of Rached al-Ghannoushi were suprised when, in one of his typical "manifestos," he declared women to have "every right to be present at all levels of decision-making in the movement." Women militants siezed upon the edict to demand equal voting rights as well as the chairmanship of some of the revolutionary cells. The male reaction came quickly and Ghannoushi was openly threatened with rebellion.

He agreed to issue a new "manifesto" canceling the previous one and urging women to return to their "original place in Islam." The move silenced many male militants but led to the resignation of scores of women, mostly university students, from the movement.

This slowly mounting challenge against the Party of Allah appeared by the summer of 1986 to have become an irreversible trend in many countries. In the Islamic Republic itself, doctors of medicine organized a series of general strikes against a government decision preventing male physicians, surgeons, and dentists from treating female patients. More importantly, Ayatollah Khomeini agreed to postpone indefinitely his dream of bringing the country under the exclusive rule of the *shari'ah*. Seven years after his Islamic Revolution almost all the laws inherited from the *ancien régime* remained in force, including the Family Protection Act, which had horrified him in the early 1970s by giving women the right to seek a divorce. The build-up of resistance to Holy Terror as a system of government was described by one member of the Islamic Majlis in July 1986: "The old society and its Western roots is proving to be far stronger than any of us imagined. . . . People prefer ordinary comforts to lofty ideals. . . . Our mosques are emptier than ever. Islamic rule has proved incapable of removing injustice or eliminating poverty. I am deeply pessimistic. Government as Allah intended it is not for tomorrow."

Very few fundamentalist leaders and activists, however, would share that view. Most would see in it little more than a sign of faint-heartedness on the part of a disillusioned revolutionary. It might take the slow build-up of resistance against the Party of Allah years to stem the tide of fundamentalism in many Muslim countries. In some countries—Egypt, for example—the Holy Terror movement and the secular forces trying to stand up to it are growing simultaneously; in October 1986 there were even signs that Holy Terror was winning the race.

In mid-1986 the Holy Terror movement was losing its grip on the intellectual elites in many Muslim countries, but many of its clerical leaders saw this as a positive development. They were content with their control of the dispossessed masses—the muscle that can storm public buildings and control the sprawling slum streets of Muslim capitals. In his message to the Mecca pilgrims on 10 August 1986 Khomeini said that the Islamic Revolution was only just beginning and that many Muslim countries would go Iran's way before "the Satanic world" could stop "this inevitable movement of history."

The Muslim world, with its deep social wounds and almost traditional penchant for violence, remained a fertile ground for the seeds of revolution sown by the heirs of Hassan Sabbah and Hassan al-Banna. "Satanic forces," represented by the rich, the westernized middle class, religious minorities, and any foreigners working in the realm of Islam, remained to be fought and destroyed at local and national levels in many Muslim countries. And the global fight against "the enemies of allah" continued to capture the imagination of the poor and the downtrodden, who compensated for their sufferings in this world by dreaming of the promised paradise of Muhammad. Nothing would shake their determination to "cleanse" the world with faith, fire, and blood.

In Egypt, militant Muslim students often put themselves at the head of gangs of paupers from the Cairo slums to eject Coptic Christians from the universities. In Iran the campaign for the forcible conversion of the Baha'is to Islam became popular at the lowest levels of society in the early 1980s. But in both instances a deep sense of disappointment replaced early enthusiam as the poor and downtrodden began to show more compassion for their fellow humans than did their educated and better-off leaders. Mullahs in the province of Yazd complained bitterly about poor Muslim peasants who refused to identify Baha'i families or to participate in shedding their blood in accordance with the rules of the Party of Allah.

The idea that poor peasants in the Muslim world provided fertile ground for the Party of Allah was by 1986 more open to question in the wake of experiences in many countries. In the Islamic Republic itself, in 1984 and 1985 more than 80 percent of the electorate in the rural areas refused to take part in either presidential or parlimentary elections, despite pronouncements by Khomeini that voting was "a divine duty." In Turkey, attempts by fundamentalist groups to brand Turgot Ozal's synthesis of Islam and modernization a "new trick by the West" failed, and his Motherland party scored unexpected victories in local elections throughout the country in 1985. Ozral's biggest successes were registered in the poorest and most deeply religious regions. Malaysia's prime minister, Mahatir Muhammad, achieved an even more impressive victory when his National Front coalition won more than two-thirds of the votes in the general election of 1986. The fundamentalist coalition, PAS, secured only one parliamentary seat and collected less than 4 percent of the popular vote. In Senegal, mullahs dispatched to make sure that African Muslim women covered their breasts and adopted the *chador* were driven out of many villages with derision, despite the fact that they had come with suitcases full of cash and promises of more to come.

In 1986, for the first time in six years, hardly any members of the Party of Allah were successful in elections held among student bodies in the occupied West Bank or in Jordanian universities. The party suffered similar setbacks in Muslim student unions in France, Belgium, the United Kingdom, and Italy. To be sure, Islam in general remained an important part of the electoral discourse and secular student unions, such as had existed in the 1960s, were nowhere in evidence. But the Islam being talked about was clearly not the same as that propagated by Holy Terror.

The failure of the Islamic Republic to improve the lives of the people, its endless war with Iraq, the all but clear refusal of Iraqi Shi'ites to rise against their government, the inability of Holy Terror economists to offer a credible alternative to either capitalism or communism—in spite of various farcical experiments with interest-free banks and "Islamic planning"—and an increasing perception of the Party of Allah as little more than an instrument of violence, are facts that can no longer be ignored in an overall assessment of the world of Islam in the 1980s.

During the 1950s and 1960s many Western observers saw the political future of Muslim countries as the outcome of a three-way fight involving European-style nationalism, best symbolized by Mossadeq and Nasser; communism, represented by powerful parties in Iran, Iraq, and Syria; and traditionalism of the kind that ruled Saudi Arabia, North Yemen (before the Egyptian-inspired coup d'etat), and Libya (before Gaddafi's seaizure of power). The Muslim Brotherhood and the Fedayeen of Islam were dismissed as marginal forces incapable of affecting the central course of events in Islam.

The imperfections of this analysis were best illustrated by Khomeini's successful revolution and the emergence of Holy Terror as a force to reckon with in many Muslim countries. But this in turn promoted an equally inadequate understanding of the political life of Islam in the 1980s. It was automatically assumed that the vast majority of Muslims wanted to be ruled in Khomeini's style, and that more than 150 years of exposure to Western ideas, as well as Western domination and injustice, had left behind nothing but a deep and gaping wound. The fact, however, is that such eminently Western ideas as democracy, socialism, the worth of the individual, and national sovereignty still enjoy an important measure of support in most of the socially more advanced Muslim countries—Egypt, Turkey, Iran, Lebanon, Tunisia, Algeria, and Pakistan. Some Western observers expressed surprise when women politicians emerged as national opposition leaders in both Paskistan and Bangladesh in 1986, despite much grumbling from the local mullahs and Partisans of Allah.

It is often forgotten that during the past three decades millions of Muslims have been educated in the West or in Western schools in their own countries, and that no fewer than fifteen million workers, mostly from Turkey, the Muslim regions of Yugoslavia, and North Africa, have gained direct experience of the West in the same period. Such first-hand contacts did not always lead to hatred of the West, as happened with some militant students who attended American universities in the 1960s and 1970s. In many cases, Muslims who came into direct contact with the West resented it not because of the freedom and prosperity in Europe and America, but because the Western powers were seen as the protectors of corrupt and dictatorial regimes in many Islamic countries.

The Party of Allah presented a program for "re-becoming ourselves" at a time when Western ideologies were suffering a tactical retreat, mainly as a result of a universal trend toward pragmatism but also because their local representatives in the world of Islam did not practice what they preached. But those who tried to "re-become" themselves through the recipe offered by Holy Terror became "someone quite different."

The central political problem in the Muslim world is that of every other contemporary society: the distinction between people's private lives and their public ones. The Party of Allah proposes to solve the problem simply by allowing public life totally and irrevocably to annex the area set aside for private life. The attempt to do so has led to violence and failed wherever it has been made—most dramatically in the Islamic Republic. The question of democracy and the separation of the mosque from the state is very much alive in every Islamic society today. Even the Party of Allah is obliged to pay lip service to democratic values by organizing elections—something totally alien to Islam.

Islamic fundamentalism had lingered in the background of Muslim political life for generations, making occasional bloody eruptions. It resembled Count Dracula, the prince of the "undead," who rejected the past while haunting the present. Because it was believed to belong to the realm of the "undead," fundamentalist Islam did not cause much alarm among westernized Muslim elites until the mid-1980s. Khomeini showed that the "undead" was in fact very much alive and capable of killing in order to prolong its own life. From the mid-1980s the Party of Allah and its network of Holy Terror could not be dismissed. They had to be faced and fought, and must eventually be defeated by forces of life in the Muslim world itself before Islamic societies can tackle the inescapable problem of modernization.

Maxime Rodinson, the distinguished French Islamicist, prophecied in the 1950s that the global duel between socialism and capitalism would one day have to be fought in the realm of Islam as well. In 1979 Rodinson appeared like a false prophet, but in 1987 one could no longer be so sure. Islam as a civilization has proven rich, resilient, and sufficiently receptive to change not to fear its current political upheavals. It is the background of all culture in every Muslim country, and the intellectual home even of those of its children who have the courage to reject its claim to possess divine authority. The reduction of Islam to the level of a political ideology can only lead to its rejection as a religion also—especially by the masses in the long run. Every attempt at turning Islam into a doctrine of political power inevitably leads to terrorism: the Kharejites, the Qarmathians, the Assassins, the Muslim Brotherhood, and the Fedayeen of Islam all attempted what Khomeini's movement of Holy Terror offered in the 1980s. The path charted by the Party of Allah is an impasse that would leave Islam with the problem of terrorism for many years to come.

From a strategic point of view the current movement of Holy Terror is at once stronger and weaker than its predecessors. It is stronger because neither the state structures inside the Muslim countries nor the foreign powers threatened by Holy Terror are capable, for obvious reasons, of meeting its violence with a corresponding measure of counter-violence. It is weaker, on the other hand, because it has to compete with many other ideologies from a position of weakness. Holy Terror has no answers to the political, economic, and social problems of today. It does not even know how to ask the pertinent quesitons. Unable to offer a life worth living, it advocates death as man's highest and noblest goal. Despite attempts by some Western professors (of the type who enjoys other people's revolutions from a suitable distance) to bestow on the political and economic writings of Holy Terror theoreticians some semblance of rationality and consistency, what we are offered is nothing but half-understood quotations from the Qur'an and dubious Hadiths or sayings of the Prophet sprinkled with pseudo-Marxist jargon. The attempt to elevate protest into a theory of state cannot be dignified merely by its presentation as "Islamic philosophy," The fact is that the very expression "Islamic philosophy," as applied to the writings of Khomeini, Baqer Sadr, Ragheb Harb, Qutb, Mawdoodi, Lajevardi, and Khalkhali, is a contradiction in terms. The Party of Allah admits to no doubt and no speculation. It does not recommend thinking, but "repeating" the "Truth as revealed once and for all" in the Holy Book.

The claim by some Western admirers of Holy Terror that the government of the Party of Allah is precisely the type of rule desired by a majority of Muslims had by 1987 been exposed as an exaggeration. It must nevertheless by emphasized that Muslims have never rejected the choice of a pluralist, democratic society based on the Universal Declaration of Human rights and "other such Satanic Western values." Muslims have never freely chosen death over life, war over peace, and terror over the rule of law. Those who claim that Islam, being "the religion of the sword," can lead only to violence and war forget that less than a third of Muslims live in countries converted to Islam by conquest.

The idea that the Muslim world could or should cut itself off from the contemporary world in order to live in accordance with its traditional spiritual values seems to some Muslim intellectuals an invention of Western Islamicists. The precursors of the Islamicists of the 1980s in the West, known as the Orientalists, were partly responsible for the invention of various brands of nationalism in Muslim countries. Persians in the 1930s, for instance, were invited to push Islam into the background in order to claim the heritage of Cyrus the Great, of whom they had not heard before the arrival on the scene of European archaeologists and Orientalists. Arab nationalism, traced back to the *Epic of Gilgamesh*, was also invented for the most part by Western romantics. As for Turkey, Mustafa Kemal imported large numbers of European scholars in order to help him invent the myth of a Turkish nation related to the Celts. In every case the Orientalists achieved some success, and Western-style nationalism did become part of the overall political tradition of the larger Islamic states.

Islamic fundamentalism of the 1980s, referred to by some writers as Islamism in order to indicate the essentially Western mode of expression it has adopted, is certainly not an invention of Islamicists. But it remains a result of the original clash and subsequent fusion of Western-style "Third-Worldism" of the type best symbolized by people like Franz Fanon and the tradition of terror within Islam itself. Also present within it are strong Marxist and fascist influences that have nothing to do with Islam either as a religion or as a political doctrine. Some Muslim scholars see the Holy Terror movement as a twisted version of "secularization in the name of Islam." In their view it is the totalitarian state that turns religion into an appendix of itself, while claiming to aim at the exact opposite. In the Islamic Republic, for example, the day-to-day political needs of the state are invariably given precedence over the exigencies of the Faith. The argument is ingenious in its simplicity as put by Khomeini himself: the Islamic Republic must be preserved, otherwise Islam will be destroyed, while our republic cannot exist if Islam vanishes.

In a sense, therefore, what we are witnessing is not a religious revival in the Muslim world but the inclusion of religion in political life after decades of separation. The future of Islam will not be decided by theological debate concerning Qur'anic principles and the finer shades of meaning in the sayings of the Prophet. It will be decided by Islam's ability to adapt itself to the hopes, needs, aspirations, and realities of the contemporary world. It may be the only "Divine Truth," but it still has to cope with the facts of life concerning nearly a billion human beings from many different, and often even irreconcilable, historical backgrounds. The idea that the Senegalese, the Persians, the Malaysians, and the Arabs can shape a single and unique future within Islam is as absurd as tying together the political future of the Poles and the Filipinos simply because both are Christian nations. And in both Poland and the Philippines Christianity was as alive and active as Islam was in any Muslim country in the 1980s.

Islam cannot ignore the Renaissance, the French Revolution, the Industrial Revolution, the dramatic technological progress of the past three centuries, and its own violent contact with Western colonialism have led to the creation of a global system in which it is virtually impossible for a single nation or group of nations to wall themselves in with the hope of shaping a separate destiny. Until even 150 years ago "the perfect harmony of form and content" enabled Islam to live in relative tranquility and be content with its own ghetto in a changing world. That harmony was destroyed by colonialism, war, the infiltration of Western ideas among Muslim elites, and the growing economic interdependence of all countries. As Shayegan put it:

While the West entered into history through the dramatic changes of the nineteenth and twentieth centuries, the other part of humanity [Islam] remained untouched by all that movement. It was to receive its effects much later in the form of fully made packages: fully made machines as well as ideologies and ideas—positivism, and later Marxims also. . . . Third World revolutions in the twentieth century, like the one in Iran, made of the rejection of the West a symbol of their quest for authenticity. But the West has, paradoxically, avenged itself thanks to its ideologies, and [Third World] revolutions have fallen into what is called "the ruses of reason." By trying to deny history they have historicized themselves, and by wanting to spiritualize the world they have secularized themselves. And in wishing to reject the West they have become Westernized. (In an interview with *Nouvrel Observateur*, September 23, 1982)

In other words, in wanting to distance Islam from a world that it considers "satanic" because it is created and dominated by the West, the Party of Allah has done more to push Islam into that world than any other movement in Muslim countries during the past 150 years. Ever since its divine revelation more than fourteen centuries ago, Islam's central "slogan" has been the celebrated formula known to every Muslim: "There is no God but Allah, and Muhammad is the Prophet of Allah." The movement of Holy Terror has added to it other slogans, including "Death to America," "Death to Russia," and "Death to Israel." They have made millions of Muslims aware for the first time of the existence and reality of these "enemies of Islam." By wishes them dead, Khomeini brought them to life even in the remotest villages of the Islamic world. Another effect of Khomeini's revolution was the re-definition of Islam as a faith concerned not with the broader and permanent issues of human existence but with the existing balance of political and military power in the Middle East.

The discovery of "the other," even when it comes in the violent and twisted form offered by Holy Terror, is the first step toward eventual self-doubt. In hating "the other," one is bound to end up seeking the reasons for this "otherness." Neither the generals nor the rank and file of Holy Terror could escape the inevitable questions: Why do we desire the death of those whom we wish to see destroyed? What makes them different from us? Why can we not defeat them in the existing context of our relationship with them? Do they really deserve to be so hated? Would it not be wiser for is to become like them, at least in some respects? Is a return to Medina both desirable and feasible, or do we have to look to a future we may be able to shape rather than to a past which now belongs more to history than it does to us?

ISLAMIC FUNDAMENTALISM IS WINNING VOTES

PARIS—Eleven years after Ayatollah Ruhollah Khomeini was swept to power in the Iranian revolution, Islamic forces in Algeria, Egypt and Jordan have peacefully secured footholds on power at the ballot box. Elsewhere, Islamic fundamentalists are seeking or consolidating power through the use of arms and intimidation.

In the Sudan, a military dictatorship is implementing religious edicts by force. In Lebanon, Egypt, Tunisia and Morocco, armed fundamentalists are seeking to overturn secular regimes. Fundamentalists are challenging the Palestine Liberation Organization for leadership within the Arab uprising in the Israeli-occupied West Bank and Gaza Strip. Even in Saudi Arabia, where strict Islamic laws are already enforced, princes and technocrats privately complain that religious leaders are obstructing the ever-so-slow pace of modernization.

Now, since elections in May put Islamic fundamentalists in local offices in Algeria, and elections in Jordan earlier this year gave 36 to 80 seats in Parliament to parties linked with fundamentalism, it has become clear that two distinct tendencies have

---

[4]Reprint of an article by New York Times reporter Youssef M. Ibrahim. Copyright © 1990 by The New York The Times Company. Reprinted by permission.

emerged in the movement: the electoral option and the armed military option.

Western diplomats have begun developing contacts with some groups that take part in elections. Among the many unanswered questions, however, are what the West can gain from such contacts, how effectively the fundamentalists would govern if they were elected to full national power, and whether they would preserve democracy, given that their basic demand is for a guarantee that the country be run by their religious rules.

"Islam, Not Revenge"

"The Algerian people have chosen Islam, not revenge," was the response given by Sheik Abassi Madani, the leader of the Islamic movement in Algeria, when asked in a recent interview whether his movement will seek to ban alcohol, end mixed bathing on beaches, and require women to wear veils. "These matters come through education and not otherwise," he said.

The remains to be seen. In Iran similar promises were made and broken. There are, in each Islamic movement, hard and moderate tendencies. What the fundamentalists share is a dream: to break with secularism and install Islamic regimes.

On June 12, that dream was expressed in Algeria with the Islamic Salvation Front's triumph over the ruling National Liberation Front in voting for local and provincial offices. The offices have some authority over education, cultural and social activities, public beaches and the licencing of places that serve alcohol. The victors have been vague about their policies beyong saying they support free trade and Algeria's merchants.

"The Algerian elections proved that Islamic movements are not necessarily 'Khomeinist' in nature, limited to Shiite Islamic societies," said Ghassan Tueini, publisher of the Lebanese daily newspaper *Al Nahar*. "These movements will manifest themselves more and more as they represent the rejection of the present order and the desire for a change." Western diplomats are not blind to this. Since the Iranian revolution, American embassies in the Middle East have been told to seek dialogue with fundamentalists. In Algeria two weeks ago, Western diplomats quickly arranged meetings with Sheik Madani.

The distinction between fundamentalists willing to run for election and those committed to violence is clear in Egypt, where the Government tolerates the Muslim Brotherhood but fights almost weekly clashes with the more militant Islamic Cells. The Muslim Brotherhood was barred from running in recent parliamentary elections as a party, but many of its candidates ran—and won—as allies of other opposition groups.

Why is fundamentalism making such headway? Its biggest boost in the 1980's probably came from hardships visited on the Arab middle classes since oil prices collapsed. With sons and daughters unable to find jobs or housing while privilege remained in the hands of governing elites, many turned to religion as a political force.

In the 1950's the Lebanese historian George Corm notes, the United States encouraged an Islamic alliance of Saudi Arabia, Pakistan, Turkey and Morocco as a bulwark against Communism and non-aligned nationalism. The Iranian revolution of 1979 radicalized the concept of Islamic rule by making it a cause for the socially disenfranchised and spurning ties to either superpower. Later, fundamentalists who accepted Western aid fought the Soviet Army in Afghanistan, solidifying Islam's reputation as a fighting ideology.

The overall result was that for many Arabs, Islam emerged from the 1980's as the solution to the quest for national dignity and cultural identity. Not even the severe economic and political problems faced by Iran seem to have stemmed the tide. "The demand for change is based on a popular appeal rising from the bottom against ruling cadres seen as ideologically bankrupt and in a cultural vacuum left by dictatorship, inefficiency and lack of vision," says Fahmy Howeidi, an Egyptian columnist. "In Algeria fundamentalists were facing the ruling party which is a zero. Similarly, in Iran Khomeini was up against the Shah, who had also become a zero. The question is how do you deal with this fundamentalist force: with the mind or with the whip."

Professor Corm argues that the West may have little alternative but to expand contact with fundamentalists. "What can be done is encourage the Muslim tendencies that are moderate," he said. "Ignoring Islam, or, worse yet, assaulting it as a religion, only adds fuel to the fire."

BIBLIOGRAPHY

The Islamic revival is a subject much better understood by referring to books than to periodicals. The many and complex causes of the revival are seldom noted in accounts found in weekly or monthly magazines. This bibliography concentrates on recent books that best describe the revival's origins and course. The periodical articles listed at the end, with their abstracts, are examples of recent journalistic commentary.

An asterisk (*) preceding a reference indicates that the article or part of it has been reprinted in this book.

BOOKS AND PAMPHLETS

Ahmed, Ishtiaq. The concept of an Islamic state. St. Martin's. '87.

Ahmed, Manzooruddin. Islamic political system in the modern age. Saad. '83.

Ajami, Fouad. The Arab predicament. Cambridge. '81.

Antonius, George. The Arab awakening. Hamish Hamilton, '45; Putnam, '65.

Anderson, Benedict. Imagined communities: reflections as the origin and spread of nationalism. Verso and New Left. '83.

Askari, Hasan. Society and State in Islam: an introduction. Islam and the Modern Age Society. '78.

Ayoob, Mohammed. The politics of Islamic reassertion. Croom Helm. '81.

Aziz Ahmad, Muhammad. The nature of Islamic political theory. Maaref. '75.

Bani Sadr, Abolhassan. The fundamental principles and precepts of Islamic government. Mazda Pubs. '81.

Bannerman, Patrick. Islam in perspective: a guide to Islamic society, politics and law. Routledge. '88.

Banuazizi, Ali, and Weiner, Myron, eds. The state, religion, and ethnic politics: Afghanistan, Iran, and Pakistan. Syracuse. '86.

Bennigsen, Alexandre, and Broxup, Marie. The Islamic threat to the Soviet state. Croom Helm. '83.

Carlsen, Robin W. The Imam and his Islamic revolution. Snow Man Press. '82.

Carré, Olivier, ed. Islam and the State in the world today. Manohar Pubs. '87.

Cleveland, William. The Making of an Arab Nationalist. Princeton. '71.

Dekmejian, R. Hrair. Islam in revolution: fundamentalism in the Arab World. Syracuse. '85.

Dessouki, Ali, ed. Islamic resurgence in the Arab World. Praeger. '82.

Dhawan, R. K. Three contemporary novelists: Khushwant Singh, Ghaman Nahal, Salman Rushdie. Classical. '85.

Enayat, Hamid. Modern Islamic political thought. Texas. '82.

Engineer, Asghar Ali, ed. Islam and revolution. Ajanta. '84.

Engineer, Asghar Ali, Ed. The Islamic state. Vikas. '80.

Esposito, John L., ed. Islam and development: religion and sociopolitical change. Syracuse. '80.

Essaid, Abdul Aziz. Le réveil de l'Islam. Marseilles. '85.

Etienne, Bruno. L'islamisme radical. Hachette. '87.

Gauhar, Altaf, ed. The challenge of Islam. Islamic Council of Europe. '78.

Geertz, Clifford. Islam observed: religious development in Morocco and Indonesia. Yale. '68.

Hadi Hussain, Muhammad. The nature of the Islamic state. National Book Foundation. '77.

Hairi, Abdul Hadi. Shiism and constitutionalism in Iran. Brill. '77

Halliday, Fred, and Alavi, Hamza. State and ideology in the Middle East and Pakistan. Macmillan Educational. '88.

Haq, Inámul. Islamic bloc: the way to honour, power and peace. Haq. '68.

Hassan, S. Farooq. The Islamic republic: politics, law & economy. Aziz. '84.

Hassan, S. Farooq. The concept of state and law in Islam. Univ. Press of America. '81.

Heper, Metin, and Israeli, Raphael, eds. Islam and politics in the modern Middle East. St. Martin's. '84.

Hunter, Shireen T., ed. The politics of Islamic revivalism: diversity and unity. Indiana, in association with the Center for Strategic and International Studies. '88.

Khomeini, Ruhalloh. Islam and revolution: writing and declarations of Imam Khomeini. Mizan. '81.

Lapidus, I. M. A history of Islamic Societies. Cambridge. '87.

Lippmann, Thomas W. Understanding Islam: an introduction to the modern world. Meutar. '82.

Malik, Zahid, ed. Re-emerging Muslim world. Pakistan National Centre. '74.

Maudoodi, Syed Abul Ala. Human rights in Islam. Islamic Foundation. '76.

Mortimer, Edward. Faith and power: the politics of Islam. Random House. '82.

Mozaffari, Mehdi. Authority in Islam. M.E. Sharpe. '87.

Nasr, Seyyed Hossein. Science and civilization in Islam. Harvard. '68.

Parameswaran, U. The perforated sheet: essays on Salman Rushdie's art. Affiliated East-West Press. '88.

Pipes, Daniel. In the path of God: Islam and political power. Basic. '83.

Piscatori, James P. Islam in a world of nation-states. Cambridge. '86.

Qutb, Sayyid. Milestones. Unity. '81.

Rodinson, Maxime. The Arabs. Chicago. '81.

Rodinson, Maxime. Islam and capitalism. Allen Lane. '74.

Rodinson, Maxime. Marxism and the Muslim world. Monthly Review Press. '81.

Shah, Amritlal B. Challenges to secularism. Nachiketa. '68.

Siddiqui, Abdul Hameed. Theocracy and the Islamic state. Islamic Book Centre. '76.

Siddiqui, Kalim, ed. Issues in the Islamic movement. Open Press. '81 to date.

Siddiqui, Mohammad M. Islam and theocracy. Institute of Islamic culture. '53.

Sivan, Emmanuel. Radical Islam: medieval theology and modern politics. Yale. '85.

Smith, Wilfred Cantwell. Islam in modern history. Princeton. '57.

Taheri, Amir. Holy Terror: inside the world of Islamic terrorism. Adler & Adler. '87.

Vatikiotis, P. J. Islam and the State. Croom Helm. '87.

Weatherby, W. J. Salman Rushdie: sentenced to death. Carroll & Graf.

Zubaida, Sami. Islam, the people and the state: essays on political ideas and movements in the Middle East. Routledge. '89.

ADDITIONAL PERIODICAL ARTICLES WITH ABSTRACTS

For those who wish to read more widely on the subject of Islamic politics, this section contains abstracts of additional articles that bear on the topic. Readers who require a comprehensive list of materials are advised to consult the Reader's Guide to Periodical Literature and other Wilson Indexes.

ARAB NATIONALISM: THE FAILURE OF THE SECULAR IDEAL

Egypt: the Islamic issue. Mohamed Sid-Ahmed *Foreign Policy* 69:22–39 Winter '87/'88.

The forces of Islamic fundamentalism have hobbled Egyptian President Hosni Mubarak's efforts to achieve stability through policies designed to maintain equilibrum between the military and the civilian establishments. When Mubarak took office in October 1981, he managed to defuse the crisis that followed President Anwar el-Sadat's assassination without abandoning the fundamentals of Sadat's policies. In an attempt to bolster domestic support for the regime, however he has emphasized Egypt's traditional Arab, Islamic, and African affiliations and has sought to isolate only the dangerous Islamic extremists. Faced with a wide range of opposition forces, Mubarak has focused on revitalizing the three-party system and has tried to counterbalance political forces, limiting his freedom to maneuver. Because the army and the fundamentalist movement operate on a deeper level than political parties, Mubarak must take a different tack in his second term.

Jordan votes the Islamic ticket. Stephen Hubbell *The Nation* 249:786+D 25 '89.

The November 8 general parliamentary elections in Jordan, the first since 1967, resulted in landslide victories for some of King Hussein's worst enemies and defeat for many of his allies. Voters gave 34 of the 80 seats to members of the fundamentalist Muslim Brotherhood and other Islamic extremists. Leftists and Arab nationalists received enough of the remaining seats to give the opposition a fragile majority. Suprisingly, ethnic Palestinians did not fare well. Fahed Fanek, a senior researcher at the Arab Thought Forum and economic columinist for the Arabic-language daily *Al Ra'i*, says that many Palestinian feared creating a large delegation in parliament that would undermine the Palestine Liberation Organization's position as the sole representative of the Palestinian people. The new parliament will have to formulate a coherent policy to deal with the country's $8.3 billion debt and a high rate of unemployment.

Ballots for Allah. Jill Smolowe *Time* 135:26–7 Je '25 '90.

The fundamentalist Islamic Salvation Front took a majority of the municipal provincial councils in Algeria's first multiparty election since the country's independence from France in 1962. The election represents the first time that Muslim fundamentalists have obtained a majority in a free vote in an Arab country, and fear is spreading throughout the Arab world that the electoral process is giving radical fundamentalists an opportunity to seize power.

The roots of Muslim rage. Bernard Lewis *The Atlantic* 266: 47–54+ S '90.

The virulent anti-American sentiment that has emerged in much of the Muslim world must be seen in a context of an East-West struggle that has been going on since the advent of Islam in the 7th century. The Judeo-Christian West has dominated the struggle for the last 300 years. Islamic fundamentalists correctly perceive that Western institutions like capitalism and democracy represent the most compelling challenges to the political, economic, social, and cultural structures that they want to retain or restore. Thus the United States, which is seen as the legitimate heir of European civilization and the unchallenged leader of the West, has become the target of pent-up hate and anger that far transcends any specific issues or policies. Westerners must resist an irrational reaction against this trend and aim toward a better appreciation of other religious and political cultures in the hope that they, in turn, learn to understand and respect ours.

Iran: the impossible revolution. Fouad Ajami *Foreign Affairs* 67:135–55 Winter '88/'89.

The summer of 1988 marked the point at which Iran realized that its Islamic revolution would not spread beyond its borders. When Ayatollah Khomeini announced that he would accept the poisoned chalice of peace with Iraq, ending the long war between the two nations, it signaled an end to the larger conflict between Iran and its Arab adherents and the Arab status quo. After a decade of zealous proselytism and some measure of force, the leaders of Iran's revolution failed to spread their brand of faith throughout the Arab world as they had hoped. Iraq withstood the toll of the war and the conservative Arab states of the Gulf, having learned the correct lessons from the fall of the Shah, managed to avoid the chaos of 1970s Iran and wait out the peaking of fervor for the revolution. The theocratic state founded by Khomeini will survive the troubled present and Khomeini's death, but his successors will inherit a cynical and weary nation.

Spreading the faith. Bob Levin *Maclean's* 100:14–17 Jl 27 '87.

The fundamentalist brand of Islam preached by the regime of Iran's Ayatollah Ruhollah Khomeini has touched nerves throughout the Islamic world. Since coming to power in 1979, Khomeini has attempted to unite fellow Shi'ite Muslims and mainline Suni Muslims. While Iran continues to engage in its long, bitter war with Iraq, Khomeini has found support among Shi'ites in Lebanon, and his influence has spread into other Middle East countries. Kuwait, which has supported the bordering country of Iraq, fears that it will face an Iranian attack if Iraq loses the war. As a result, Kuwait has enlisted a US and Soviet escorts to assist its oil tankers through the Persian Gulf. Experts are split on the extent of Khomeini's power in the region, but it seems clear that his revolution will continue to gain ground.

The March of Islamism. *World Press Review* 36:30–2+ Jl '89.

A special section examines changing attitudes among Muslims and the role of Islam in the politics of the Middle East.

THE SALMAN RUSHDIE CASE

Why the Ayatollah is whipping up a new wave of fanaticism. Susan Carter *Business Week* 47 Mr 6 '89.

The Ayatollah Khomeini's death threat against author Salman Rushdie is an attempt to subvert a push by Iranian pragmatists to end Iran's isolation and economic insolvency by expanding ties with the industrial West. Charging that Rushdie's book *The Satanic Verses* blasphemes Islam, Khomeini called on Islamic zealots throughout the world to kill Rushdie, a Muslim-born British citizen, and his publishers. The Ayatollah's confrontation with the West will only temporarily support the political position of Iran's fundamentalist radicals, and it may delay or derail plans by Tehran's oil minister and others to borrow badly needed funds for reconstruction. If Khomeini causes a serious crisis between Iran and the West, Western economic ties could be cut off, which would prove disastrous for Iran.

The Ayatollah, the Novelist, and the West. Daniel Pipes *Commentary* 87:9–17 Je '89.

To understand why Ayatollah Khomeini found Salman Rushdie's *The Satanic Verses* so offensive that he precipitated an international incident by calling for the author's death, it is necessary to view the novel through Muslim eyes. An overly literal interpretation of portions of the book and a misunderstanding of its title led Muslims to the conclusion that Rushdie was denying the validity of their faith. Moreover, Khomeini saw the novel as part of a deliberate Western conspiracy to weaken the Islamic world by seducing Muslims away from the laws of their religion. In light of the trepidation and self-censorship that the ayatollah's reaction inspired in the West, he may not have been irrational to make so much of the Rushdie affair.

Beat the devil. Alexander Cockburn *The Nation* 248:366–7 Mr 20 '89.

The Salman Rushdie affair raises some disturbing questions about the nature of free speech. Rushdie deserves sympathy, but one wonders whether the intensity of the support that he has received from other writers would be as high if he had written a consciously blasphemous work on Jewish or Christian religions rather than on Islam. Because the offense caused by *The Satanic Verses* to pious Muslim sensibilities is barely under-stood in America, support among writers for Rushdie has been nearly unanimous, yet defenders of free speech have shown little support for other writers of contentious material in the past. Noam Chomsky, for ex-ample, has been ostracized and censored at various times for holding con-troversial political views. The Rushdie affair should prompt free speech advocates to ask themselves whether they have ever endorsed the notion that some writer may have unnecessarily gone too far and abused the right of free speech.

Rushdie furor highlights the nature of Islamic faith. (interview with S. Johnson). *Christianity Today* 33:38–9 Ap 7 '89.

In an interview, Steve Johnson, former executive vice-president for the American Islamic College in Chicago, explains why many Muslims are an-gered by Salman Rushdie's book *The Satanic Verses*. He notes that Rush-die's book has called into question basic tenets of the Islamic faith. According to Johnson, Muslims believe that Rushdie has committed an act of *fitnah*—the creation of chaos within Islam—which is punishable by death under Islamic law. Johnson notes that not all Muslims should be viewed in light of the fundamentalist Islamic movement, whose members are the Muslims most angered by Rushdie's book.

FUTURE OF ISLAMIC POLITICS

Hating America. David Toolan *America* 163:236 O 13 '90.

Irrational Islamic hatred and resentment of the United States has a long history and will continue for the foreseeable future. Three centuries of Western dominance have left Islam defensive and humiliated, and resur-gent Islam is an attempt to restore Muslim greatness. The United States would do well to avoid cornering Iraq and assist it in saving face to avoid a confrontation with Muslim groups in solidarity against the United States.

When the dust settles, Iran may be facing west. Stanley Reed *Business Week* 50 Je 19 '89.

Fierce competition for power following the recent death of Ayatollah Khomeini could heat up anti-American rhetoric in Iran over the next few months, but the likely victors are more pragmatic and politically responsi-ble than the late religious revolutionary. Speaker of Parliament Hashemi Rafsanjani, the only announced candidate in presidential elections sched-uled for August 18, is expected to emerge with the most power. He and current president Ali Khamenei, who is likely to succeed Khomeini as Iran's spiritual leader, are said to favor a greater role for private enter-prise in the economy and improved relations with the outside world.

A brand new kind of politics. Richard A. Falk *The Progressive* 54:20-1 Ja '90.

A new kind of revolutionary politics has begun to take shape in the past decade. Events such as the Palestinian uprising in the occupied territories, the popular movement that brought Corazon Aquino to power in the Philippines, the Islamic revolution in Iran, and the drive toward democratization in China all exhibit certain common elements: reliance on the general population, a refusal to use violence as a main revolutionary tool, and a reluctance to embrace state power. The experience of the 1980s should not be interpreted too optimistically, as there were defeats like the massacre in Tiananmen Square. Nevertheless, the decade's events showed that the new revolutionary politics can challenge the militarized state even when the latter deploys its power brutally.

Iran after Khomeini. Nikola B. Schahgaldian *Current History* 89:61-4+ F '90.

Part of an issue on the Middle East. Iran's political situation is more unsettled since the death of Ayatollah Ruhollah Khomeini on June 3, 1989, but a number of stabilizing forces are in place. Shared objectives, similar backgrounds, internal religious solidarity, and skillful manipulation of traditional Iranian political behavior have enabled Iran's clerical establishment to consolidate its power in a way that is agreeable to the Iranian majority. Extreme factionalism continues to plague the Muslim leadership, but these cleavages are more often personal than ideological in nature. The new leadership now faces urgent challenges, including economic reconstruction, military demobilization, and the fulfillment of long-promised political and socioeconomic reforms.

The challenge of reclaiming Islam from extremists. Jean-Pierre Langellier *World Press Review* 36:30-1 Jl '89.

Part of a special section on Islam. An article excerpted from *Le Monde* of Paris. The Muslim world must reclaim the vision of Islam from the extremist zealots of Islamism. Traditional Muslim theology does not distinguish between church and state, nor does it lend itself to democratic pluralism. The Iranian Shi'ites and other Islamist extremists take sharia, the Islamic law based on the Koran, as a social and legal model for the world. Lately, as in the case of Salman Rushdie, they have even tried to enforce their views in the West. Nevertheless, the larger Islamic world, which is predominantly Sunni, is secularizing. A younger generation of Western-educated Muslim intellectuals may find ways to reconcile the teachings of the Koran with progress and democracy.

Will Algeria become a second Iran? *World Press Review* 37:33 Ag '90.

An article excerpted from *Der Spiegel* of Hamburg. Algeria has the potential to become another Iran. In Algeria, as in Iran, extremists are waging a campaign to expel Western culture from the country. Insiders consider Abassi al-Madani, a professor of the University of Algiers and the head of the fundamentalist Islamic Salvation Front (FIS), to be more powerful than President Chadli Benjedid. According to one Western diplomat, al-Madani has the characteristics of a terrifying fanatic. The FIS's support comes mostly from Algeria's young people, who make up more than two-thirds of the country's 25 million people. Half of these young people are unemployed. According to al-Madani, the young, who have suffered from a lack of ideals since the socialist dictatorship came to power, are finding answers in Islam. He maintains that the FIS will build an Islamic power in which laws are derived only from the Koran and from Islamic law.

State and civil society under Islam. (adaptation of address, 1989) Bernard Lewis *New Perspectives Quarterly* 7:38–40 Spr '90.

An article adapted from a speech given by a professor of Near Eastern studies at Princeton. The intolerant regime in Iran represents a departure from Islamic history. The office of ayatollah was created in the 19th century, but the rule of Ruhollah Khomeini was unique to the 20th century. Within certain limits, Islamic government throughout history was willing to tolerate most non-Islamic religious practices. Reforms whose origins were in the West increasingly affected the way Muslims lived, however, and they began to feel so threatened by Christian minorities that traditional measures of tolerance ceased. Today, these traditional measures would seem insufficient to minority elements schooled in modern notions of human, civil, and political rights. The best hope for renewed coexistence in Iran is establishment of some form of civil society.